INSIGHT GUIDES

THE RHINE

Edited by Kristiane Müller
Photographed by Erhard Pansegrau and others
Translated by Tony Halliday, Jane Michael-Rushmar
and Thomas Fife

APA
PUBLICATIONS

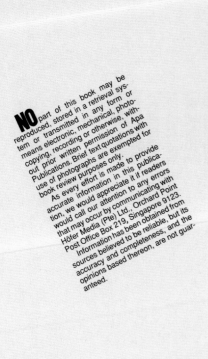
THE RHINE

First Edition

© 1991 APA PUBLICATIONS (HK) LTD

All Rights Reserved

Printed in Singapore by Höfer Press Pte. Ltd

ABOUT THIS BOOK

People still come from all over the world to gaze at its castles, visit the many historical cities which are strung out along its banks, to indulge in its wines and its festivals. The River Rhine has managed to maintain its fascination and appeal as a major travel destination; despite the environmental scandals of the last few years praise for the river continues to be sung in many languages.

The Celts and the Germani once settled on its banks. The Romans constructed its first bridges, so creating a river of immense importance - a key player in war and peace in Europe. Napoleon gazed across to the opposite shore in both advance and retreat. Queen Victoria once took a cruise downstream in torrential rain and bitter cold, and longed for home. Others, like Lord Byron and Victor Hugo, stayed longer on the Rhine and waxed lyrical about its romantic appeal. The longest resident of all, of course, is the Loreley, that fictitious blonde who led the fisherman to his death, in this river of myth and legend.

The Authors

The first vision that Project Editor **Kristiane Müller** had of the Rhine was in dotting its course on the map of Europe at school at the tender age of ten. Since then, she has assembled experience as author, translator and editor of a number of books and articles, covering a wide spectrum - from cookery to the history of art.

For this book she travelled and walked the entire length of the river, from the villages where the story of the Rhine begins high up in the Swiss mountains, to those where it ends as it spills into the North Sea - through five countries all told; Austria, Switzerland, France, Germany, and Holland.

Few have ever written about the Rhine with so much sentiment as Nobel Laureate **Heinrich Böll** (1917-1985), a keen observer of contemporary history, committed writer, an author whom many regard as the greatest German narrative writer of the post-war era. Two of Böll's essays make up the introduction to this book.

Geographer and journalist **Dr Richard Brunnengräber** takes a look at the history of the river itself, from the time when it was born through millions of years of upheaval, of constant change. He looks at the mighty barriers that dictated where the river could flow and where it couldn't, the landscape which it in turn helped to shape.

Kirsten Kehret studied German Language and Literature, Political Science and History. This variety of subjects coupled with her intimate knowledge of the area enabled her to write about the early history of settlement on the Rhine and all those hordes who determined its historical course.

History and politics were always the favourite subjects of **Susanne Urban** who provided an insight into later developments on the Rhine in her article "River of Destiny". Heinrich Heine and other notable German and French poets are the subject of her other article on Literature.

In times past the Rhine was often a bone of contention between the French and the Germans, even French and German writers. It was largely the oeuvre of the English poets of the 18th and 19th century that established the river's international romantic appeal. A summary of their collected Rhine works is contained in the article by **Ilona Esche**.

K. Müller   *R. Brunnengräber*   *S. Urban*   *E. Urban*   *M. von der Grü.*

A one time book seller and today a producer of calendars in Frankfurt, **Eberhard Urban** also translates and writes about locomotives, ships, cars, art and history for both children and adults. He writes about art in this book too, and also carries the reader away into a different world - a world of fairytales and myths and legends.

Hailing from the Ruhr Basin, that vast industrial conurbation just to the east of the Lower Rhine, **Max von der Grün** spent 13 years of his life working in the mines. He turned his hand to writing some twenty-five years ago, and has since dealt with many topical themes concerning his native territory. His article "The Ruhr Basin" deals with a region accustomed to drastic change, though he makes it quite clear that, come what may, the people themselves remain constant.

Amongst other activities, **Dr. Herbert Heckmann** is President of the German Academy of Language and Literature. As a connoisseur of food and drink, he gets involved with his favourite pastime wherever and whenever he can, whether by travelling, reading or indeed writing. His article "Food and Drink" deals with one of the most important of all Rhine topics.

Dr. Hans Joachim Aubert has worked as a travel journalist and travel book author for more than ten years. He is constantly on the move but always at home in his native Bonn on the Rhine. He describes the Rhine as it flows from its sources to Lake Constance and from Strasbourg to Worms.

Nina Köster studied in Hamburg and worked as an editor for seven years before launching out as a freelance journalist. She, too, spends a lot of time on the move and here describes the Rhine from Lake Constance to Strasbourg. She also wrote the article on the Rhine as an industrial river, as well as examining some of the flora and fauna which can still be found along the banks of the river.

Journalist **Michael Bengel** came to Cologne when as a child and learned his trade on the feature supplement of a local newspaper. He is both a literature critic and commentator of cultural events, as well as author of a long-running serial on walking in the Rhineland. Here he describes the many points of interest along the Rhine all the way from Mainz to the Estuary.

Johann Albrecht Cropp is a photographer and travel journalist. He has authored numerous travel books, including one about hiking through Germany and another about boating through France. For his contribution to this book, he trekked all the way from Karlsruhe to Duisburg.

Anne Modersohn ("travelling is my profession") prefers to go by bike and has put together a number of cycling guide books. Here she discovered the nicest bicycle routes along the length of the Rhine, from the sources (almost) to the North Sea.

The Photographers

The majority of pictures in this book were taken by **Erhard Pansegrau** from Berlin. He has made a name for himself not only by his large-sized wall calendars or the numerous shots he has had published in other APA Guides, but also by those which have appeared in his colour volumes on China, Japan, Hong Kong and Korea. Further high-quality contributions come from **Rainer Kiedrowski** and Cologne-based **Wolfgang Fritz** who has also published many of his photographs in other APA Guides.

H. Heckmann   *J. Aubert*   *N. Köster*   *M. Bengel*   *E. Pansegrau*

CONTENTS

DOWN THE RIVER

TRAVEL TIPS

HEINRICH BÖLL
THE RHINE

The Rhine is a masculine river; its name is Celtic, but the towns along its banks are Roman in origin. The Romans brought stone, paved roads, and built palaces, camps, temples and villas. They brought stones as a symbol of their own futile dreams of permanence; they left the stones behind as witnesses of their bygone power. To the succeeding German emperors they bequeathed a legacy: that to rule is synonymous with building and law-making. The Romans loaded blocks of marble onto rafts and floated them down the Rhine and up the adjoining tributaries; they carved pillars, capitals - and the Lex Romana. The Rhine served simultaneously as road and boundary. It was not the German border, nor was it a language frontier; it kept apart far more than mere languages and nations. The river has nothing of the so-called obliging nature proverbially attributed to the Rhineland. Until modern times, when a 600-metre wide waterway ceased to be regarded as an obstacle, it maintained its position as a barrier. In 1945 it was no less of an adventure to cross from one bank to the other than it must have been in Roman times.

The Romans, experienced conquerors, thought they knew how to tame this broad, wild, fast-flowing river: by means of bridges. They built some; they constructed bridgeheads - and yet, north of the Main confluence, they somehow failed to establish themselves on the right bank. Bridges are expensive and vulnerable; in a flash the two banks can be separated again by axes and fire, by bombs and explosive charges. The victorious army, in rebuilding the bridges, exacts a relentless toll: control. A bridgehead is like the eye of a needle; thousands of people can thread their way through each day, one at a time. Six hundred metres of grey, swiftly flowing waters separate families, lovers. "Once upon a time there lived a prince and princess." The fake goddess of fate has assumed a variety of disguises during the course of history: Roman mercenary,

Merovingian bandit, captain of the Elector of Cologne's private army, Napoleonic sergeant, watch-dog of the German Wehrmacht, American lieutenant. "Identity card, Ausweis, discharge papers!" A yellow powder sprayed all over your clothes: DDT. No louse was permitted to cross the Rhine alive; this was the border. Ferries, pontoons - technically scarcely superior to those the Romans must have used - became instruments of power, sources of wealth. Longingly one stood and gazed across at the opposite bank. The water was far too deep.

Big rivers are merciless. With the exception of Basle, no city has managed to straddle the Rhine properly, with one foot on each side - as do the cities on the Seine, the Tiber or the Thames. Prague is not Warsaw, Pest is not Buda - and not even today's administrative organization has been able to remove the last traces of the division between Cologne and Deutz (the Roman bridgehead Divitia). It was a hazardous business, marching across the Bailey bridge on the site of the Romans' first bridge. Muddily flowed the primeval waters of the Rhine in the autumn of 1945, north-west past the ruins of Cologne, whilst we - furnished with identity papers and DDT - struggled between tanks and jeeps over the slippery, parapetless bridge towards the longed-for left bank. The wooden supports thudded dully beneath us, as they once thudded beneath the feet of the warring Germanic tribes: the Chatti and the Cherusci, the Bructeri and the Sugambri.

The Rhine does not flow through the cities along its banks; it flows past them - past Strasbourg and Mainz, Koblenz and Bonn, Cologne and Düsseldorf. The towns of Roman origin all lie with their centres firmly on the left bank, where the Romans presented the intimidated and amazed Germanii with the sight of stone buildings, paved roads and walled camps - and the Lex, which subjected to severe punishment all those who attacked that which meant so little to the Germanii: the state, property, possessions. On the right bank, the ultimate crime was cowardice; it was punishable by death. Corpses buried in peat, thousands of years old, bear witness today to the way the Germanii administered

Preceding pages: at the source of the Rhine, winter on the Lower Rhine, river freight, near the estuary in Holland. **Left,** dressed up for the carnival.

justice. In 1945, with the retreat across the Rhine, barbarism reached its zenith. Wotan ruled the right bank; the marshes had long ago been drained, had long since fallen prey to progress - and yet Wotan still reigned. The corpses of deserters - and all those who were considered as such - hung from trees and telegraph poles. Germani ignavos in paludem praecipitabant - thus it stands written in the schoolboy's Latin primer. Only the Rhine could stem the torrent of German Wehrmacht soldiers fleeing from France in the autumn of 1944; the few bridges were easier to keep in check than the thousands of villages, side roads and woods. And - in spite of the bombers - the allied advance across the Rhine is also named after a bridge: Remagen.

Cossacks and Spaniards, Swedes, Romans and Huns all stood on one bank or the other, gazing down at the majestic river flowing by which in the first instance checked their progress. Napoleon made one final attempt to make of the Rhine a boundary between two nations; he re-drew the frontier neatly along the left bank of the river, from Basle to Cleves. His attempt was doomed to failure. The word "nation" is too feeble an expression to define the distinction between the different elements separated by the Rhine. German is spoken in Cologne and in Deutz, in Bonn and in Beuel - and yet, if you happen to be born on the left bank, you will find that the journey from East to West across one of the bridges will evoke emotions older than the experience of any single individual. The imponderable aspect of the Rhine's function as a boundary is precisely that which made Napoleon's attempt so pointless; it is also the reason why separatism has found so little favour in the Rhineland. As it flows from South to North, the Rhine divides so many things; and yet there are also many secret links joining East and West. Different languages, different kinds of bread, religious differences, which are often divisions within the individual faiths; boundaries between the ancient electorates and bishoprics; here Trier, there Cologne; the one, rural Catholic, devote, almost baroque - the other more urban, democratic. Once the Rhine is declared a national frontier, primeval emotions are aroused - emotions rooted not on a North-South, but on an East-West axis. North of Bonn the Baroque only exists as an isolated dream - an alien element which has never

truly been realized, neither as an architectural style nor as a *Weltanschauung*.

The Lower Rhine, between Bonn and Rotterdam - the least-known stretch of the river - is by no means the least significant if one judges it by sheer length alone. Language, lifestyle and humour imperceptibly assume the characteristics of the Netherlands: beer and schnapps gain the upper hand in the pubs - the drinks of people for whom mist and rain are a part of life. It all sounds as atypical of the Rhine as the sleepy villages of the lower Rhineland; with their church towers à la Brueghel, their chances of being acknowledged as truly Rhenish seem remote. And yet, does not the Basler Fastnacht take place on the Rhine, just like the Cologne Carnival? One celebration is bizarre - hidden behind the masks of monsters and demons, ungainly and rigid in its rhythms. The other is vulgar, its dances modern, its wit political and up-to-the-minute - and yet as old as the hills. The common folk makes a laughing-stock of those in power in a country where absurdity is a capital offence. And yet, with unerring instinct, it omits from its buffoonery one single source of power, the Church. The Cologne Carnival has nothing in common with the Basler Fastnacht - and yet they are both Rhenish.

Today, the administration of justice is the same on the right as on the left bank; stable bridges link the two sides together, seemingly for ever; the barges chug merrily, busily, indefatigably upstream and then back down again, from Basle to Rotterdam. No toll cannons fire warning shots across their bows, no greedy city fathers, no bankrupt electoral princes practise the right to stockpile. The robber knights' castles are in ruins, the Nibelungs a wonderful dream. Occupation is a permanent state of affairs; each and every army, even if it speaks the local language, will always be regarded as an army of occupation. Often enough, three or four armies were involved; they all spoke the same language, fighting at first side by side, and then against each other, changing allegiances; who could be expected to keep track of it all?

It was the nineteenth century which first brought the bosom friend and arch-enemy: the tourist. The Rhine became a marketable commodity. The indestructible countryside allowed itself to be translated into ready cash. Millions of pairs of eyes have gazed from the Drachenfels down on the Rhine below; the view has not changed one iota. Millions of pairs of eyes have gazed up from the passing steamers at the ruins of the robber knights' castles: they, too, have all remained standing. An irreplaceable panorama, sung by every poet who ever put pen to paper. "I know not what it meaneth." Hard hearts, cold brains - strong men became soft, warm and weak, as they travelled by steamer from Bonn to Rüdesheim through this bleakly magnificent primeval landscape, formed by the Rhine and still under its sway. The Rhine remained sovereign, making everything taking place on its banks seem transient. When the muddy flood waters rise over the prom-

curred along its banks seems like a jest which has only lasted for a couple of millenia - like a second, third, fourth dream of permanence: even the powerful industrial complexes which spring up ever closer, ever more obtrusively in their foolish optimism. Not even the industrial filth, which has made the Rhine the dirtiest river in Europe, can rob it of its majesty.

For centuries the rhymesters have determined what is typical of the Rhine, and what not. For them, the Rhine actually began at Rüdesheim and ended at Bonn. This section of the river actually comprises barely one tenth of its total length. Stefan George, with his stern intellect, was a Rhinelander in spirit;

enades and quays into the tourists' inns and cafés, when the jetties lead not downwards to a friendly steamer but upwards towards a slate-grey sky, the only sound to be heard is the droning roar of the water. North of Bonn, where the Rhine emerges from the restricting clutches of the mountains into the plains, it pours its flood waters across a wide area. Darkly menacing, it rolls past anxious villages, even threatening Cologne, its secret queen. Everything which occurs or has oc-

so, too, was the poet Elisabeth Langgässer - gentle, melancholy and with her deeply-rooted sense of humour, familiar with both angels and demons. Rhenish, too, are the sleepy tobacco-growing villages of the Upper Rhine, or pairs of towns as different from each other as Cologne and Duisburg, Düsseldorf and Mainz.

What the rhymesters regard as truly Rhenish is not even typical of the stretch they love to extol in song. Wine-growing means hard work, and the tourist season is short; for most of the year the locals do not wear their make-up, living as they do in dark, cramped villages - erstwhile serfs' settlements in the

Above, artists and their havens are all part of the Rhine landscape; here near Lake Constance.

shadow of the castles. When they dress up à la Bacchus, with a wreath of vine leaves round their brow, they will keep one Rhenish eye firmly fixed on the cash register. The books must be balanced, and even their sense of humour has long become a saleable commodity.

The lovely Rhenish maidens, who stood model for so many Madonnas, must have revealed a cold twist around their mouths, or a mocking toughness in their eyes. Amidst all the devotion and tenderness there still remained a trace of the rational good sense which was once borne northwards along the left Rhine bank, along with the stones and the Lex. Neither wine nor dancing nor song can

To The Woodcutter
For H.A.P Grieshaber

One way of doing the Rhine justice is to imagine what would happen if it did not exist, or if it dried up. If there were no Rhine, Cologne would be a desolate market place for cattle and vegetables set in a gloomy plain - and the puritan zeal of the Ruhr or the Wupper would not have crowded in on us to such an extent. And if it were to dry up - abandoned by the Main and the Nahe, the Lahn and the Moselle, the Ahr, the Agger, the Ruhr and the Sieg, left in the lurch by all the little tributaries, by the Dhünn, the Sauer,

ever quite extinguish it, this reason. The soldiers of every army ever to march through the Rhine valley have learned just how sensible the Rhineland maidens are: marriage dictated reason, and they settled where they were. It may seem a bold theory to maintain that the Rhine also represented a frontier when it came to affairs of the heart; it must be mere chance that the boundary for the official "Venus Quarters" runs along the river. The irrational aspect of love is thus held in check by reason at the Rhine. There are limits not even extinguished during the Carnival, regarded elsewhere as a time for taking leave of one's senses. (1960)

the Niers and the Erft - there would be a veritable avalanche of after-effects. Were this the case, the Rhinelanders would be able to gather up the remains of their history from the dried-up river bed; they are no separate people, but, at the very most, a tribe - and not a merry one, either, as outsiders erroneously believe. They would find the odd head of a river god, thrown as a sacrifice into the green waters - the odd Hitler bust, sacrificed by somebody; neighbours and children; as an extra, the decorative trivia with which citizens are wont to demonstrate their sense of belonging, making clear to each other, "I hereby make a sacrifice; you are the victim".

Of course there were also stainless steel insignia - golden ones too - and a mixture of German artefacts of bronze, which only need washing and derusting for all the embarrassment to be revealed. But where are the billions of fetishes belonging to Max and Moritz? Old Father Rhine is wide and darkly flowing enough to be a safe and long-suffering grave for fetishes which one would rather hide, forget, or get rid of. One would find few ribbons and medals - they were the last currency of the vanquished: cigarettes, bread, a drop of wine or whisky. The Rhine Watch could be bought for a song. Of course, we are all fed up with some things; if the Rhine bursts its banks only a little, it washes the

nounced, unopposed), was, until 1918, almost more xenophobic in its attitude towards the West than the East. Nowadays it is as tame as a wise eunuch as regards the West; regarding the East, the newly heralded nationalism behaves like a cross between Puss in Boots, Lucy Locket and a dog in the manger. We have always had enough of the wrong thing.

I noticed it, dear Mr. Grieshaber: on your woodcut Cologne Cathedral has no towers. It would be much more beautiful without the towers; buildings like that are not meant to be finished. Not only did the Romantic dream of the united nation and the Rhine Watch plan this embarrassingly perfect Gothic

walls of the Federal Parliament; perhaps it would like to wash away everything which annoys us there. The Rhine has swallowed so much already - even the tanks which careered off the bridge at Remagen. Only an experienced phrenologist could say whether there were negroes amongst those who were the first to cross "Germany's river, not Germany's frontier"; the liberators (no inverted commas!).

German nationalism (the renaissance of which has meanwhile been officially an-

Left, in the vineyards. **Above**, a float parades at one of the many Rhine wine festivals.

structure; they then went and carried it out as well - in an orderly manner, finished down to the last detail - in spite of the fact that the Rhine is the river of Romanticism, and Cologne a city of Romanesque churches. And the merciless bombing of the war was guilty of the ultimate act of mercilessness in failing to correct the accident of history which the cathedral towers represent. The cathedral towers naturally meant something to the others - a tourist's dream, a taboo for guides, these completely un-Rhenish forms. The Romanesque churches were destroyed without mercy; they lie not more than five minutes' walk from the cathedral.

It is true that the French have proclaimed the Rhine and the Rhineland to be French from time to time, but they never considered it really to be so. The Prussians, on the other hand, thought it French - and treated it as backward, corrupt, slovenly and Catholic. Berlin's freedoms during the Romantic period were dreams which no one dared to dream in the Rhineland. (My grandfather moved to Baden in 1848, in order to fight as a nineteen-year-old at the side of Hecker and Struve.) Of course every child knows that, when the forward defence has become an "elastic" front line once more, the bombs no one talks about will fall where Europe's heart lies - on the Rhine. No belt will help then - neither one of cork nor of mines, when the Rhine - polluted, deformed in many of its branches to a lake, pond, mere or swamp - checks the progress of the fugitives. And every child knows that all survivors must be instantly shot - alas, alas. (They might otherwise conceive the insane idea of fleeing to Switzerland or the Côte d'Azur). And so - only the forward defence counts, of something we're sick of already; sick to death.

When I was a boy I believed for a while that the Rhine was composed of dragon's blood flowing from the Odenwald. I liked Siegfried, who was also a Rhinelander; I never took his guilelessness for stupidity, and thought that his vulnerability - his vulnerability unto death - was what made him great. Only industry is steeled in slaves', soldiers' and dragon's blood (and not even the pea blossom fell from the heaven of German history, in order to create a weak spot - and no star will ever fall from the heaven of the board of directors!). Yes, industry. In Germany, at least, it is clearly feminine, and even in Moscow, Warsaw and Peking they kiss her invulnerable innocent little hand...(1966)

These essays are printed with the kind permission of the publishers, Kiepenhauer & Witsch, Cologne.

From: Heinrich Böll, Lectures and Writings, Vol.I and II.

<u>Left</u>, The Rhine in Flames; the great summer firework display in the Rhinegau attracts visitors from far and wide.

"Near Bingen the Rhine has miraculously succeeded in threading its way between the confining valleys. At first sight it seems difficult to fathom why the river had determined to squeeze between slate-rock faces rather than expanding in the direction of the level region near Kreuznach. Yet, on closer examination, it soon becomes evident that yonder the level of the countryside gradually rises and actually constitutes the slope of a hill. If it is deemed meet for a natural scientist to deduce from the given reality the prevailing circumstances of the past, it seems conceivable that just prior to reaching Bingen, the waters of the Rhine, cramped and contained by the rock face as they were, first swelled, flooding the whole level expanse, then rose up over the level of the rocks of the Binger Loch (Bingen Hole) only, perforce, to flow northwards in the direction which the river still follows to the present day. Gradually the water excavated its own river bed and the level area thereupon re-emerged. Presupposing that this was the case, perhaps the Rhinegau, part of the Palatinate and the area from Mainz to Oppenheim and Darmstadt was once a lake, until the dammed-up waters had surmounted the rocky valley near Bingen and the river eventually found a release."

Georg Forster (1754-1794), geographer, circumnavigator and political agitator, wrote these lines in 1790 when he travelled down the Rhine together with the 21-year-old Alexander von Humboldt, the foremost geographer of his age. At the time Forster could not know that a good twenty years later his contemporaries would meddle with the natural course of the Rhine, with consequences so dire that they have not been solved to the present day.

"If the course of the Rhine is straightened, everything in the immediate vicinity will change for the better" a lieutenant, one Johann Gottfried Tulla, had claimed full of enthusiasm when in 1812 he presented his plans

for a comprehensive rectification of the Rhine's course to the administration of Baden.

The local inhabitants were thereby to be protected from the floods as well as the resultant destruction of valuable farmland in the more susceptable areas down near the river. However, in the course of time the population had learnt to cope with the swampy ground, the high water and the floods. They refused to condone any interference with this - as they believed - divinely ordained, albeit irksome, order of everyday life.

In 1928 the economist Gustav Adolph Dehlinger wrote: "Just how the intolerable state of affairs in the lower-lying areas can be alleviated and the yield from the land be vouchsafed for the benefit of all is not exactly a new question. In order to prevent any newfangled attempts, we have to go far back into the history of our land of Hesse. We will then realize that the inhabitants of these areas had already objected to sundry dehydration measures 700 years ago."

At the turn of the 19th century the Rhine was three to four kilometres wide, meandering gracefully through the Upper Rhine Plain from Basle to Mainz. The plain was so broad that there were few obstacles to prevent the river from constantly changing its course, thus creating vast expanses of boggy, marshy land. An immoderate number of inhabitants suffered from the dreaded marsh fever. Typhoid and dysentery were rampant and occasionally decimated whole regions. Yet, in spite of all this, the peasants had come to terms with their hard mode of existence and objected to each and every novel concept that the authorities came up with.

Tulla's team undertook rectification measures to compel the Rhine to carve out a new river-bed. The river was constricted by means of transverse dams, loopings were severed, inflows to tributaries and bogs were cut off. The local inhabitants feared the consequences of such large-scale interference. In some areas, resistance was so vehement that the tasks at hand could only be effected with the aid and protection of the military.

But by 1876 work had finished and the course of the Upper Rhine had been straightened. Its length had been shortened by 82

Preceding pages: an oriel window of a half-timbered building, richly decorated with wine motifs. **Left,** Bacchus raises his goblet.

kilometres and its width had been funnelled into a 200 metres-wide channel. Prior to these developments, the main source of worry for the local population had, quite naturally, always been the large-scale destruction caused by the continuous flooding and high ground water. But now that the authorities had chosen to ignore their objections, they were faced with far greater problems than these; they are problems which the people of the Upper Rhine have had to contend with to this day - water shortage due to the lowering of the ground water table.

Dire consequences: The idea had been to contain the high water, and, as far as this was concerned, the measures succeeded. But regular shipping was still not possible because the river bed had become steeper and within a few years the river bed between the Swiss border and Breisach had deepened by seven metres. The result: the currents intensified and tons of silt - 1000 cubic metres per day - were now swept northwards and new gravel banks and islands emerged. With the lowering of the river bed, the ground water table in the adjoining areas was reduced too and various river basins dried up altogether.

Nevertheless, Tulla's achievement was initially lauded by all and sundry. The flooding had been reduced, 10,000 hectares of fertile farmland had been gained by the elimination of what had once been Rhine tributaries. The quality of deciduous trees on the Rhine pastures could now be enhanced through the planting of ash-, elm-, oak- and poplar trees.

Before these developments, on 25th August 1797, Johann Wolfgang von Goethe crossed the little river Weschnitz, a tributary of the Rhine, on his way from Heppenheim, via Weinheim and Heidelberg to Switzerland. He subsequently wrote: "The Weschnitz has been the first river of any importance I have crossed for quite some time. During a thunderstorm it tends to carry an enormous quantity of water." Times have changed. To quote the Munich comedian Gerhart Polt: "A meandering river - what a dreadful thing for nature to do."

Man has abolished this "dreadful" course of nature, because it obstructs the advantageous development of our civilisation. These days local farmers have installed pumps in the ground of the Rhine Valley in order to raise the ground water.

But let's take a look at the past, to the time when the Rhine area was fashioned, millions of years ago. The Rhine - a river that separates and joins peoples - runs like a continuous thread through the history of the earth and through the most diverse scenic areas - from the high ranges of the Alps to the wild waters of the North Sea.

The evolution of a river: In the eons of its history, the Rhine has changed course many times. It has been a main provider of water for all European oceans. During the Tertiary period, about 50 million years ago, at the time when the Alps were being created, the "High Rhine" flowed through the Burgundische Pforte (Burgundy Gate) into the Mediterranean. Prior to the Ice Age, approximately two million years ago, what is now the Alpenrhein was the most important tributary of the Danube and its waters thus flowed into the Black Sea.

The present course of the Rhine was determined during the Ice Age. Shifting northwards from the Alps, huge glaciers carved out a new course for the waters of the River Rhine. When the ice piled up in the most northern part of what is now Lake Constance, resulting in the creation of a new watershed, the waters of the Rhine were finally severed from the catchment area of the Danube and forced to penetrate the mountain range near Schaffhausen, and to skirt the southern slope of the Black Forest, to Basle.

The Rhine had thus reached the Southwest German Basin and was free to flow northwards between the Black forest and the Vosges, until the *Rheinische Schiefergebirge* (Rhenish Uplands) to the north presented yet another barrier to its progress, which it duly overcame in the manner previously described by Georg Forster.

The geological evolution of the Rhine was thus a tumultuous process. An alpine river which originally flowed into the Mediterranean and later fused with the Danube before flowing into the Black Sea, now became joined with the rivers of central Germany. Today, the whole Rhine Basin is fed by a number of separate catchment areas. Firstly: the rivers in the Swiss mountains that originally flowed towards the north-east (the erstwhile Aare tributaries that flowed into the Danube, the Aare being the primary river). Secondly: streams and rivers, such as the Neckar, originating in the Black Forest and flowing down into the Upper Rhine Plain. Thirdly: The River Main and its tributaries flowing from the east. Fourthly: The streams and rivers flowing northwards from the Rhenish Uplands.

The multifarious forms of landscape relief in the Rhine region, and the large number of scenic beauty spots from the Alps to the North Sea are primarily due to the great diversity of geological formations, which, particularly in the Alps and the Lower Rhine Plain, were later subjected to the abrasive treatment of huge glaciers and sheets of ice hundreds of metres thick.

During the last ice age, the Rhinelands must have had a particularly strange counte-

The Alps: In geological terms, the Alps are a "young" range of mountains having been created in the Tertiary period some 60-100 million years ago. Their precise evolution was a complex process and has given rise to a great deal of hot debate. Back in the 18th century, for example, the "Neptunists" and the "Plutonists" argued vehemently. The Neptunists propounded the theory that all rocks and boulders of the earth's crust had been left there by the receding water masses. The Plutonists, in turn, maintained that all vital formation forces of the earth, including mountain building, issued from deep within the earth, from the molten fire as it were. It was their opinion that this fire dictated the

nance: from the Alps in the south, the Rhine glaciers covered the area from the confluence of the Aare to the southern slope of the Black Forest. From the north, Scandinavian ice masses extended almost as far as Cologne. Signs of this are found right up to Duisburg and Krefeld. The region of the Middle Rhine, however, remained almost totally ice-free, only being subjected to a few localised glaciations. Let us now take a look at this geomorphological development in some detail.

Above, The meandering Middle Rhine viewed through a fish-eye lens.

hardness and stability of rock masses, their folding and their shattering, the protrusion of whole mountain ranges and continents, as well as volcanic activity.

Today, despite the state-of-the-art geophysical and geological equipment and working methods, there remains a great deal of contention as to how exactly the Alps were formed, although the basic "moving plate" theory has long been settled. 100 million years ago, the Mediterranean was substantially larger than it is today and formed the southern boundary of the great "northern landmass". The sediments laid down here, in the *Tethys,* provided the material for what is now the Alpine massif. When the Adriatic micro-continental plate, a portion of the much larger African continent, advanced in a northerly direction, it duly collided with the northern landmass. The sediments of the old sea bed, where the collision had taken place, were forced to fold and were consequently thrust upwards and northwards. The resulting "wave" of folding rock strata submerged the prevalent rock masses and created a chain of "fold" mountains. It was all part of a much greater upheaval stretching all the way from Gibraltar to the eastern Himalayas, known as the Alpine Orogenesis.

The glaciers set to work: "If we cross one of our alpine passes in winter, we come across

could come about if the Föhn were ever to absent itself for some reason.

The abrasive action of the ice and its ability to transport huge volumes of debris has always been the most important factor in shaping the mountains and valleys, in the morphology of the alpine area. Basically, there were four different ice ages: Günz, Mindle, Riß and Würm. There are scientists who maintain that there were two even older ice ages, a pre-glacial Danube and a Biber Ice Age. The ice ages were interspersed by warm periods. The advance of an ice age must have provided an impressive spectacle. Five huge slabs of ice moved northwards from the alpine ravines: The Salzach-gla-

astonishingly large snow drifts piled up at various places by the storm winds. Returning to this area two months later, we hardly recognise it. Now we see huge mountain faces, separated from each other by heaps of rubble and pastures, of whose short-grown, yet succulent, grass the sheep partake. How, one asks oneself, is such an incredible metamorphosis possible in such a short time and at such a height?"

"That's because of the Föhn" answers the shepherd. For the geologist Heinrich Dove in 1867 there was a direct link between the warm Föhn winds and the thawing of the glaciers. He even believed that a new ice age

ciers on either side of the Salzach, the Inn-Chiemsee glacier between Traun and Mangfallknie, the Isar-Loisach glacier, beside it the Iller-Lech glacier and finally, between Iller and the Swabian Alb, the Rhine glacier. Each was subdivided into several ice streams, separated from each other by moraine dams of sand and rubble. The meltwater from the glaciers flowed off in the direction of the Danube.

When the ice ages came to an end and the climate became warmer, this was by no means tantamount to an end of the glacial development in the alpine regions. Again and again "post-glacial" (smaller) glaciers oozed forwards, changing the landscape that had been formed by the larger tongues of ice, creating new moraines. They also created an over-steepening of the valley sides resulting in landslides which blocked the valleys and led to the formation of lakes. Rivers were forced to cut deep gorges through the layers of the valley. The geology of the Rhine and its alpine water catchment area affords ample evidence of all these developments.

Through lower mountains: The Alps are not the only range of mountains through which the Rhine flows on its journey to the North Sea; there are many lesser ranges in Germany, the so-called *Mittelgebirge*, some of which accompany the river on its journey and provide it with a backdrop of constantly changing scenery.

Having left its east-west course and started to flow northwards below Basle, the Rhine passes along the broad valley, the South-west German Basin which was also formed during the Tertiary Age, when tectonic forces had caused a huge block of the earth's crust to sink along the fault lines which separated it from the adjacent strata. A huge rift valley, a *Graben* was thus formed, flanked by two areas of high ground, the Black Forest and the Vosges to the east and the west.

But it was a counter process occurring further to the north which produced the mightiest range to directly confront the Rhine on its journey to the sea, namely the range to which the river itself gave its name, the *Rheinische Schiefergebirge* (Rhenish Uplands). It is characterised by wholly diverse landscape regions: Hunsrück and Taunus in the south, which drop steeply to the Rhine and Main Valleys; northwards from there is the Westerwald with its central basalt plateau, surrounded by the Sauerland, Bergisches Land and the Rothaar range; in the north-west there is the Eifel with its characteristic peaks like the "Schnee Eifel" or the "Hohen Venn".

During the ice ages, these lower mountain ranges, situated as they were between the northern ice and alpine ice, were largely ice-free. Only a few "local glaciers" on the highest peaks (those of the Black Forest, the *Herz* and the *Riesengebirge*) had formed. But

Left, **the river flows through the varied scenery of the German Highlands. The houses nestle between the mountain slopes and the river.**

these glaciers had a much less drastic effect on the landscape than the alpine glaciers. Evidence of glacial activity is provided by the lakes which now fill the ice hollows. The *Mittelgebirge* were not totally covered by ice then, but lay in a "peri-glacial" zone. The outflowing water etched itself deeply into the landscape and the characteristic indented valleys that are still found everywhere were formed. The Rhine retains its special romantic appeal as a river of the *Mittelgegirge*, if we think of that broad Upper Rhine Plain with the Black Forest and Odenwald rising above it, and, to the north, the much more confined, picturesque nooks and loops of the Rhinegau north of Mainz and Wiesbaden, which the river enters at Bingen Hole.

The North German Lowlands: The region that follows the highlands in the north and stretches to the North and Baltic Sea, is about 300 kilometres across. It is a vast expanse of flat, low-lying terrain that was formed almost exclusively by the activity of ice. These vast ice sheets, often several hundred metres deep, levelled off virtually everything in their path, and the ground level sank under their weight. In this region, the North German Lowlands and the Netherlands, the often melancholy, misty, Lower Rhine atmosphere is especially evocative.

The coast: In the course of time, the North Sea that greets the estuary of the Rhine in the Netherlands has repeatedly changed its shape. In post-ice age times, the North Sea coast extended to the northern flanks of the Dogger Bank. About 8,000 years ago, the coast began to move farther and farther south, Dogger Bank was gradually submerged, and the sand dunes that had been formed along the coast were eventually turned into islands. Flats and marshland were formed, and finally settled by man, who, for the last 900 years, has endeavoured to protect himself against the North Sea floods by constructing dams and dykes. Thus, on the North Sea coast, it is the tides and the waves which have always been the most influential landscape architects.

The Rhine seems to have an uncertain fate. At the source one does not quite know where it begins to flow, and at the estuary one does not know where it stops. Many scientists therefore call the whole estuary complex with its rivers, brooks and canals the "Netherlands stream corridor" - an almost European term for a mighty European river.

TRIBES AND TRIBULATIONS

The oldest remnants found in the vicinity of the Rhine are tools dating from the stone age - 2,500,000 - 30,000 years ago. Nothing remains of those who used those tools. Neither do we know anything about the migrating groups of hunters. In 1856 however, skeletal remains of early man were discovered in the Neandertal, near Düsseldorf. Neandertal man died out approximately 30,000 years ago, lived in caves, tents or huts, practised certain burial rites and communicated by linguistic means.

During the Stone Age, human way of life changed, not least because of the change of climate and the development of the living and production patterns. The people in the Rhineland were fishermen, hunters and gatherers. They founded settlements and used more and more highly developed utility and artisan tools. An important change in the living pattern of these people was brought about by the slow transition to arable farming and stock-rearing which encouraged the populace to establish permanent settlements. The use of metals for the manufacture of tools and weapons during the bronze and iron age triggered a further development of human communities.

Celtic and Germanic tribes: On the Rhine, later civilisation was partly characterised by Celtic influence on the left bank of the Rhine, and partly by Germanic influence, largely on the right bank of the Rhine. The Celts were the first people north of the Alps to migrate from East to West and for about 200 years they played a leading role in Europe. They settled in Southern Germany, migrated as far as the Upper Rhine region and eventually beyond it. They settled throughout the Rhine Valley and and moved farther north until they occupied Gaul. Eventually they spread throughout Europe up to Asia Minor and the British Isles - a huge migration movement long before the great migration of the Germanic tribes. The word "Rhine" (Celtic:

Preceding pages: a view from Drachenfels Castle, houses on stilts in Unteruhldingen on Lake Constance. **Left**, this tower was constructed by the Romans.

Renos) and also the names of many old Rhenish cities date from this time.

The origins of the Celtic tribes can be traced back to the ancient European population that was already familiar with the applications of iron. Irish sources, too, confirm that the Celts had a high level of civilisation that resulted in immortal works of art, highly-developed social structures as well as their own religion.

The Celts conquered other European peoples, forcing their rule upon them. Exactly the same happened to the Celts themselves later, when the Germanic tribes from the area around the North Sea coast spread throughout Europe, mingled in some areas with the Celtic predecessors or displaced them. Some peoples that had long been under Celtic influence, were "germanized" as late as the pre- Roman Iron Age.

The classification "Germans" referred to a tribe on the Lower Rhine and was later applied to all neighbouring tribes to the east. It was a term which Julius Caesar also used, although the Germans themselves had no name for their tribe. They worked the land and bred cattle, lived in consolidated settlements, hamlets or isolated habitats, mostly in the immediate vicinity of the river.

The river as a Roman frontier: For around 400 years, the history of the Rhine was determined by the policies of the Roman Empire. Since about 100 B.C. the Romans had penetrated Celtic territory as far as the river. At the same time Germanic tribes from the north and north east bore down on the Celts. The resultant clash between Romans and Germans was to have a considerable effect on the development of the political and geographic conditions along the Rhine.

Before he crossed the Rhine in the Neuwied Basin twice around the year 60 B.C., Julius Caesar had already subjugated the Celts during the Gallic Wars. After the integration of the new Roman province of Gaul, Caesar deemed the Rhine to be the natural, eastern boundary of the Roman sphere of influence. The crossing of this boundary was to be a warning to any peoples in the adjoining regions that might have harboured expansionist ideas. The bridges over the Rhine near present-day Neuwied - in the eyes of the Germanic inhabitants miracles of technology - were intended to demonstrate the superiority of the Roman Empire.

Despite the fact that the Empire basically ceased at the west bank of the Rhine, the Romans still had a great influence on the artistic and cultural development of the tribes to the east of the river. The Germans carried out extensive trade with the Romans (amber, fur, glass and metal receptacles). The production of artisan and household objects (pottery and weaving) flourished.

A thorn in the flesh: As time went on, however, the relationship between the Romans and the Germans declined. The Germans were naturally attracted by the greater economic prosperity of the land to the west of the Rhine, and there were constant invasions during which the Roman legions were often routed. The Germans increasingly became a thorn in the flesh of the empire and under the Emperor Caesar Augustus the Romans planned a massive offensive across the Rhine into "free" Germania in order to protect the borders from the danger of further raids once and for all.

The attack on the German tribes was carried out in several phases and led to the establishment of provincial Roman administrations in the conquered territory. However, military rule could not be consolidated in Germania, as the Roman legions continuously had to ward off new attacks from the German tribes. The Roman campaign resulted in huge losses at the famous battle in the Teutoburger Wald in 9 A.D. when the allied German tribes, led by Arminius, the chieftain of the Cherusker, beat back the Roman legions led by Varus.

The Romans withdrew from Germania and the Rhine once again constituted the north-eastern boundary of the Roman Empire, a state of affairs which continued until the downfall of Roman rule north of the Alps. To the east of the Rhine, the Romans were only in complete control of the territory to the south of the Danube. In order to speed up the transport of food supplies and weapons, they now attempted to push this boundary farther towards the north.

The war Domitian waged against the Chats in A.D. 83 further increased the area under Roman sovereignty and resulted in the construction of the *Limes Imperii Romani*, the 548 kilometre long, consolidated and guarded border, which began between Bad Hönnigen and Rheinbrohl, included the area between Rhine-Main and the Danube and was to prevent further German raids. This aim was achieved - albeit temporarily. The respect of the German tribes for the military ability of the Roman legions dwindled even further and their attacks and raids increased proportionately. The Limes were further consolidated and castels and camps were established along the main routes.

The Celts had assimilated better into the life of the Roman Empire than the Germans. The "Barbarians" had become acquainted with the municipal constitution of the Romans and Roman law which now also applied to them. They became familiar with the Roman way of life, their economy and culture. The tolerance of the Romans towards Celtic cus-

increasing threat from central Germania. Some Germanic tribes now banded together to form large strike forces, in order to prepare their attack: In the south the Alemannians and Burgundians, in the north the Franks, were the main forces. While earlier forays of the Germanic tribes into Roman territory had been mainly for looting purposes, now it was a matter of finding new homelands, either within the Roman Federation or as sovereign occupiers of their own territories.

In the time of the great migration, many Germanic and Asiatic tribes crossed the Rhine, occasionally penetrating deep into Roman territory. There followed the Franks, Alemannians, Burgundians, Visigoths, and

toms and cultural traditions accelerated the integration of the Barbarians from the border regions into the Empire. In addition, the victory of Christianity over the heathen Roman Empire during the second and third centuries had an immediate effect on the inhabitants of the adjacent provinces; the new religion was slow to spread in the border provinces along the Rhine, however.

Since the third century the inhabitants of the Rhine area had lived in fear of the ever-

Above, classical reliefs and sculptures are displayed in a Bonn museum.

other tribes with which the Romans concluded treaties and alliances in order to elicit their assistance in combating other, hostile German tribes.

The development of the German Empire: The increasing instability of the Roman Empire facilitated the advance of the Germanic tribes into Roman territory. Roman rule on the Rhine finally ended with the victory of the King of the Francs, Chlodwig (Clovis), over the last Roman army in Gaul in 486 A.D. The Franks had evolved from a fusion of several West-Germanic tribes on or near the Rhine, which, until the fourth century, had been individual tribes within a federation, with their own names and chieftains. Eventually they were united under the leadership of Chlodwig. The Franconian Kings from the Merovingian dynasty increasingly subjugated their fellow German kings, so providing the basis for the establishment of a unified empire.

But the opposing interests between the various Franconian regions and disputes between the king and the nobility eventually weakened the authority of the Empire and the power of the Merovingian rulers. Its top officials, the stewards from the Franconian house of Carolingia were increasingly responsible for guiding the fate of the Empire, while the Merovingian rulers were reduced

by the Pope. On his way back from Rome, Charlemagne went to Ravenna. He saw there the mosaics of Justinian and Theodora in the church of San Vitale and realised just how magnificent an Emperor could be. Thus, when he returned to his residence at Aix-la-Chapelle he decided to build a replica of San Vitale as his own palace chapel. As the ruler of an empire that stretched from Denmark to the Adriatic, he collected treasure from all over the known world - jewels, cameos, ivories, precious silks. Ultimately only the books matter - and the craftsmanship of the works of art produced under the influence of Charlemagne's revival are masterpieces. In their own day these books were so precious

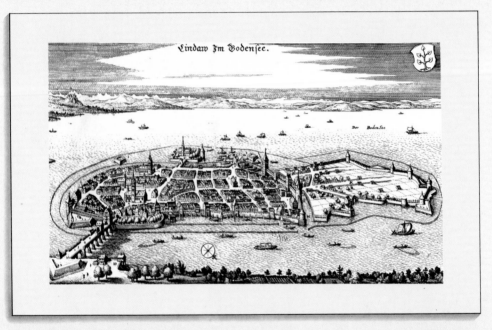

Lindaw Jm Bodensee.

to mere puppets. Eventually the Carolingians forced them to abdicate and, with the consent of the Pope, they assumed the Royal throne.

The alliance of the new kingdom with the Pope was of great importance for the development of the European Middle Ages. The Carolingian dynasty integrated further tribal chiefdoms into the Empire. At the same time, they had to ward off threats from the Arabs.

Under Charlemagne, the realm of the Francs reached its greatest expansion. He led bloody raids against the Saxons and Langobards, whom he forced to convert to Christianity. On Christmas Day 800 A.D. Charlemagne had himself crowned Emperor

that they were given the most elaborate bindings conceivable. Charlemagne's grandson, the historian Nithardt, wrote about him: "In wisdom and virtue he was superior to all his contemporaries, to all equally avuncular and equally terrible, revered by high and low."

After the death of Charlemagne, the Franconian Empire disintegrated. Diverse hereditary claims had shattered its unity. Its death knell was rung in 877 A.D. with the final division into the Western and Eastern Franconian *Reich*. The power of the Franconian Kings, who could no longer defend their countries against the usurpers from the north and east, dwindled more and more, thus enabling tribal potentates to once again take control of their territory. They chose a king from their own ranks after the Carolingian dynasty had finally died out in the East Franconian Reich.

It was only with the accession of the Saxon Duke, Otto, who had been crowned King in 936 in Aachen and in 962 had been crowned Emperor in Rome, that the German rulers once again began to call themselves Emperors. They regarded themselves as the successors of the Roman Caesars of old. From now on the empire had a noble name: Holy Roman Empire of German Nations.

Remnants from the past: The few pre-historic remnants along the Rhine are mostly toric times include Neandertal near Düsseldorf, where skeletal remains of Neandertal man were discovered. Two Stone-age settlements were unearthed in Cologne-Lindenthal and Andernach. Tools as well as skeletal remains were discovered in Bonn-Oberkassel, and at the excavation site at Urmitz (south-east of Neuwied), an earth fortification with a burial ground was found.

The Romans left a plentiful supply of memorabilia from their time at the Rhine. After all, they had ruled the area for several centuries. Many of the great German cities along the Rhine - Xanten, Neuss, Bonn, Cologne-Deutz, Andernach, Koblenz, Boppard, Bingen, Neuwied, Mainz - were

exhibited in museums. Only settlement and burial sites are found on location, but for archeological laymen these are of little interest. Not until the time of the Romans were there more extensive sites and buildings.

In what was once Feldkirchen-Gönnersdorf (now Neuwied), a stone age settlement was discovered some years ago with an unusually large number of well-preserved objects. Excavation sites with objects from pre-historic

Left, an engraving of the Old City of Lindau on Lake Constance. **Above**, a coloured steel engraving of Basle by J.M. Kolb, from a drawing by L. Rohbock.

founded by the Romans. What were once legion camps, castels or provincial capitals were in later epochs centres of political, cultural and religious life. Apart from the remnants of city walls, castels and guard towers (Limes) there are also special points of interest for the students of civilisational developments like the aqueduct in Brey, roads, religious and cult sites and object d'arts (numerous mosaics).

The Dionysos Mosaic in Cologne, on display in the Roman-Germanic Museum next to the Cathedral in the former Roman city, was discovered during work on a construction site.

THE RIVER OF DESTINY

Old Father Rhine not only witnessed the ebullitions of German history, sometimes he even determined their course.

In the 11th century, the Salier, a noble Franconian family, ruled the region of Worms and Speyer. This Rhenish area did not suffice, however, and so, by means of a skilful marriage policy, they extended their sphere of influence, until, from 1027 onwards, they ruled as Imperial family over the whole area of what then constituted the German realm. Not least because of family disputes as well as the proclamation of various counter kings and an enforced abdication, the power of the Salier was weakened. On top of that came disputes between the emperors and the church concerning the nomination of the clergy. This power struggle, also known as investiture dispute, ended in 1122 in Worms am Rhein. In 1127 the Salier dynasty died out.

From the end of the 12th century, the German King was nominated by a chapel of six (later seven) electors. Three (later four) of these electors were the rulers of the German states which had emerged after the disintegration of the Franconian Reich, and included the Count Palatinate of the Rhine. The remaining three electors were all drawn from the ranks of the clergy; the archbishops of Mainz, Cologne and Trier. These three Rhenish cities consequently wielded an enormous amount of power right through the German Middle Ages and beyond; they didn't actually lose their voting rights in the royal nomination until 1803.

Principalities and cities: In the late Middle Ages, the German King granted these electorates and other principalities more and more power and sovereignty. Their rulers were able to consolidate their power during the "emperor-less" era (1254-1273). The first League of Rhenish Cities (*Rheinische Städtebund*) evolved in 1254 as a counter-reaction against the resultant despotism of the territorial counts especially concerning the customs posts on the Rhine and their

Preceding pages: Napoleon's army near Düsseldorf, 6th September 1795. **Left,** Gutenfels Castle and the statue of Marshal Blücher, who crossed the Rhine on New Year's Day 1813/14.

detrimental effect on Rhine shipping. In 1256, one year before its disbandment, this league already included 70 cities. The second Rhenish League was founded in 1381 and its purpose this time was to combat the impoverished knights who had cast a beady eye on the wealthy cities on the Rhine. This envy soon escalated to armed disputes and not until 1388, when a peace treaty was signed, was the League disbanded.

Worms, one of the oldest cities on the Rhine, became ever-more important during the Middle Ages. Not least because of the frequent assemblies held in Worms, the city was decisively involved in the establishment of the first League of Rhenish Cities, as well as begun in the name of Luther but was soon castigated by him.

Constant warfare: By 1550, despite the quarrels, many of the principalities along the Rhine had disassociated themselves from Catholicism and had embraced the cause of the Reformation. The Thirty Years War (1618-1648) which was caused not least by contrary religious positions, resulted in death, starvation, diseases and devastation throughout Germany. The Rhine Palatinate was one of the most embattled regions. In accordance with the "Westphalian Peace Treaty" of 1648 which was to have settled the disputes, part of Alsace was ceded to France. But the 1648 treaty did not bring peace for long. Difficul-

as in many German policy matters. The reform of the Reich in 1495 was decided upon there, as was the famous edict dating from 1521, in accordance with which the authorities banished Martin Luther and prohibited the reading and dissemination of his writings. The Reformation started by Martin Luther nevertheless soon established itself in the Rhinelands and, in 1529, the Imperial Diet in Speyer vehemently protested against its prohibition. In Worms, Speyer and Mainz, the rebels had, in fact, assembled to support the demands posed by Luther and there were diverse rebellious centres between Mainz and Basle at the time of the peasant revolt

ties within the Reich and the French annexation policy caused storm clouds to gather, pre-empting any kind of permanent peace. In order to safeguard it at least for a brief span, in 1658 the various south and west German principalities combined under French leadership to form the first Confederation of the Rhine. By 1668 the Conferation no longer existed. In the period between 1672 and 1697 the "Peace" broke down completely and war was again rampant in various parts of Europe. The military leaders and armies used the Rhinelands as a troop assembly area and as a battle ground. The Palatinate was devastated several times - this time by troops of the French King - and not before 1697 did the rulers decide to negotiate a peace treaty. This was signed in the Dutch city Nijmegen.

The subsequent years proved once again that the rulers could not keep the peace for very long. A number of royal succession problems, the aggressive expansion policy of some kings as well as the opposing interests of Austria and Prussia caused the Rhenish population to become participants, witnesses and victims of military disputes. When in 1763 the last of these wars, the Seven Years War, came to an end, peace was restored for all of thirty years in Germany.

Changing hands: The French Revolution in 1789 caused trepidation throughout Europe, signed in 1801 under the auspices of Napoleon Bonaparte, at that time still First Consul. The stipulations were: the whole region to the left of the Rhine was to become part of French territory.

The princes who had hitherto ruled there were recompensed. In exchange they received the ecclesiastical principalities that had meanwhile been secularised as well as smaller territories previously ruled directly by the German Reich. The princes were thus appeased and therefore revised their adverse opinion of revolutionary France. In 1806 the principalities on the right side of the Rhine joined to form the Second Confederation of the Rhine under the protection of Napoleon,

at least as far as royalty was concerned - so much so that, for a while, the Prussian-Austrian conflict became secondary. In its stead a call resounded for military intervention in France. In 1792 the French declared War on Prussia and Austria. In the course of the war, the area on the left bank of the Rhine changed hands several times, being ruled by the French and by the Germans alternately. Eventually the peace treaty of Luneville was

Left, Rheinstein Castle, a painting by Johann Bachta from 1837. **Above**, Rheinstein Castle today, viewed from a pleasure steamer.

who had meanwhile had himself crowned Emperor of the French.

The Rhine Confederation States declared their autonomy from the German Empire and promised Napoleon military aid for his campaigns. On 1. August 1806 they seceded from the German Reich and on 6. August 1806 an empire that since the 12th century had been known as the "Holy Roman Empire of German Nations" ceased to exist when the German Emperor, Francis II resigned the imperial crown. Thereupon, a number of other states joined the Rhine Confederation. In the federal states, in accordance with the "Code Napoleon", a reform of the judiciary and taxation laws was carried out and the feudal and dietary rights were reduced; suddenly every citizen actually seemed to have been granted a legal status.

Blücher crosses the Rhine: The Prussians were no to be subdued for long, however. Anti-French revolts all over Germany broke out in the spring of 1813, and supported by Russia, England and Sweden, Prussia finally declared war on a France that had been weakened by the Russian campaign. German patriots, mobilised by the king for the so-called "wars of liberation" against Napoleon, fought, suffered and died for the cause of freedom in a united Germany.

The battle of Leipzig in 1813 represented a turning point in world history: Napoleon's army was beaten and the Rhine Confederation ceded from France. Blücher crossed the Rhine on New Years Eve 1813/14 and marched into his place in history. Germany's fate, too, was decided one year later, when most of Europe's nobility, including two emperors, six kings and over a hundred princes came together at the glittering Congress of Vienna. The hopes of the German people, who had fought for "King and Fatherland", were not to be fulfilled. The conservative forces at the congress, notably Prince von Metternich of Austria, ensured that the German states remained fragmented, and under the control of the feudal powers of old. The authorities founded the German Confederation, an unwieldy conglomeration that consisted of 39 states, 35 princes and four free cities.

Revolution: The promised civil liberties were forgotten in the subsequent restoration. Demonstrations for democracy were suppressed, student's groups were persecuted. Heinrich Heine wrote: "When I think of Germany at night, then I am robbed of sleep". The French July revolution of 1830 was the signal for a general outbreak of dissatisfaction throughout Europe. German democratic forces began to grow in self-confidence. Because of the proximity to France, the Rhinelands were politically wide awake and the influence of the revolutionary movement increased. Eventually constitutions were established in the various principalities. Some 30,000 people gathered at the Hambach Festival of 1832 - only a stone's throw away from the Rhine - to lend their voice to a powerful declaration of democracy. Patriots demanded unity, justice and liberty. The organisers were arrested by Metternich's police, and their black, red and gold colours were banned.

The Festival was one of the most important events in the run up to the bourgeois German Revolution of 1848/49, which occurred when a further revolutionary upheaval in France in February 1848 had spread to the Rhinelands and then to the rest of Germany. The most important centres of rebellion in the Rhineland were Karlsruhe, Mannheim, Cologne and Düsseldorf. After the disastrous end of the revolution in 1849, some courageous people again took up arms. Regular troop associations were mobilised against them and so in Rhine Hessen, in the Palatinate and in the Cologne region many of these true democrats died in their fight for liberty. After that a new phase of oppression started. Many Germans, including thousands of Rhinelanders, turned their back on their home country and took their chance to emigrate, primarily to America.

After the German War of 1866, the Prussians, who had beaten the Austrians, further extended their territory: the Rhine from Wesel to Mainz was now part of Prussia. Because the German authorities could not desist from playing their favourite game, a new war broke out in 1870, once again between Germany and France. After a victory over France in 1871, long glorified by Germany, it was specified in the peace treaty signed in April in Versailles that Alsace-Lorraine should become part of the "German Reich", a fact which further intensified the enmity between the two neighbouring countries.

The First World War: In 1914 the First World War broke out. Imperial Germany made quite sure that the relations between the two countries plummeted to a new low. Fortunately, the Rhineland itself was spared the senseless battles of the First World War. For the French, however, the Rhine was of great interest. Before the war was over, discussions had already begun as to how the expected restructuring of the territory should be carried out. This developed into the so-called "Rheintheorie", something that occupied the minds of many Frenchmen during the war, until the capitulation of Germany.

In 1918 Imperial Germany had been beaten and the Treaty of Versailles was signed that same year. As is well known, permanent peace did not come about. Instead the revanchistic forces in Germany grew, Alsace-Lorraine was ceded to France, a 50 kilometre strip of land on the right bank of the Rhine was declared a de-militarised German Zone, and the left Rhine bank was occupied by allied troops.

In November 1918 the revolutionary wave finally swept away what was left of the German Empire. In Düsseldorf, Koblenz, Mainz and Mannheim, worker- and soldier councils were established and the Weimar Republic, a crisis-torn democratic state now took over. In 1923 Belgian and French troops marched into the Ruhr on the right bank of the Rhine because Germany had not paid the

reparation sum stipulated by the Allies. The resistance of the population and a new regulation of the reparation question led to an evacuation of the Ruhr area. The Young plan of 1929 prescribed that the Allies would withdraw their troops from the occupied regions on the left of the Rhine earlier than originally planned.

The rise of Hitler: During this time the National Socialist Party under Adolf Hitler had won a considerable number of votes at vari-

Above, Konrad Adenauer, who became the first Chancellor of the Federal Republic of Germany in 1949, lived in Rhöndorf near Bonn.

ous elections. The elections in 1932 were the first steps to a barbarism officially legalised when Hitler was appointed *Reichskanzler* on 30th January 1933. The election results of the Rhineland proved that the National Socialist strongholds were not here - on the contrary, above Cologne the Communists (KPD) were very firmly entrenched. The 1000 year *Reich* only lasted for 12 years but naturally had a profound influence on the history of the Rhine. In 1936 Hitler had given orders for three Wehrmacht battalions to march into the Rhineland, which had been declared a demilitarised zone in accordance with the Treaty of Versailles; this breach of international treaties was denounced by the other countries in Europe but did not result in any measures that might have cut Hitler down to size. In 1939 Hitler's ideology and politics inevitably led to the Second World War. The Rhinelands and the Rhinelanders were directly affected this time. In 1942 the bomb attacks on cities like Mainz, Mannheim, Cologne and the Ruhr area caused enormous numbers of casualties among the civilian population.

The Allies arrive: After the allied troops had liberated the left bank of the Rhine in Febuary 1945, the Americans crossed the Rhine over the bridge near Remagen on 7th March. The bridge was the only one that had not been dynamited by the retreating German troops. Within 24 hours more than 8000 US soldiers had crossed to the east bank of the Rhine. It was the first time since 1805 that foreign troops had crossed the river. Eighteen days later all the Western Allies had left the Rhine behind them.

On 8th May 1945 the unconditional capitulation of the Third Reich was signed. The terror of National Socialism had come to an end and peace was finally restored to the Rhine area. The restructuring of Germany was one of the points that had been discussed by the Allies during the war. Alsace-Lorraine, the area that had constantly been shifted hither and thither between France and Germany was - this time for good - declared part of France. The Rhine flowed through the three occupation zones of the Western Allies who had fixed the boundaries in 1945.

Since the end of the Second World War the leading representatives of France and Germany have ensured that former enemies are now European allies.

THE ENGLISH ROMANTICS DISCOVER THE RHINE

Around the turn of the 18th to the 19th century, it was the done thing in England for a young man of good breeding to travel to Italy - either via France or along the Rhine, thus commencing on his "Grand"- or "Continental" Tour. In the course of time, the English not only began to prefer the Rhine detour as the route to Italy, the region itself began to be considered a worthwhile vacation area for educated, above-all, romantically inclined people. The restiveness of the English, combined with a typical bent for sight-seeing excursions to ruins and the national predilection for eery places like cemeteries and haunted castles was well-known on the continent, long before the Germans themselves began to laud the fascinating castles of the Rhine Valley. The ground had thus been prepared for rapidly expanding tourism and the Rhine became one of the first regions for mass tourism. The Rhinelanders were much enamoured of the itinerant Englishmen, not least because they brought desperately needed revenue to the country. It is even reported that some hoteliers substituted portraits and busts of the British monarch for the portrait of the local ruler.

The English enthusiasm for the Rhine was the result of a changed attitude to nature and a corresponding openness towards landscapes and buildings.

In the last decades of the 18th century, enthusiasm for the Rhineland was an aristocratic pastime. Here were the picturesque and splendid ruins that had traditionally fascinated the English and which they subsequently rebuilt back home at vast expense.

The connoisseur who went on his "grand tour" was mostly a man of letters. He was well-read, collected etchings or dabbled in the art of painting, was widely travelled, took pains to landscape his garden in accordance with the latest fashion, replete with rivulets and waterfalls cascading down rocks, so that his landscape garden resembled the paint-

ings by Claude Lorrain and Salvador Rosa that he admired so much. The educated Englishman spent his time in coffee houses, salons and art exhibitions and, on seeing a landscape, he could immediately say whether it was "picturesque". The "picturesque", ever after the epithet much in favour for book titles, determined the travel impressions and sensibilities of many an Englishman. Prime criterion for the picturesque was diversity of landscape, naturally, in the case of the English garden, with a little assistance from landscape gardeners.

The Rhineland and especially the Rhinegau, with its rocks, mountains, vineyards and castles was the incarnation of everything romantic. The countryside resembled that ideal depicted by Italian landscape painters. The romantic interpretation of Germany and the German past - so prevalent in the legends, sagas, fairy tales and folk songs - was soon part of English Rhine romanticism.

Beginning with the Nibelungs, the Rhine was a microcosm of the world in which all the chivalrous events of long ago had taken place, where castles and ruins were relics of another age. The river inspired many English writers and painters. However when Queen Victoria travelled along the Rhine in August 1845, the impression she got was anything but romantic. During her tour it rained the whole time - all the way from Cologne to Mainz.

Enterprising art dealers brought back paintings and etchings of the Rhinelands which they had purchased locally, thinking them to be priceless originals, only to learn in England that they were forgeries. More often than not the subject matter of a picture was a daring combination of beauty, horror and immensity. The river and its environs were an inexhaustible romantic font for all lovers of the "picturesque".

John Gardnor (1726-1808) in his book "Views taken on and near the River Rhine" (first edition 1788) depicted various views in the then customary manner of picturesque illustrations. He and William Turner, who between 1817 and 1844 visited the Rhine eleven times, had a decisive influence on the style of Rhine illustrations.

Preceding pages: a coloured engraving of Pfalzgrafenstein Castle with Gutenfels Castle in the background. **Left**, water-nymphs in the rushes wonder at a passing paddle steamer - the romantic Rhine of the last century.

Samuel Prout (1783 - 1852) immersed himself in medieval architecture on the Rhine, Robert Batty - much influenced by Gardnor and Turner in his book "Scenery of the Rhine, Belgium and Holland" (1824 - 1826) - also produced superb work. He published the first collection of steel engravings of the Rhine area. The influence of Turner is also evident in William Womblesons's book "Views of the Rhine" (1835), which included steel engravings of various Rhine landscapes.

The early 19th century was very much the period of the Gothic novel. Through the depiction of intense emotions and situations, similar states of mind were to be aroused in the reader. Locations like monasteries, cas-

enlightenment, simple folk and their more humane, more amicable style of life were juxtaposed with one's own society - a society that had paid for its culture with "repression". Keate waxed eloquent about the population of the Swiss Alps: "In Switzerland the Rhine flows through the traditional land of democratic freedoms in which the peasants under the maple trees - so dear to Rousseau - practise self-government, in the highlands that for centuries have remained untouched by civilisation."

William Lisle Bowles (1762-1850) became famous primarily because of his book "Fourteen sonnets written chiefly on Picturesque Spots during a Tour." The last son-

tles and ruins as well as wild, picturesque landscapes played a vital role in the intensification of emotional states of mind. The anti-rationalistic attitude prevalent at the time went hand in hand with a predilection for the Middle Ages and religion, primarily, of course, Catholicism, with its variety of emotional characteristics, which were frequently combined with a preference for supernatural events and exotica.

In 1762 George Keate romanticised the craggy Alpine scenery in his poem "The Alps" describing the source of the Rhine, following its course and idealising the dwellers of this region. Contrary to the age of

net is entitled "On the Rhine" and glorifies the river. For Bowles the Rhine landscape was quite simply a beautiful painting. The legends and the splendid view of the castles overwhelmed him. "T'was morn, and beauteous on the mountain's brow/Hung with the blushes of the bending vine/Stream'd the blue light, when on the sparkling Ryne/We bounded, and the white waves round the prow/In murmurs parted."

In 1794 Robert Gray had started on his Continental tour and wrote enthusiastically about the Rhine Falls at Schaffhausen. "The river appears almost surrounded by a fine amphitheatre of hills richly covered with trees." In 1794 Thomas Cogan penned a description "The Rhine: On a Journey from Utrecht to Francfort". He was primarily interested, however, in historical fact rather than sagas and legends associated with the castles he saw.

One of the first important Rhine romantics was William Beckford (1760 - 1844). He travelled along the river in 1782 and subsequently wrote a book of poems and travelogues called "Dreams, Waking Thoughts and Incidents" (first edition 1783). Beckford, like many subsequent writers, was particularly fond of the region between Bonn and Koblenz. "Let those who delight in picturesque country repair to the borders of the Rhine, and follow the road which we took, from Bonn to Coblentz". Beckford was especially impressed by the castles on the craggy hilltops. He mentioned a lady in white that had appeared to him, her hair suffused with glow-worms. She was rushing hither and thither so that the contours of her figure remained vague. Sometimes he even heard her sigh. He claims that he did not know whether the figure was a real human being, an apparition or merely a figment of his imagination.

For Beckford the Rhine was an evocative fairy-tale landscape which he described so tellingly that many of his countrymen were moved to come and share his delight themselves.

Ann Radcliffe (1764-1823) travelled along the Rhine in 1794 and wrote about it in "A Journey made in the summer of 1794 - Through Holland and the Western Frontier of Germany with a Return down the Rhine". She described the war catastrophes not from their political aspects but rather as a human tragedy. The wounded soldiers and civilians, loneliness, moonlight, storms, ruins, craggy hills were the very essence of her book. The war did not exactly make travelling easier, the inns were frequently poorly furnished, sometimes there was not even enough cutlery for the guests.

The romantic description of the Rhine landscape is also evident in one of the most famous Gothic novels of the 19th century,

written by Mary Wollstonecroft Shelley (1797-1851), the wife of the poet Percy B. Shelley (1792 - 1822). He accompanied his wife to the Rhine in 1814 and again two years later together with their friend Lord Byron (1795 - 1821) who had a profound literary influence on both.

Byron's Rhine description in "Childe Harold" was soon to become famous. "The castled crag of Drachenfels/Frowns o'er the wide and winding Rhine/Whose breast of waters broadly swells/Between the banks which bear the vine/And hills all rich with blossom'd trees/And fields which promise corn and wine/And scatter'd cities crowning these/Whose far white walls along them

shine/Have strew'd a scene, which I should see/With double joy wert *thou* with me."

At that time the Rhine romanticism also began to become popular in Germany, especially because of the books written by Brentano, Arnim and Schlegel. Amicable relations were soon established between English and German romanticists. In 1818 appeared Mary Shelley's "Frankenstein or the Modern Prometheus". The plot of the novel has since been used for many a horror film. A physician, Dr Frankenstein, carries out experiments until he eventually creates a humanoid creature. Contrary to the homunculus in Goethe's "Faust", this is a giant

Left, the Rhine in flood near Osterstai. **Above**, it rained cats and dogs when Queen Victoria travelled down the Rhine in 1845.

monster, ugly and frightening. Because everybody finds him repulsive and no-one loves him, he sets out on his murderous rampage.

Frankenstein's trip from Geneva along the Rhine to London had been made by Mary Shelley herself. Her descriptions were thus based on the real, not an imaginary, landscape. In 1842 she enthused about it in the "Rambles" when she described the Rhine Falls at Schaffhausen. "What words can express the feeling excited by the tumult, the uproar and matchless beauty of a cataract, with its eternal, ever-changing, veil of mistry spray..."

Lord Byron saw the Rhine through the eyes of Rousseau - beautiful and uncorrupted. Untamed nature was rejected for a mixture in which - as was the case with the Rhine Falls - delightful and wild, tranquil and lofty beauties fused; it was this very contrast that attracted English writers.

For a time Napoleon's continental blockade had dampened the travel enthusiasm of the English; after 1814 both banks of the Rhine were German territory again and the steamer (the first steamed down the Rhine in 1816) contributed considerably to making the Rhine a tourist attraction once more.

In 1821 the Prussian government introduced the first stage-coach postal service Koblenz-Cologne-Düsseldorf and from 1844 onwards the first railway linked Cologne and Bonn. Travelling thus became less expensive and much more comfortable. Numerous wealthy sons of the merchants, the new aristocracy, travelled down the Rhine.

F.K. Hunt, an author who in 1845 had written a book about the Rhine called: "The Rhine, its Scenery and Historical and Legendary Annunciations" soon became a noted travel author. He praised the rapid travel now possible between London and Cologne: "Cologne is but a day's journey from London; as near as the English Lakes, and nearer than the Highlands of Scotland!...the Grand Tour is no longer the privilege of the few; for steam has thrown down the barrier of cost, and offers to all the teachings of the travel lessons in the Great School of the world ... its brave knight and fair ladies; its ancient warriors, its mischievous... and graceful mermaidens..."

Not all the Englishmen that travelled to the Rhine at the end of the 18th century immediately metamorphosed to Rhine romanticists.

Only those who had definite associations with Rhine romanticism like the Gothic novelists Beckford, Lewis, Radcliffe or landscape poets like Keate and Bowles enthused about the romantic Rhine.

Other 19th century English writers who mentioned the Rhine in their works were Crabb Robinson (1755-1844) and Thomas Campbell (1777-1844).

Robinson was especially keen on the Rhinegau. He was a great friend of Ernst Moritz Arndt and lived with the Brentano family for some time. The war had a decisive influence on Campbell's writings, nevertheless it was primarily the "romantic-picturesque" Germany which Ann Radcliffe and

other authors had popularised and Byron's poems had lauded, that prevailed.

The Rhine was further idealised by Byron in the ballad "The Child and the Hind" and later, once again, in the epic poem "Childe Harold's Pilgrimage": "The river nobly foams and flows/The charm of this enchanted ground /and all its thousand turns disclose/ some fresher beauty varying round/The haughtiest breast its wish might bound/ Through life to dwell delighted here... and later: "Adieu to thee, fair Rhine! How long delighted/The stranger fain would linger on his way/This is a scene alike where souls united/Or lonely contemplation thus might stray/And could the ceaseless vultures cease to prey/On self-condemning bosoms, it were here/where Nature, not too sombre nor too gay/wild but not rude, awful yet not austere/Is to the mellow Earth as Autumn to the year."

Southey, in turn, did not bother with romantic aspects of the Rhine - he had no liking for ruins and castles. Instead he mocked the Catholic beliefs in Saints and legend of the virginous maidens. Not even where it might have been apposite - in his ballad "Roprecht the Robber" - did he make use of Rhine motives.

Other writers resorted to parody - for example Meredith and Thackeray, who jibed at a love story in which a sulphurous devil threatened the city of Cologne. This was probably an allusion to the various odours of the city that many had commented upon adversely.

William Thackeray heaped scorn on the spooky-sentimental legends: "A legend of the Rhine" (1845) mocked the Rhenish legends. Sarcastically he described all those Rhine tourists and sneered at their romantic credulity.

These romanticists who swarmed to the beauty spots to compare what they had seen in their mind's eye with reality were the butt of his wit..."How you see people asleep in the cabins - at the most awakened when they

Byron's chivalrous tales. As a child George Meredith (1828-1909) had attended a denominational boarding school in Neuwied for some some years (1842-1844) and thus had some knowledge of the area and its inhabitants.

In 1857 he published his book "Ferina, A Legend of Cologne" a mixture of parody and Gothic horror. Many associated the name "Ferina" with the well-known "Eau de Cologne". For Meredith, Ferina was the hero of

Left, too much of the sun. **Above**, an engraving of Strasbourg, from a painting by Tombleson.

fire off those stupid guns for the echos!" Thomas Hood (1799-1845) was the most prolific of the Rhine parodists. In his book "Up the Rhine" (1840) he warned all the tourists about the cut-purses that lay in wait everywhere. He even found the landscape mundane. "Why, Tourist, why/The seven Mountains-view? Any one at home can tint/A hill in Prussian blue".

In the mid-19th century, the flood of English travel and illustrated books dealing with the Rhine petered out. Two of the last were "Scenery on the Rhine" by Charles Raleigh Knight and "The Rhine and its picturesque scenery" by Henry Mayhews.

"Ich weiß nicht, was soll es bedeuten,/Daß ich so traurig bin?/Ein Märchen aus uralten Zeiten,/Das kommt mir nicht aus dem Sinn." ("I cannot divine what it meaneth/This haunting nameless pain/A tale of the bygone ages/Keeps brooding through my brain.") That is the first verse of the famous poem *cum* song "The Loreley", which many Germans take to be a traditional folk song, not least because the oeuvre of its author, the Jewish poet Heinrich Heine, was banned during the National Socialist era. This song (set to music by Friedrich Silcher in 1837) was so popular, however, that it just couldn't be prohibited and so the Nazi's simply forbade any mention of the author's name. It is also wrong to think that the famous legend of "The Loreley" is particularly old. The sorceress, this "loveliest maiden, combing her golden hair" who causes "the pitiless billows to engulf the sailor and his bark" is a figment of the romantic poet Clemens Brentano, who probably gleaned the idea from the stories of the Rhenish mermaids on the rock of the Lure Ley, opposite St. Goar.

In the course of his long life, Old Father Rhine has garnered a vast store of legends: beautiful, romantic fairy-tales, exciting, noble sagas and ugly and spiteful legends. One instance of the latter is the story of St. Werner. This Christian youth, thus runs the spiteful lore, was savagely murdered by the Jews in Bacharach. Despite the fact that this anti-semitic story was quite obviously unhistorical, Werner was canonised in due course and the persecution of the Jews intensified immediately. A chapel dedicated to St. Werner was erected on the path leading to ca Stahleck Castle. This chapel can still be seen, albeit as a ruin.

Let us turn to the sagas and lores of genuine heroes. Siegfried, the hero of the *Nibelungenlied* is certainly a case in point. This epic poem, in which actual events are inextricably entwined with legend, is set at various locations along the Rhine. The thirty-nine

Preceding pages: a moonlight view of the Old Castle in Meersburg on Lake Constance. **Left,** the "Loreley", a painting by Eduard Jacob von Steinle (1864).

adventures link the fate of Siegfried as outlined in the *Edda* (a heroic epic dating from the early 13th century) with the downfall of the Rhenish Kingdom of Burgundy during the battles that ensued during the "migration of nations" period. "Uns ist in alten Mären viel Wundersames gesagt" (In ancient tales much wonder prevails) begins the first of more than 2,300 verses, also written in the 13th century, discovered in 1755 in Hohenems Castle on the Alpenrhein. Various sections of the manuscripts are now attributed to copyists and editors. The Romantics declared the *"Nibelungenlied"* the national epic, the German "Illiad". Blond Siegfried became the epitome of the German hero and was a suitable embodiment of Germanic man for the propaganda of the German Nationalists and, especially, the National Socialists. And yet - how splendiferous were his origins.

Siegfried was the son of Siegmund, the powerful King who ruled in Xanten on the Lower Rhine. The young hero went out in search of adventure and travelled up-river. In the land of the Nibelungs he was to assist in subdividing the immense treasure trove among the two sons of the local ruler. As adjudicator he was entrusted with the legendary sword "Balmung". But his decision satisfied neither party, a quarrel ensued, Siegfried slew not only twelve giants but also the young princes and 700 of their followers. From Alberich, the dwarf, he succeeded in wresting the magic helmet that afforded invisibility. Subsequently he appointed Alberich guardian of the treasure. Travelling farther up the Rhine to Königswinter, he witnessed - much to his ire - how the locals led a bound maiden up to the top of the rock as a ritual sacrifice.

On the Drachenfels (dragon's rock) there lived a dragon with a insatiable appetite for virginous maidens. Siegfried climbed the craggy rockface and slew the fearful beast. Bathing in the dragon's blood he became invincible, except for a tiny place between his shoulder-blades where a linden tree leaf had fallen. Returning to Xanten, the maidens and young women tried to woo him but Siegfried had heard that in Worms, the capital city of the Burgundy realm, the beautiful Kriemhild lived, the sister of King Gunther (a historical personage, as it happens) as well as the royal heroes Gernot and Giselher. Siegfried instantly fell head over heels in love with the maiden and together with his companions, he continued his travels up-river to woo the noble Kriemhild. Hagen von Tronje, King Gunther's grim henchman, recognised Siegfried, the Lord over the land and treasure of the Nibelungs and future King of the Netherlands.

Yet a King such as Gunther does not give away a sister that easily. Siegfried first of all had to assist the Burgundians in their wars and acquire a consort for the King. Gunther

tied up her spouse and hanged him on a peg in her bedchamber. Thus Siegfried had to fight for his King a second time. Making use of his magic helmet, he once again over-whelmed the mighty maiden. Thereupon he took the ring and the belt as a token of his victory. Now King Gunther was able to force his lust upon her. Siegfried and Kriemhild travelled to Xanten, where King Siegmund abdicated in favour his son. All's well that ends well?

After an interim of ten years, the story continues! Throughout this time, Brunhild had considered Siegfried to be one of her husband's vassals. While on a family visit in Worms a dispute arose between the two

had heard of the mighty warrior-Queen Brunhild in Iceland and his heart pined for her. They sailed down-river in a sturdy vessel, traversed the seas and Gunther, Siegfried, Hagen and Dankwart reached the castle of Queen Brunhild. She, in turn, was only willing to surrender her maidenhead to a man who could evince greater prowess in jumping, hurling spears, stones and the like. Invisible because of his magic helmet, Siegfried man-aged to deceive the Queen, who deemed herself vanquished by Gunther.

A resplendent double wedding ceremony was duly arranged. While Siegfried and Kriemhild celebrated their nuptials, Brunhild

Queens concerning the question who was allowed to proceed into the Minster first. Who was more royal? Kriemhild accused Brunhild of being her spouse's concubine, as Brunhild had first been wooed by her hus-band Siegfried. To prove her point she showed the ring and the belt.

First tears started flowing, then blood. Hagen wanted to avenge the insult. He ar-ranged a hunting expedition in the Odenwald. Pretending solicitiousness, he asked Kriemhild about the vulnerable spot between Siegfried's shoulder-blades, which she, in her guilelessness, duly marked with dainty embroidery work. When Siegfried wanted to quench his thirst after the tiring hunt and bent over one of the fountains (to this day called *Siegfriedsquellen*) Hagen's spear pierced his back. Kriemhild's suffering was immense as was her desire for revenge. 8,000 vassals were sent to fetch the treasure from the foggy land of the Nibelungs on the Rhine estuary. Twelve huge carts brought the treasure to the ships; three days and three nights it took to load the treasure onto the ships and each cart went to and fro thrice a day. In Worms Kriemhild distributed the treasure to the needy and, in addition, hired many new heroes.

Gunther and Hagen sensed danger. Hagen stole the treasure and cast it in the Rhine. Was it near Lochheim? Was it near the

remained a widow. Then the King of the Huns, Attila, (in the *Nibelungenlied* called Etzel) sought her hand in marriage. Kriemhild moved away from the Rhine and the remainder of the *Nibelungenlied* is not set on the banks of the Rhine. The Burgundians were massacred at the Danube whence they had been invited by the Queen, and Kriemhild was slain too.

The death of the Nibelungs and Burgundians is not the end of the saga however. Siegfried, the dragon slayer, had killed one of the monsters. But eventually another beast on the Drachenfels terrorized the area, again partial to virgin maidens. The heathens, who housed in this region, proffered him a plen-

Bingen Hole? Or did Hagen immerse the Nibelungen treasure near Gernsheim, some distance upriver? Or was it near Germersheim after all, where as late as the 18th century Rhinegold was discovered in the sands of the river? Is the treasure still in the Rhine, waiting to be raised one day, like the legendary treasure of Troy?

Hagen von Tronje, perhaps a descendant of the Royal house of Troy, eventually got his just desserts. For thirteen years Kriemhild

Left, an early morning mist hangs above the Rhine. Above, virgins lying in wait. Was it they who lured the dragon to Drachenfels?

tiful supply of Christian maidens as a repast. One day, the fearful serpent with his baleful breath sidled up to a Christian virgin. From her bodice, the girl took a crucifix which she brandished at the serpent. The dragon took fright, lost his dragon-footing, slid down the mountain face and sank in the waters of the river. The power of the crucifix over the dragon was so convincing that the heathens were instantly converted to Christianity. One of their leaders was Rinbod. He wooed the courageous maid and she immediately consented to his request. And as their residence they built the mighty Drachenburg on the craggy rock.

Just as the sky and clouds are reflected in the river, the history of the peoples and the legends, sagas and fairy-tales recounting love and passion, hatred and vengeance are an integral part of this mighty river.

The Swiss peasants once found consolation in the heroic deeds of one of their compatriots. He lived near Zillis and opposed the local governor. The tyrant wanted to annoy the poor peasant and invited himself to dinner. Scowling at the meagre meal, he spat into the bowl. The peasant got hold of the governor, pressed his face into the bowl and said that he should eat what he had prepared for him. Thereupon he stabbed the governor. All the neighbours sang his praises, the peasants took up arms, stormed the castles of their overlords and slew them one and all.

Not far from Zillis is the once dreaded gorge called the Via Mala. It so happened one day that the local lord of the manor kidnapped a beauteous maiden of lowly birth who was betrothed to a poor but honest man. The peasants gathered in fury and stormed the castle overlooking the gorge, down which the lord wanted to throw himself and the girl. The maiden was freed - and the lord thrown off the cliffs.

The exemplary actions of the courageous men who fought dragons and tyrants became well-known. When news spread that on the banks of Lake Constance there lived a monster, seven brave Swabians set off to liberate their land. Quaking with fear in spite of themselves, they managed to chase the monster away. Spiteful locals soon after claimed that the monster had had long ears and that it had hobbled away.

The common bond of the people on the Rhine is their love for their home country - wherever they originally hailed from. On the Rhine the Romans and the Germanic tribes, the Burgundians and Nibelungs, descendants of the sacked cities of Troy and Jerusalem intermingled.

When the Jews were first dispersed 2,600 years ago, some of these God-fearing people settled in Worms. They had brought sanctified earth from the Holyland along with them, which they mixed into the foundation of the synagogue and the soil of the cemetery. So the Jews had their Jerusalem in Worms on the Rhine. Had the Christians not forgotten the fifth commandment, had they not again and again attacked and killed their fellow men, the region of the Rhine would surely be sacred territory today.

One particularly base man living in this area was Archbishop Hatto of Mainz. He ruled the city with an iron hand. The citizens of the "golden city of Mainz" - some say it was founded by a magician who had been driven out of Trier, others that Moguntius, a hero from Troy - were starving, while Hatto and his followers lived a life of plenty. The famished citizens begged for food, were driven away, persecuted and slaughtered by the bishop. When the people are starving, the mice have nothing to nibble either. The rodents, too, had gathered in Hatto's palace begging for grain. The bishop tried to escape the rodent pest and fled to castle Ehrenfels, and, from there, to the tower on an island in the river - ever since known as Mäuseturm (MouseTower). In Wave after wave swept the mice to the tower. Eventually they attacked Hatto and feasted on him.

Passing the seven hills, where Snow White and the seven dwarfs lived until the prince brought her to his palace, the traveller will come to the sacred city of Cologne, where the bones of the Three Magi are kept as relics. Cologne is also the city of the "Heinzelmännchen" (brownies) who assiduously and secretly helped mankind until the inquisitiveness of a tailor's wife drove the helping spirits away.

The fairy-tales, myths and sagas of the Rhine harbour many a secret. One such is the legend of the Swan knight of Cleves. Here lived Elsa von Brabant, who had lost both her parents and her brother. The evil Telramund had cast a beady eye on her wealth. Elsa prayed for the help of a knight, who promptly arrived in a bark drawn by a white swan. The Swan Knight drove Telramund away, fell in love with Elsa and married her.

Never was she allowed to ask whence he had come. For many years they and their three children lived happily but eventually the uncertainty of her husband's origin plagued Elsa so much that she posed the forbidden question. A bark immediately drew nigh, pulled by a swan, and Lohengrin, the Knight of the Holy Grail, disappeared forever.

Right, Hagen disposes of the Nibelungen treasure; an engraving by Julius Schnorr von Carolsfeld (1843).

 Ê daz der künec rîche
wider wære komen,

die wîle hete Hagene
den schaz vil gar genomen.

er sancte in dâ ze Lôche
allen in den Rîn.

er wande er solde in niezen:
des enkunde niht gesîn.

A Literary Survey of The Rhine

"The Rhine combines everything. The Rhine is swift as the Rhone, wide as the Loire, deeply embanked like the Meuse, winding as the Seine, limpid and green as the Somme, historic as the Tiber, royal as the Danube, mysterious as the Nile, spangled with gold like a river of America, covered with fables and phantoms like a river of Asia."

These beautiful thoughts were written in 1838 by the French novelist Victor Hugo (1802-1885). Not only Hugo was fascinated and inspired by the Rhine. Many illustrious names are linked with the splendid river. The cities along its banks brought forth famous and not so famous authors, others came just to see it and all had to write about it. Bettina von Arnim, Johann Wolfgang von Goethe, Heinrich Heine, Thomas Mann, René Schickele, Carl Zuckmayer, Heinrich Böll - a long list of those who, each in their own way, have immortalised the river in their oeuvre.

Even Julius Caesar (100-44 B.C.) had found time, in spite of his conquests, to write about the Rhine and the Germanic tribes living there. In his book "Commentarii de bello Gallico" he lists the peoples and tribes that lived along the Rhine: "The Rhine rises in the country of the Lepontii, who live in the Alps, and flows swiftly for a great distance through the territories of the Nantuates, the Helvetii, the Squani, the Mediomatrici, the Triboci and the Treveri. As it comes near the Ocean it divides into a number of tributaries, forming many very large islands ...and finally flows into the Ocean by several different mouths." Apart from the names of the inhabitants living there, the description of the course of the Rhine holds true to the present day.

No longer topical, in fact better forgotten because it is detrimental for international understanding, is the so-called "war of the poets" that excited the nations in the 19th century. The disputes triggered in 1812 by

Left, the Nobel Laureate, Heinrich Böll, demonstrating against the deployment of nuclear weapons in Mutlangen in Autumn 1983. Böll died in 1985.

German bards centres around the Rhine as a symbol of traditional enmity between the Germans and the French.

Max von Schenkendorff (1783-1817) an occasional, albeit secondary, poet full of nationalistic ire during the Napoleonic occupation wrote the "Song of the Rhine" in 1814, in which he claimed that the Rhine was a wholly German river and at the same time castigated the French for "scorching the soil of the revered Palatinate".

After Schenkendorff's death, the poet and publicist Ernst Moritz Arndt (1769-1860) wrote the following verses in homage: "Er hat vom Rhein/Er hat vom deutschen Land/ Er hat vom welschen Tand/richtig geklungen"

(He sounded true about the Rhine/He sounded true about the land/He saw no reason yet to praise/the Frenchies' dastardly forays). Arndt, who published such jingoistic propaganda throughout his life, wrote a slogan on a pamphlet in 1813 that subsequently gained notoriety: "Der Rhine - Teutschlands Strom, aber nicht Teutschlands Gränze" (The Rhine - Germany's river but not Germany's boundary). The poet demanded, couched in "romantic nationalism", that language and customs alone should be the criteria for what constitutes "Germany".

From this linguistic nationalism derived the claim for possession of Alsace and Lorraine. Another contemporary poet who made use of the Rhine for his own dubious political ends was Joseph Görres (1776-1848). Initially a fervent adherent of the French revolution, he soon renounced his high-flying ideals and published anti-Napoleon diatribes in the "*Rheinische Merkur*". In his francophile adolescence he had spoken of the Rhine as constituting France's border. Now, after his volte-face, he saw the matter from an ideological point of view. From the source to the estuary it constituted the "German frontier, the river itself is the moat, the Alps and the man-made consolidations in the Netherlands are the bastions and citadels" - against France and the French, of course.

Around 1840 the "war of the poets" culminated, after the French side picked up the gauntlet. Nikolaus Becker (1809-1845) who hailed from Bonn had written the notorious verse: "Sie sollen ihn nicht haben, den freien deutschen Rhein" (They shall not have it, the free German Rhine) - to which the French poet Alphonse de Lamartine (1790 - 1869) promptly replied with the "peaceful Marseillaise" by means of which the poet wanted to ask for tolerance among the nations. Alfred de Musset (1810-1857) in turn jibed at the German pretences: "We've had it, your "German" Rhine!" Max von Schneckenburger (1819-1849) published the "Wacht am Rhein" in 1840 - not much more than a jingoistic battle cry - full of Germanic sound and fury, signifying nothing.

Heinrich Heine (1797-1856) was born in Düsseldorf but, after his studies in Bonn and other German cities, he chose to live in France. He thought less than nothing of the pseudo-literary drivel about German-French enmity and countered that neither the Germans nor the French nationalists could lay claim to the Rhine - the only ones justified to do so were the Rhinelanders themselves. Heine's poetic cycle: "Deutschland - Ein Wintermärchen" recounts a conversation between the author and Old Father Rhine. The object of Father Rhine's complaint is primarily the above-mentioned poem by Nikolaus Becker: "Zu Bibrich hab ich Steine verschluckt/Wahrhaftig, sie schmeckten nicht lecker!/Doch schwerer liegen im Magen mir/Die Verse von Niklas Becker/.../Wenn ich es höre, das dumme Lied/Dann möchte ich mir zerraufen/Den weißen Bart, ich möchte fürwahr/Mich in mir selbst ersaufen!"

(I swallowed stones near Bibrich, they were no dainty morsel, but far more indigestible are the verses by Niklas Becker. When I hear that stupid song/I'd like to tweak my white beard/and actually drown in myself)

Apart from ironic political poems, Heine also wrote romantic poetry: "Berg und Burgen schaun herunter/In den spiegel-hellen Rhein/Und mein Schiffchen segelt munter/Rings umglänzt von Sonnenschein/.../Freundlich grüßend und verheißend/Lockt hinab des Stromes Pracht/Doch ich kenn ihn, oben gleißend/Birgt sein Innres Tod und Nacht" (Hills and castles look down/on the mirroring Rhine/and my little bark sails merrily/steeped in sunshine /.../greeting me joyfully and enticingly/the splendour of the stream beckons/but I know it - entrancing on the surface/beneath lurks death and night). Heine's "Rabbi von Bacharach" affords the reader a wonderful description of the power and the glory of the Rhenish landscape.

The philosopher Friedrich Nietzsche (1844-1900) was impressed by the Rhine too. In a lecture dating from 1872 he recalled a trip down the Rhine when he was a student. "Suddenly refreshing, breathless solace of nature! The shadows had already lengthened and from the green, sparkling waves of the Rhine, a slight breeze wafted our hot faces."

Karl Simrock (1802-1876), another author who studied in Bonn, wrote a book about the Rhineland: "Wanderungen durch das Rheinland" (Hikes through the Rhineland). "What is it that has this magical effect on the mind? Is it the scent of the vines ...or the noble spirit of the wine...? Or are we wafted by the fresh breeze from the Rhine valley, the bracing alpine air, that hails from the glaciers? Is it the majestic...river itself, with its clear, green waves...that course from Switzerland to Holland? Is it the historical recollection or the old, familiar legends?" Simrock continued in this vein for many pages, trying to fathom the magic of the Rhine.

The greatest German classicist, Johann Wolfgang von Goethe (1749-1832), of course felt the urge to describe the Rhine and its beauties (not least the female beauties he encountered there) too. While staying in the area, Goethe had not only fallen in love with Friederike Brion, the daughter of a local priest from Sesenheim, but had also studied in Strasbourg.

In 1797, many years after his salad days, Goethe wrote in his diary about the Rhine Falls at Schaffhausen: "I travelled along the right Rhine embankment; on the right lay beautiful vine-covered hills and gardens, the river gushed across rocky shallows. Continuing farther upriver, I saw in the evening sun the Rhine Falls from the top and behind...face to face with it is a splendid, but conceivable, wholly interesting...scene of nature: the river gushes past noisily, and then cascades down." Goethe never forgot the

Rhine, the beautiful river was always a source of inspiration for him. It is mentioned in "The Feast of St Roch at Bingen" in the Rhine Hymn "*Mahomets Gesang*" as well as in other, smaller poems.

A contemporary of Goethe, who must also be counted a classicist, was Karoline von Günderode (1780-1806). She was born in the area and committed suicide in Winkel im Rheingau, aged only twenty-six. She wrote to Bettina Brentano (1785-1859), whose family lived in Winkel: "If one's alone on the Rhine, then one becomes quite melancholy." It wasn't actually the Rhine that made her sad, rather it was an unfortunate love affair

Left, the great German poet and publisher Heinrich Heine (1797-1856). Above, René Schickele, a writer from Alsace, a mediator between French and German culture.

which caused her to stab herself on the banks of the Rhine.

Karoline von Günderode, Bettina Brentano - later the wife of the poet Achim von Arnim (1781-1831) - as well as other poets and authors are known in German literary history as the "Heidelberger Romanticists". This was a group of authors whose work associated them closely with the Rhine. The river was not only the subject matter of lofty poetry; there were also numerous drinking songs and ditties in praise of its noble wines.

Matthias Claudius (1740-1815) whose songs and poems are a constant delight because of their child-like effusiveness, wrote the following song in praise of Rhenish

wine: "Bekränzt mit Laub, den lieben, vollen Becher/Und trinkt ihn fröhlich leer!/.../In ganz Europa, Ihr Herren Zecher/Ist solch ein Wein nicht mehr!/.../Am Rhein, am Rhein da wachsen unsre Reben/.../Da wachsen sie am Ufer hin and geben/Uns diesen Labewein/.../und wüßten wir, wo jemand traurig läge/Wir gäben ihm diesen Wein". (Garland the wondrous, brimful goblet with vines/and quaff it cheerfully/There's nothing like it anywhere, gentlemen throughout Europe/On the Rhine where our vines grow/affording us this soothing wine/And if we knew where someone pined/we would hand him this wine).

If the Rhine wine gladdens the heart, then perhaps Old Father Rhine might like a sip himself - considering the state of the polluted water, he must be quite depressed. Indeed Old Father Rhine is said to be quite a melancholy soul, as Joseph Victor von Scheffel (1826-1886) wrote in his epic "Der Trompeter von Säckingen" (The trumpet player from Säckingen): "Und wenn ich im Sand von Holland/Müd'die müden Wellen schleppe/Und die Windmühle trocken klappert/.../Und es tönt ein dumpfes Rauschen/Weithin durch die kahlen Felder/Weit hinaus bis an die Nordsee/Aber keiner dort versteht mich/.../Und im Sand, den ich so tödlich/Hasse, schlepp ich müd' mein Dasein/Und ich bin schon lang gestorben/Eh'das Meeresgrab mich aufnimmt". (And when to the sands of Holland/I drag my tired waves/And the windmill creaks dryly/.../And a muffled hissing/resounds through the bare fields/far away to the North Sea/No-one understands me/.../And through the sand/which fills me with such deadly hate/I drag my tired existence/And I died long before/The sea, my grave, enfolds me). This sad sigh of a proud river, shaken by grief because its majesty must, perforce, flow into the North Sea, does that not tug at your heart-strings?

The tears of sympathy shed for the Rhine might turn to tears of laughter, if one reads the adventures of the Rhinelander Felix Krull. Thomas Mann (1875-1955), the author of the "Confessions of the Imposter Felix Krull" has his eponymous hero say: "The Rhinegau bore me - that favoured tract of land, surely one of the most delightful spots in the inhabited world, mild and without roughness in terms of both weather and soil, richly provided with towns and villages and cheerfully populated."

Carl Zuckmayer (1895-1977) was born of a wine merchant in Nackenheim and attended school in Mainz. His play "Der fröhliche Weinberg" (the cheerful vineyard) is set in the Rhine-Hessen region. This somewhat raunchy comedy is in sharp contrast to what Heinrich Böll (1917-1985) who hailed from Cologne wrote about the river. "I am ready to believe anything of the Rhine; but I have never been able to believe in its summer serenity. I have looked for this serenity but never found it; My Rhine is dark and melancholy; it is too much a river of tradesmanlike cunning for me to believe in its summer-like young man's face..."

Kurt Tucholsky (1890-1935) just like Böll criticized the conditions prevalent in Germany. The target of his satires were the political conditions during the time of the Weimar Republic. At a relatively early date he sounded a warning about the rise of the Nazis. In one of the satires mocking the debates after the First World War concerning the question of whether or not the Rhineland should become autonomous, the Rhine bridge in Cologne was the crux: "There is a big railway bridge that crosses the Rhine. Cars and trains cross this bridge because it's on the route to Paris. This bridge has seen quite a bit of traffic or rather trafficking ...all those millions of banknotes with which the Rhineland was flooded so that it wouldn't become autonomous...it was quite an auction; Paris made an offer, and the autonomists made one, so did Prussia, poor as it was..and when the hammer fell, it turned out that Prussia had once again won the bid for the Rhineland...Yes, below this bridge flows Father Rhine; transfused by legends, garlanded with *kitsch* ..." Tucholsky, who watched these events with trepidation, was ultimately so horrified about the developments in Germany during the Nazi era that he committed suicide while in exile in Sweden.

The Alsatian author René Schickele (1883-1944) wanted to mediate between the Germans and the French, which, because of his birth place, he was predestined for. His trilogy "The heritage of the Rhine" he called "Evolutionary Novel of a country". The left bank region of Alsace was to be the cradle of a new, peaceful spirit: "The level street jutted straight into the Haardtwald, as if it had been a park, and the Rhine forest did indeed resemble an overgrown park with its mass of trees...A certain, conscious solemnity, a touch of barely visible architecture distinguished it from all other forests of the country...At the end of the remaining, fairly steep, section of the street flowed the Rhine...On a day like this the people might well come from either bank of the Rhine and recognise each other as brothers and sisters...torrentially the dark green Rhine flowed, bearing along great loads of sunshine..."

Left, Karoline von Gunderode (1780 - 1806), a German writer, committed suicide on the Rhine. **Above**, Anna Seghers (1900 - 1983) was born in the city of Mainz.

The hope that the Germans and French would settle their differences and become friends remained unfulfilled for a long time. The barbarous era that soon started in Germany after the publication of Schickele's trilogy drove many, including the novelist Anna Seghers (1900-1983) into exile.

Anna Seghers was born in Mainz. After her university studies in Cologne, she joined the German Communist Party. This and the fact that her father was Jewish would have sufficed for her to be arrested in 1933. Anna Segher emigrated that same year. In 1957 she wrote: "I hail from the Rhine and every day I regarded the Rhine with envy because in Holland it would suffuse with the sea."

The Rhine played a central role in her life and oeuvre. In her novel "The Seventh Cross" seven convicts escape from a concentration camp on the left bank of the Rhine, and, after a long Odyssey, the river is eventually the men's route to Holland, the gateway to liberty.

The desire to see the Rhine free from Nationalism, was the common bond of literary men in the neighbouring countries for centuries. The river was symbol for some, for others it was a medium to further understanding among peoples. Some love it for the wines, others because of its romantic charm. Its fascination continues to the present day.

FROM THE SOURCES TO THE ESTUARY

When the writers of antiquity wanted to define the length of the Rhine, they usually resorted to quoting Ptolomy, the Greek geographer, although he, too, must have made different calculations in his time, because the statistics he cites for the length of the Rhine vary from 550 to 1100 kilometres. Meanwhile, as the "Rhine studies" in the Rhine museum in Koblenz document, the official length has been determined as 1237.6 kilometres.

For the section from the Alps to Lake Constance it is 163.0 kilometres, from Lake Constance to Konstanz it is 43.0 kilometres and from there to the North Sea estuary 1031.6 kilometres.

The sources at St Gotthard: Now that the question of the length of the Rhine has been settled, we must decide on its source - or rather sources. No easy matter, as it happens.

Many a school textbook mentions Lake Thoma as source and thus considers the Vorderrhein (Rhaeto-Romanisch Rein Anteriur) the sole source. Others, in turn, point to the Hinterrhein (Rhaeto-Romanisch Rein Posteriur) below the Paradise Glacier on the eastern face of the Rheinwaldhorn (Mt Adula). This confused history of the sources might well be symptomatic for the river itself, which, in its subsequent course was always embroiled in dispute and could never be wholly claimed by one or the other political camp. Let us, however, agree on there being two sources - the Vorder- and the Hinterrhein - as well as the other more or less significant inflows from the St. Gotthard massif.

Let us examine the source area of the Vorderrhein - the glacial edge between Lake Thoma and Lake Curnera: here the "Rein da Maighels" flows from the glacier mouth. This region is wild and unruly, not tamed as is the case with the Main and the Danube, which have a precisely locatable source, or even the Seine, where the source is in fact marked by a grotto. No, in the case of the Rhine what we have is untrammelled nature,

Preceding pages: a bird's eye view of the Rhine, Cologne Cathedral at carnival time, a mixed choir from Stein am Rhein. **Left**, Black Forest costume.

when it springs forth from the inner ice fields as a milky-green glacial rivulet and cascades down to the valley. Here, in the solitude of Graubünden, there is, as yet, no inkling of the noise and dirt that will be associated later on with the Rhine.

The Hinterrhein - its source is 35 kilometres away from the Vorderrhein, and both are 2,345 meters above sea level - hardly changes course until it is dammed at Sufers. It now flows from east to north and cuts its way through the *Roflaschlucht* (Rofla Gorge). And soon we come to the Via Mala (literally "Evil Road") one of the most famous ravines in the world. The Via Mala, situated between Schams and Domleschg, is six kilometres

the gory story of a bibulous woodmill owner who for years terrorized his family in a truly despicable fashion - so much so, in fact, that one night the whole family conspires to murder him. And yet... who may presume to dabble in, what should the rights be, divine retribution? Even the murder of a monster is a monstrous act - especially for the woodmill owner's daughter Sylvia who, as storyteller's imagination would have it, marries the very lawyer in charge of investigating the case. (John Knittel's novel is generally deemed to be a masterpiece popular fiction and has been adapted for a number of cinema and TV films. Since the first publication of the novel in 1934 it has enjoyed innumerable

long, and the chasm goes down to a depth of 600 metres at one point. The traveller may still shudder if his gaze travels up the craggy rock face or down at the tumultuous cauldron of the Hinterrhein.

What must the Romans then have felt when they saw this awe-inspiring sight? When they had got to this forbidding region, they chose to level a path high above the gorge, leading from the Heinzenberg to the Schamserberg. In 1473 the first road through the gorge was built.

This was the inspiration for John Knittel (1891-1970) to write his novel "Via Mala" (1934). This perennial bestseller recounts

editions and has been translated into several languages). The present road that leads through the Via Mala was built by the citizens of Graubünden in 1822 and the spooky ambience is clearly an ideal setting for a story of crime and passion.

With gorges such as this, nature shows its awful power. Through the course of millenia the combined forces of water, frost and wind have pounded and eroded the rockface to create the bizarre rock forms that can be seen today.

We now come to the point where the Vorder- and Hinterrhein fuse to form the Rhine proper - the valley area of the Imboden, below Castle Reichenau, which is built on a chalk layer created by the Flimser landslide, and towers above the surrounding countryside. The Imboden, the valley between Bonaduz and Chur is a fertile region, the soil being the rich infil provided by several landslides. The land is not only highly suitable for arable farming but it is also ideal for the cultivation of fruit trees.

Before the Rhine proper starts, the Vorderrhein has had to overcome a height difference of 25 metres per kilometre. Along its 70 kilometres course it drops from 2,345 to 1,750 metres above sea level. The Hinterrhein falls the same amount in the even shorter distance of 61 kilometres, and thus gathers

Bregenz. Lake Constance is also the final destination for the immense mass of debris and silt carried along by the Alpenrhein.

200 years ago the estuary was an extensive area of marsh and bogland; the snow-melt and the resultant high water phases in spring and early summer caused the river to constantly change its course and flood. Only a few marsh and reed areas as well as peat bogs remain. In 1834 dams were constructed and around the turn of the century the unruly Rhine was "regulated". Since then it has flowed along a man-made, 120 to 200 metre wide riverbed, which even partly runs above the level of the surrounding land.

In the "bathtub Lake Constance" the eco-

considerably more force to dig deeply into the mountain range, as is proved so impressively by the Via Mala gorge.

Lake Constance: Lake Constance has been termed a huge, water-filled bathtub. The main source of water supply is, of course the Rhine, which, after the sources have combined, flows past such historic towns and regions as Chur, the Principality of Liechtenstein or the monastery city St. Gallen, before flowing into the "Swabian Ocean" at

Left, a promenade on the Rhine in winter. **Above**, the same promenade some weeks later at the time of the spring floods.

logical system still functions, despite all human interference. The ecology is worth looking at in some detail. Both in and around the lake there are a number of biological processes at play, which all interact to promote ecological stability. Nutritives, water and oxygen flow into the lake from many inflows - the most important of which is the Rhine itself.

Lake Constance is divided into two distinct parts, the "Obersee" and the much smaller "Untersee" to the west of Konstanz. In ecological terms they vary greatly. The Obersee is not only larger but also much deeper. It is termed an oligotrophic body of water; near the surface, it is virtually devoid of nutritive substances, whereas at a deeper level the oxygen supply is plentiful. The Untersee is eutrophic, i.e. productive on the surface level and without much oxygen at a lower level. The fact that the Untersee is considerably shallower means that organic substances can reach right down to the bed of the lake and consume most of the available oxygen.

Ecologically, the nature reserves of Lake Constance are jewels of great price: The Wollmatinger Ried near Konstanz is a paradise for curlews and cattle egrets, souchet shovelers, terns and nightingales. The Mettnau pond is considered the best water-

When the Rhine takes leave of Lake Constance shortly before Stein am Rhein, it does so at an average rate of 365 cubic metres of water per second.

The Rhine Falls at Schaffhausen: Here, at the largest waterfall in Europe, the Rhine proffers a final grandiose natural spectacle before its riverbed takes on a virtually interchangeable, modern physiognomy.

Victor Hugo wrote in 1839: "The Rhine Falls roar like a tiger - terrible noise, frightening cascades, water dust, smoke and rain simultaneously. At one of the most frightful spots on the Falls, a huge boulder appears and disappears again and again - like the skull of a drowning giant who has had to

fowl area on Lake Constance: red-crested- and common pochards, tufted ducks and gadwalls are found in abundance. In 1975 the nature preserve Mindelsee was included in the list of the most important international biotopes. It offers crested grebes, black kites and barn owls a suitable habitat. One could continue this list to include rare flora. In the past years much has been done to improve the ecology of Lake Constance. A decrease in the amount of phosphates discharged into the lake, largely due to a phosphate reduction in washing powders, has led to a considerable improvement in the water quality compared to the 1960s.

undergo this terrible torture for the past 6,000 years."

The Rhine Falls at Schaffhausen now provide a favourite excursion area. A boat will take you right up to the Falls, but its more fun to walk along the path from Castle Lauffen.

15,000 years ago the Rhine flowed diagonally to its present course - right below the rapids. Apparently its present course is the result of an "error". After an ice age the river could no longer find its original riverbed. Huge moraines blocked its path. Meanwhile this former riverbed has been discovered - 500 metres away. These days the river - the width is 160 metres at this point - falls 23 metres. Every second, 600 cubic metres of foaming water chunnel between four limestone cliffs in five separate rapids.

Poets and philosophers have praised the Falls - enthusiastically or tepidly, as the case may be. Goethe was subdued in his praise. He regarded his description to be more of an exercise in diary writing and quotes a Frenchman who said that this was all very well but it wasn't quite as beautiful as everybody said it was. Nevertheless he penned an impressive description: "More splendid was the kaleidoscope of colours at sunset, although the movement of the water also suddenly seemed to become more rapid, wilder and more tumultuous. Slight gusts of wind

At the level of Basle, the "High Rhine" turns north and begins its long course through the the Upper Rhine Plain. In Basle the Rhine becomes an "industrial river" - a description that can be used until its waters finally disperse in the North Sea. For Basle itself the river has long become an indispensable lifeline. In 1832 the first steamer docked here, and in 1904 the first train of barges - suitably welcomed by pealing bells.

The city is home to one of the highest concentrations of chemical factories in Europe. The concentration of chemicals in the Rhine is said to have decreased in recent years, although the explosion at Sandoz in 1986 illustrated just how vulnerable the river

caused more crinkles in the seams of the cascading foam, mists seemed to combat each other violently, and because the awe-inspiring spectacle remained steadfastly the same, the viewer feared to succumb to the excess and expected a catastrophe at any moment." That was in September 1797, but about 200 years later it is still a wonderfully apposite description of one of the glories of the Rhine.

Left and above, the arts flourish along the Rhine: a symphony orchestra tunes its instruments and a restorer puts the finishing touches to an afternoon's work.

still is. It hasn't yet fully recovered from this particular disaster.

The Upper Rhine Plain: Below Basle, where industry is less prevalent, the river has been "technologized" in a different fashion. At kilometre 173 the Rhine is dammed up by a weir, and the water is diverted off to a Rhine canal. During dry periods the river is not much more than a trickle, from here right up to Breisach, while the water on the French side flows along the "Grand Canal d'Alsace". This canal is more than ten metres deep and 150 metres wide.

The Upper Rhine Plain is blessed with the mildest climate in Germany. The annual average temperature is 10.3 degrees Centigrade and is thus 1.2 degrees higher than the German average, the result of the fact that the low-lying basin affords protection from strong winds and that the slopes of the vine-clad hills are bathed in sun.

A plentiful supply of important natural resources is to be found in the region. On either side of the Rhine there are deposits of potassium salt formed around 50 million years ago when the ocean which was once here began to dry out. In Alsace the exploitation of the salt deposits started before the Second World War; in Baden, on the right bank of the Rhine, after the War. Farther north in the middle section of the Upper

tryside and the people who live in the Upper Rhine Plain is concerned. Life is pleasant here - the toils and tribulations of the past, with the bogs, high water and the floods are now no more, although in recent years the Upper Rhine Plain has had its fair share of modern environmental problems.

The Rhenish Uplands: At the level of Mainz and Wiesbaden the Rhine begins to flow through the Rheinische Schiefergebirge (Rhenish Uplands) - through the Rhinegau, the hills of the Taunus, which drop down to the river between Wiesbaden and Rüdesheim. Here sweet-chestnut and almond trees flourish as does as a particularly noble wine. Near Bingen at the Nahe estuary, the Rhine forces

Rhine Plain, oil and gas deposits have been found near Pechelbronn in Alsace as well as in the region of Karlsruhe and Heidelberg right up to Darmstadt.

Despite the mild climate - already in the first weeks of April the almond and peach trees are in blossom, soon followed by cherry and plum trees; the cherries are harvested in early June - in the wintertime, while the sun shines in the upper reaches of the Black Forest and the Vosges, the left and right banks of the Rhine are often shrouded in fog and it is frequently very cold.

Yet in spite of this, the Rhine has made a good choice as far as the climate, the coun-

its way through the Bingen Hole into a (self-made) terraced, narrow valley, 100 kilometres long all the way to Bonn. Because of its numerous reefs, Bingen Hole used to be perilous for shipping. Meanwhile quite a number of reefs have been dynamited to enable an easier passage. On both sides of the Rhine, the rockfaces rise steeply to a height of 300 metres. At the same time the Rhine narrows to a width of 115 metres at the Loreley. The depth at this point is an impressive 26 metres. It is this unique geological constellation that has, over the centuries, provided the inspiration for so many sagas and folk tales. The romantic Rhine.

Beyond Koblenz the mountain ranges start to recede and the remainder of the stretch up to Bonn is scenically no longer as interesting as the preceding stretch from Wiesbaden. The Neuwied Basin begins to take over. It is a level and fertile area formed around 50 million years ago with immense pumice deposits, useful as the primary ingredient in the production of artificial bricks for the construction industry.

When the Rhine enters the Lower Rhine Plain below the confluence of the Ahr, the river passes the last mountain range on its journey to the sea: the Siebengebirge (seven hills), a group of hills consisting mainly of basalt outcrops, with the famous Drachenfels

Rhine knows that he is now old, tired and that his end is imminent.

"He is the most powerful ruler of the Lowlands" wrote the geologist Albert Kardas. "Long before man built hamlets and cities along his banks, his incessant modelling had helped to shape the contours of the Lower Rhine region. As the river winds its way across the plain with enormous force, he not only jostles the waters into the sea, but he also drags and rolls debris, masses of gravel and sands along, to deposit everything somewhere: gravel and stones from the Rhenish mountains, white quarz pebbles and sandstone from the Rhenish Uplands, bright-red, black and yellowy pebble slate from the

- perhaps the most-climbed mountain in Germany. When the river reaches Bonn it bids farewell to the mountainous and hilly landscape that has accompanied it for hundreds of kilometres.

Lower Rhine, the Estuary and the North Sea: Below Bonn the Rhine changes. Nothing remains of the unruly splendour of the Alps, nothing of the acrid elegance in the narrow ravines of the Rhenish Uplands. As if Father

Left, business transactions complete at a horse market in Stein am Rhein (Switzerland). **Above**, the cabbage harvest on the island of Reichenau, Lake Constance.

Lahn, Main, Mosel and Neckar region, red iron ore stone from the Taunus, porphyre and melaphyre from the Nahe, trachyt from the Drachenfels, granite from the Black Forest and Odenwald, black basalt from the Siebengebirge, sandstone from the Ruhr and sundry other matter".

Near Millingen, to the north of Emmerich, the Rhine reaches the Netherlands - and immediately divides into the river arms Waal and Lek. Here the Rhine Delta starts. Man's increasing interference with the natural flow of the Rhine becomes more and more apparent - not only has the river been canalised and diverted, he has even been re-named.

MAX VON DER GRÜN: THE RHINELANDERS

No river has been celebrated in as many drinking and love songs as "Father" Rhine, which the Dutch rather curiously call Waal. On the banks of the Rhine lived the Celts, here dwelt the Nibelungen and of course the Romans, who established their famous *Limes* to protect their empire from the threat of the German hordes. Behind them they built what for the times were large towns such as Colonia, present-day Cologne, and military camps such as Xanten on the Lower Rhine which has been excavated and splendidly reconstructed.

From their warm homeland the Romans however brought something else with them for which we are still grateful today: wine.

And the wine led inevitably to the proverbial Rhineland jollity, or rather carefreeness. The revered German poet Heinrich Heine, himself a Rheinlander, wrote: "The Rhine wine still shines with a golden light in its green rummer glass as before; and if you should chance to drink too much, of its punishment you may be sure".

During my life I have probably travelled by train along the Rhine several hundred times, and even though I normally read during the journey, on the stretch from Koblenz to Mainz or vice versa, however, I put aside my book or magazine and look out of the window. I enjoy the view, the river, the vineyards and the castles. Then the much-praised Rhine romanticism takes hold of me, and I imagine, at least for a brief hour, that it still exists.

And yet the Rhine has become one of the busiest rivers in the world - an industrial stream par excellence, an economic factor that is not to be underestimated. Goods of all kinds are transported on the river, from Basle downriver, from Rotterdam upriver and sometimes there actually seem to be more ships on the river than there is water in the river bed.

The banks of the Rhine and its tributaries are home not only to vineyards but to industrial centres of gargantuan proportions; giant chemical concerns, huge automobile factories, machine plants and suchlike, from Basle to Rotterdam - the biggest oil port in Europe - or Duisburg Ruhrort, the largest river port in the world, where more freight is loaded and unloaded annually than in the international port of Hamburg.

The Rhine has long lost its innocence, and years ago a satirist wrote caustically: Who would choose to commit suicide by drowning in a sewer? This might sound trifle exaggerated, but the terrible catastrophe of 1986, when a Basle chemical company released tons of poison into the river, killing all the fish and polluting the adjoining fields as far as Holland, was to justify this biting comment. Fauna and flora perished, and farmers could no longer let their cows graze in the Rhine meadows.

Neither are the atomic power plants, whether in France or the Federal Republic of Germany, exactly calculated to foster Rhine romanticism. The powerful industrial works starting at Basle, Strasbourg and Karlsruhe, and continuing to Ludwigshafen, the Mannheim area, Mainz and Koblenz, to Cologne, Düsseldorf, Duisburg and into the Netherlands, are visible evidence of the economic importance of this German - indeed, of this European - waterway.

But still we sing with fervour: "Why is the Rhine so beautiful...?", still sing the musical version of Heinrich Heine's poem "Loreley": "I cannot divine what it meaneth/This haunting nameless pain/A tale of the bygone ages/Keeps brooding through my brain."

Not even the fanatical racists of the Third Reich were able to suppress this popular song; they merely made an alteration, in order to destroy the memory of Heine, the great German poet; and Heine, the unloved Jew. Beneath the poem in the song books they just printed the words: "Author unknown". I still have such a copy in my bookcase, a prime example of total stupidity and hostility towards culture.

Rhine romanticism will probably also continue to be cultivated, and the numerous castles and ruins above the sloping vineyards or rising from steep banks will also help keep

Left, every town or village has its own annual fair or wine festival. Crowds line the street as a band parades.

it intact; on both sides of the river they somehow manage to convey the impression that we are still living in the age of chivalry and that some enchanting creature will wave to us with her handkerchief from the tower window. This stimulates the longing for an allegedly better age that we today succinctly call nostalgia. It is thus as if we were visiting a legendary castle with a mixture of curiosity and trepidation, of admiration and a pleasurable shudder of fear.

From a boat travelling upstream or downstream the towers and domes of churches and cathedrals rise to view on either side of the river: Strasbourg and Freiburg (the highest church tower in the world),

Today it is both; in its upper reaches it is a border, and as the Middle and Lower Rhine it is a German river. The Dutch, as I have already said, simply call it the Waal.

In no way can one lump all the people who live along the Rhine into one pot by referring to them as Rhinelanders; today these are only the people living along the Lower Rhine. Along the banks of the river too live the people of Baden, Alsace, Württemberg, Hessen, the Palatinate and the Ruhr, who see themselves only partly as Rhinelanders; all of them have their own particular characteristics, dialect and distinctive mentality.

The people of Alsace are in addition marked by the fact that in the long and varied history

Mainz, Speyer and Worms of course, the Nibelung and the imperial towns, Koblenz, and, not to be omitted, what is probably the most-visited sacred building: Cologne Cathedral. This is not counting the many sacred buildings of the less famous places which undoubtedly deserve to be better known...

For centuries the Rhine was an object of political conflict, and this has undoubtedly had an influence on the character of the people who live along its banks: it was always a contested border. In the last century Ernst Moritz Arndt adopted a nationalistic stance when he proclaimed: The Rhine is Germany's river, not Germany's border.

of Europe they belonged several times to Germany and several times to France. They kept chopping and changing between the two, depending on which power happened to be on the rise. As Frenchmen they felt and spoke German, as Germans they inclined towards France, but though the greater majority today still speak German, or rather Alsatian, this differs considerably from the German dialect spoken on the opposite bank of the river.

Their excellent cuisine is of international renown, and gourmet restaurants world-wide try to lure away their chefs. When this is not possible they are happy to borrow them for a week or two; then, far from Alsace, there are Alsace weeks, where guests from all over the world are provided with the opportunity of sampling culinary Alsatian delights prepared by genuine Alsatian cooks.

Nowhere else in Germany are there so many gourmet restaurants (I am just going to disrespectfully call them eating joints) concentrated into such a small area as on either side of the Upper Rhine. Whether we are in Alsace or on the German side - in the Black Forest or on the Upper Rhine Plain which runs along its western flanks under the conical peak known as the Kaiserstuhl - here we come back to real culture, for, as everywhere else in the world, real culture begins with

to experience such enjoyment one does not necessarily have to splash out by going to a three-star restaurant.

At the wine festivals which take place in all the towns and villages in the autumn months, one obviously encounters many visitors who understand little or nothing about wine. In their case, as Heinrich Heine explains, the juice of the grape does not only tickle their noses but makes their heads thump too; but they can all sing, if not beautifully then loudly, and if not melodically, then at least out of tune. The main thing was to have been there, to have had a good time, whatever the glass or the bottle might have cost, since the next day one can easily convince those

food. Even the fast-food chains have been unable to get rid of it, and they will not, thank goodness, be able to do so in the future either; many people today have gone back to the way of thinking that eating is not something that can be measured and weighed by a stopwatch and a full stomach, but solely by its quality and its taste. This is what makes for the enjoyment of eating, and enjoyment, after all, is a very ncessary part of life. And

who stayed at home why the Rhine really is so beautiful and why it will remain so.

They did not even have to have been to the Drosselgasse in Rüdesheim, which strangely enough tends to draw the most foreigners. I personally find sleepy, idyllic places like Unkel, not far from Bonn, or other "nests" that can just about be found with the aid of a magnifying glass on a map, more beautiful.

The Rhine has kept its fascination and international reputation, which is both astounding and unique, particularly when one considers the adverse industrial environment and all those poison catastrophes. When years ago my English parents-in-law came to Ger-

Left, a happy crew with their cox - another way of seeing the Rhine. **Above**, a view from the quay in Langenargen on Lake Constance.

many for the first time and I asked them what they wanted to see first, I still remember how they both promptly said, "The River Rhine".

Only the ecological developments of the future will show whether it was a good idea years ago to turn almost all of the Kaiserstuhl on the Upper Rhine into a vineyard. But there is already excess production of wine, due in the main (unfortunately) to intensive use of fertilizers; this has however greatly endangered the ground water and with it the supply of drinking water, as the Rhine is, after all, also an important source of water for industry and private households. Since the water taken from the Rhine obviously cannot be drunk unfiltered, processing plants have to be built.

remain competitive and earn enough profit to enable them to survive.

In view of the industrialization on both sides of the Rhine it is today quite incredible-almost a miracle - that this region has remained a prosperous wine growing area and that the vineyards have not been built on; and the same applies to the Lower Rhine, the vegetable garden of the country, even though here the fields have to compete for space with colossal power plants, oil processing plants and oil depots, such as those at Wesseling near Cologne.

The area to the left of the Rhine, west of Cologne, has long been associated with the open-cast mining of brown coal - the largest

The investments required have long been in the order not just of millions, but of thousands of millions. We are used to turning the tap and having the water flow out. Few people think about the costs involved in having a bath, doing the washing or the washing up; few realise that water is rapidly becoming a luxury item.

Like the farmers, the small-scale wine-growers are also having to fight for their survival, since there is powerful competition from France, Italy and Spain, and even from overseas: California and Australia. As a consequence the winegrowers are obliged to join forces to form cooperatives in order to

excavator in the world is in use there - but whole villages and small towns are being eaten away in the process, as there are millions of tons of coal lying beneath populated areas. The inhabitants are thus forced to move to newly-built settlements, which creates not only material but also serious human problems. A new social environment cannot be produced overnight.

When after several decades a mining area has been exhausted, the law requires it to be recultivated, and once again thousands of millions are involved...

Once a year the country on either side of the Rhine, from Basle to the Dutch border is the scene of turmoil as singing, dancing and masked people flood onto the streets and squares of the towns and villages. Carnival is a colourful, turbulent festival that goes on for days and attracts millions of people, whether as active participants or simply as onlookers at the big processions which take place in Mainz, Cologne and Düsseldorf.

The floats are often magnificently decorated and in some cases are still drawn by horses. They feature caricatures of politicians and other public figures, either in the form of distorted masks or tableaux, which can range from the facetious to the outright derisive. For many people carnival is not just an annual festival but an ideology.

of which are beautiful, some quite frightful. However, whether in the south or the north, everywhere the people are veiled in imaginative disguise. These days of tumult of course also spread to the schools and the administrative offices, and even the ministries; the offices are closed either on the Monday before Ash Wednesday or on Shrove Tuesday, as are most schools. If schools do not close, the pupils turn up in fancy dress and lessons are out of the question.

On the Monday before Lent, public life downstream from Mainz comes to a complete standstill, and of course the shops are shut too, while on the Upper Rhine, everything comes to a stop on Shrove Tuesday.

On the Upper Rhine, however, carnival has another name: Fastnacht. Here, other elements of an almost heathen character are also involved, such as the expulsion of winter and the casting out of devils and suchlike; The Fastnacht in Basle is very different in character to the carnival on the Lower Rhine; in the south - in Baden Württemberg - it is primarily also a festival of artistic masks, each with its own special significance, some

The event is hard to describe, one just has to plunge into the crowds and allow oneself to be swept along by all the gay abandon. It is important to note that in small towns and villages carnival is more traditional than in the larger settlements, where it has become very commercialized in recent times.

Hundreds of carnival clubs prepare the year round for the final three days of the season, and take their work seriously, since fun in Germany is a very serious business. Every year new songs are born, and carnival songs have become hits - even evergreens. From time to time there is even a hit of undisputed quality.

Far left, there are still Rhine fish and Rhine fishermen. **Left**, the look of a conoisseur. **Above**, masked musicians on a carnival parade.

Art and Architecture on The Rhine

From the fissured mountain ranges at the sources to the intricate water courses at the Delta, the various regions of the Rhine have always been both a thoroughfare as well as havens for permanent settlement and civilisation. The primitive hordes - later Celts, Germanic tribes and Romans - all had their own culture, which fused and contributed to the artistic legacy of the Rhine.

The flowering of commerce went hand in hand with the flowering of the arts. A visible indication of affluence is mirrored in the diversity of the architecture: castles, churches, monasteries and trading halls are found all along the banks of the river. Roman temples and theatres are testimony to antique culture. The lake dwellings on Lake Constance date from an even earlier time; near Unteruhldingen is the reconstruction of one of the lake settlements that was built 4,000 - 10,000 years ago.

Architecture: To list each of the important buildings along the Rhine would be beyond the scope of this book. In addition, each of the ecclesiastical or secular buildings houses priceless treasures: furniture, crockery, tapestries, paintings, and sculptures. These safe havens of wealth resounded with music and poetry. The river and its landscape were lauded in verse and song. We have outlined the poetic developments in another chapter of this book. The other arts will have to make do with only a brief mention. They are indicative of the immense diversity of the Rhine - a river, as Victor Hugo once wrote, which unites everything.

The churches and cathedrals along the Rhine are of literally towering splendour. Early medieval Romanesque architecture, with its round arches, adapted certain motifs of the architectural style of the Romans for use in sacred architecture. The three cathedrals of Speyer, Worms and Mainz date from the High Romanesque period. Each of the three mighty cathedrals has six spires. Construction work on St. Martin and St. Stephan

in Mainz was begun in 975, and the main building complex was completed between the 11th and 13th century. Construction of the Cathedral in Speyer was begun around 1030. It was consecrated in 1061. In the West porch are statues of the eight Emperors who are buried in the Cathedral.

The most famous church on the Rhine must be Cologne Cathedral (see P. 232/233). Construction work started in 1248. The cathedral is built in Gothic style, which superseded Romanesque architecture from the

middle of the 12th century onwards. Building work on the mighty cathedral ceased in the 16th century. However, once the enthusiasm of the Romantics for the past was rekindled (combined with the false notion that Gothic architecture was a typical German achievement) the cathedral - one of the biggest in Europe - was completed. It is dedicated to St. Peter and Mary. One of the famous treasures of Cologne Cathedral is the Shrine of the Three Magi, a wonderful piece of craftsmanship dating from the 12th and 13th century as well as Stefan Lochner's depiction of the Adoration of the Magi, dating from 1440. The Cathedral of Our Lady,

Strasbourg Minster, is no less impressive. Built on the foundations of an early Romanesque church begun in 1015, it mirrors the organic development of the architectural styles from Romanesque to Late Gothic (12th-15th century). One of the famous architects was the master builder Erwin of Steinbach. Inside the Minster one can see the famous astronomic clock.

With its pointed arches, narrow naves, and its slender columns continuing, uninterrupted, to support the light vaulted ceilings, Gothic architecture soared towards the heavens. The Gothic era was superseded at the time of the reformation by the Renaissance, the re-birth of antiquity, which marked a return to a rigid, grave order of proportion. City halls and other secular buildings mirrored the spirit of the times. The castle in Heidelberg, some distance away from the Rhine, but nevertheless an important landmark, is a splendid example of noble Renaissance architecture.

The voluptuous style of the subsequent Baroque corresponded exactly to the excess of emotion and affluence. Apart from the splendid churches and monasteries, above all, the palaces of the new masters that ruled land and people shine like beacons through the gloom of time. The *Neue Schloß* (New Castle) in Meersburg, the residence of the Bishops of Constance is a case in point. Another instance is the huge palace in Mannheim and the one in Biebrich near Wiesbaden. There are also numerous country houses built in the playful style of the Rococo, an aberration of the Baroque.

After such emotive gestures and witty spleen it was time for normality again. The age of enlightenment at the end of the 18th century was a throwback to the sober past. Classicist architecture was back in fashion. Friedrich Weinbrenner made the city of Karlsruhe a centre of classicist art. The most important German classicist architect of the 19th century was Karl Friedrich Schinkel, who gained his inspiration from classical Greek designs and motifs. But he also rediscovered Gothic architecture and drew up the plans for a Neogothic building which was constructed on the ruins of Burg Stolzenfels. Thus - in architecture - the cycle comes full circle. Old forms found new outlets. Not until Art Nouveau and *Neue Sachlichkeit* (the austere style prevalent in Germany in the early 1930s) did new forms evolve. The observant traveller will find salient examples all along the Rhine.

Painting: Fine buildings have to be decorated and beautified. Thus the art of painting also flourished along the banks of the Rhine. Initially there were book illustrations and frescoes. After the van Eyck brothers had developed the art of painting to include oil painting on canvas in 1432, many artists were attracted by this new form of expression and gathered in the Lower Rhine and in the Netherlands.

Hans Memling from Seligenstadt was one who found work and fame here. Local artists from the 15th century worth special mention are: Rogier van der Weyden, Dirk Bouts, Gerard David. Around the turn of the century: Hieronymus Bosch, Brueghel the Elder, Peter Paul Rubens, Anton van Dijck, Harmensz Rembrandt van Rijn, Frans Hals, Jan Vermeer van Delft are stars that shine through the ages.

Oil painting spread rapidly upstream, and no less important are the Cologne masters or those from the Upper Rhine. Stefan Lochner, who came from Meersburg to Cologne and the Alsatian painter Martin Schongauer also garnered eternal fame in the 15th century. The early Renaissance was evoked in the work of Hans Holbein the Younger, who worked mainly in Basle. A superb work of art from the early Renaissance - now on display in the Unter-linden Museum in Colmar - is the Isenheimer Altar painted by Matthias Grünewald. In the Gothic Minster of Freiburg the main work of Hans Baldung is on display.

Renaissance art depicted a new image of man - the image of a newly-won self confidence, where man himself was once more at the centre of the universe. The Baroque favoured voluptuous allegories. A new style started at the end of the 18th century. It was a bourgeois art depicting emotions, beliefs, love of nature, a longing for a better world - in days of yore as in the future, in short, Romanticism with a capital R. When the centre of Romanticism shifted from Dresden to Düsseldorf, the artists found their pictorial subjects and their home on the Rhine. When Wilhelm Schadow became director of the

Right, the gracious interior of Stolzenfels Castle which was built according to the plans of Karl Friedrich Schinkel.

Düsseldorf Academy in 1826, it developed to become a vitally important centre of art.

Arnold Böcklin was born in Basle in 1827. He was a late Romantic and explored new styles of painting. Born 150 years ago, Hans Thoma not only painted his most beautiful pictures while staying on the Upper Rhine, but he also encouraged young Rhenish artists in his function as director of the Art Academy in Karlsruhe. The Dutch artist Vincent van Gogh left his home country first to find fulfilment and then his demise. August Macke, another artist associated with the Rhine, also died young. This expressionist was killed during the First World War. The young artist Max Ernst decided to give up his rational style when confronted with the horrors of the War. Together with Hans Arp, who was born in Strasbourg, he worked most of his life in Switzerland. As a surrealist he became one of the most important artists of the 20th century.

Bele Bachem also hails from the Rhine. She was born in Düsseldorf and in her pictures she has created a dream world of magic realism. Her more recent paintings depict the industrial ruins of the Ruhr.

Memorials: While there remain some wonderful sculptures on the churches and monasteries of the Rhineland, the region was not always fortunate with its statues. Monuments can remind one of a past that was not always so innocent. At the Niederwalddenkmal, which was erected after the 1870/71 war, the figure of Germania towers over the Rhine. The equestrian statue of Kaiser Wilhelm at the Deutsche Eck in Koblenz dates from the same time. It was destroyed during the Second World War. The city of Rotterdam was also devastated during the war. In the vicinity of the Leuve-hafen there is the memorial "Die zerstörte Stadt" (the ruined city) created by Ossip Zadkine.

For the sculptor Wilhelm Lembruck it was important to maintain the spirit of humanism and a museum in Duisburg is dedicated to him. Indeed, there are numerous museums and memorials along the banks of the Rhine. Some, like the Wallraf-Richartz- and the Ludwig Museum beside Cologne Cathedral are works of art in themselves.

Right, the Rhine's cultural calendar has many high points; a scene of a performance at the Bregenz Festival.

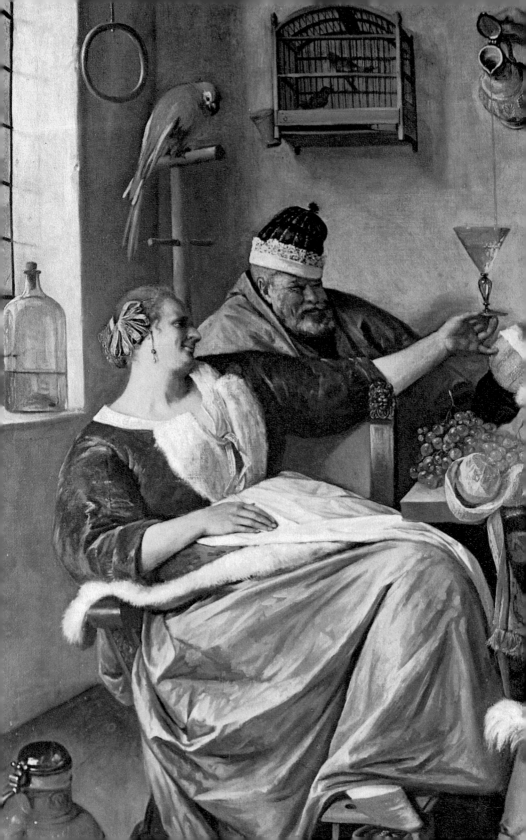

HERBERT HECKMANN:
THE PLEASURE OF EATING AND DRINKING

All the way from the Swiss mountains to the lowlands of Holland, the ways in which the people of the Rhine satisfy their hunger and thirst are every bit varied as the region's long history, as the countryside through which the river flows.

Here in the Rhineland there is a happy marriage between the refined cuisine of the French and the more down to earth, solid cuisine of the Germans; especially in Baden, which, in close competition with neighbouring Alsace, produces the most interesting food in all Germany. The wine from Baden further intensifies the pleasure of the feast. Even the writer and traveller Michel Montaigne, who travelled through Baden on his way from his native Perigord to Italy way back in the 16th century, noted that this was a region whose populace really knew how to enjoy their wine and their food.

Baden: Soup plays an important role in Baden's cuisine. It is normally served as a starter to every meal. In the morning, to make sure that nobody starves, a second breakfast is often taken at 9 am - and not only by the farmers working in the fields. It consists of Black Forest bacon and ham, crispy wholemeal bread and it is normally washed down by the juices provided by the fruit that grows so easily in this sun-soaked land.

Vineyard snails take a special place on the menu cards in Baden. They are served in herb butter and the strong taste of garlic should not be absent. As with so many other dishes in this part of the world, they are cooked in wine, which lends them a further distinctive taste.

The cooks of Baden are particularly skilled at preparing sweet water fish. The delicious pike dumplings, for example, are likely to tempt one to send for the menu a second time, as is the famous Rhine salmon which is prepared together with steamed plums. Many menus in Baden also include local trout prepared in a wine jelly.

Beef and ox meat are also an integral part of the local cuisine, as clearly demonstrated by the ubiquitous *Badische Ochsenfleisch* which is served together with horseradish sauce and cranberries.

In cafés and confectioners, one will always find the very best Black Forest gâteau, which is certainly among one of the most widespread creations of international gâteau culture. In Baden a little cherry juice is normally poured over the top. Less well known, but tasting equally good, are the *Küchle* - deep-fried fruit fritters. In Baden, there is some very inventive terminology used for sweets; the delicious *Frauenschenkli* - ladies thighs - are but one example.

But the thing that really sets Baden's cuisine apart is the wine that grows in the region. It isn't only that it is used in the preparation of the best dishes; a glass of wine (or more) drunk with the meal is all part and parcel of the the enjoyment of eating. The wines are so varied, however, that it is very difficult to identify a typical taste for Baden.

On the volcanic slopes of the Kaiserstuhl grow golden wines which get the very best of the long hours of sun: full-bodied Ruländer, delicate late Burgundies, full Silvaners, as well as Rieslings and Gewürztraminer with their fine bouquet. Note the names: Ihringen, Acharren, Oberrotweil, Burkheim, Bischoffingen, Bickensohl, Oberbergen, Sasbach and Endingen. Take time to taste everything that they have to offer. Patience is the name of the game in Baden. People have very little time for guzzlers and troughers. Wine should be sipped, taken at leisure, not hurried.

In the marches between Freiburg and Basle, the Chasselas grapes thrive on the rich loam soil. They provide a light, delicate wine known as "Markgräfler" - named after margrave Carl Friedrich of Baden who brought the grapes back with him after a visit to Lake Geneva in 1780. Famous far beyond the frontiers of Baden itself are the Rieslings of the vineyards of Central Baden, which stretches from Baden-Baden to Oberkirch and Diersburg. A spicy, elegant red Traminer which smells of roses and is known locally as "Clevner" grows on the predominantly granite slopes of the Black Forest between Bühl and Offenburg. This is home too of the very best velvety-mellow late Burgundies.

The Palatinate: North of Baden, in the Rhineland Palatinate, the gastronomic rules are rather different. Although refinement is not totally lost, good old-fashioned basic cuisine is generally the order of the day. In the Autumn, at the time when the grapes are harvested, one drinks *Federweißer* - new wine - along with freshly baked onion cake: finely chopped onions are lightly fried in butter, then mixed together with fried chopped bacon, a beaten egg yolk and cream. Salt and pepper is added to taste and then the whole lot is poured onto a yeast dough base and baked in the oven until it is golden brown. It tastes delicious.

The people of the Palatinate are very much meat and potatoes men and in the restaurants

The potato soup of the Palatinate is also famous. It was always most commonly eaten in the regions where there was no wine; potatoes were very often all there was in the poorer areas of the Palatinate Forest.

In the cherry season, the locals of the Palatinate bake *Kirschenjockel* or *Kirschenmichel*, also known as *Kirschenpolster*. It is a kind of breadpudding made with bread rolls, milk, eggs and cherries, baked in the oven. A cup of strong coffee is a good accompaniment, though the dish used to be eaten with potato soup (as did most othe dishes in this part of the world).

The Christmas goose is normally stuffed with the sweet chestnuts which grow on the flanks of the Haardt Mountains. They are also

of the region, as well as those in the Palatinate part of Baden Württemberg, one constantly comes across the term "homemade". That is normally a mark of quality and indicates, too, that the food is prepared according to the original recipe. There is, for example, stomach of pig served with sauerkraut which is the "national" dish of the Palatinate. The stomach is filled with a mixture of minced pork and potatoes. There are just about as many variations as there are people who produce the dish, each with his own recipe, passed down from generation to generation and guarded in the family like a state secret. A dry Riesling goes particularly well with this sustaining dish.

popular when they are peeled and steamed in red cabbage. The vegetable garden of the Rhineland-Palatinate plain enriches the cuisine with enormous variety. World famous is the asparagus from Schwetzingen, celebrated as the absolute "king" among many dishes. The asparagus season is in May. It is best eaten fresh, the same day that it is picked, should be *al dente* and definitely not over-cooked. It is said that there are asparagus fanatics who burst into tears when the season is over.

The people of the Palatinate have particular penchant for pork, from which they prepare a great variety of dishes, including the liver sausage flavoured with marjorie. Indeed, if you like sausage, then the Palatinate is the place to go. It isn't for nothing that one of the largest festivals in the area, the Dürkheimer Sausage Market, celebrates the sausage - and the wine - that is produced here.

The best part of the pork, namely the loin, is enjoyed by the locals as *Lummelbraten*, which they lard. Game is also very popular. But it is still the potato that holds pride of place. There are potato dumplings which are stuffed with sausage meat and known locally as *Herzdrücker* (heart squeezer) on account of the fact that one is always tempted to eat too much. *Eisknoche* - leg of pork - is eaten together with mashed potatoes and sauerkraut. As in neighbouring Alsace, sauerkraut is

a delightful and very palatable Sylvaner. It is the standard wine of the area, although the dry Riesling is becoming more and more popular among the wine growers of the Palatinate. Alongside grow the spicy Traminers as well as the mild Müller-Thurgau. The wine which grows on the gravel and basalt soils of the Middle Haardt is of a particularly high quality.

Wines from the *Beerenauslese* - where selected grapes are deliberately left on the vines until they are over-ripe - *and the Trockenbeerauslese* - where the grapes remain there until they have just about withered away to raisins - both take several years to reach full maturity. They are very much sweeter and richer and have a higher alcohol content. They

normally served as an accompaniment to many dishes. It aids the digestion.

The German Wine Road winds its way through three wine growing areas, those of Upper Haardt (from Schweigen with its wine gate to Hambach), Middle Haardt (from Neustadt to Ungstein) and the Lower Haardt (from Ungstein to Grünstadt). A huge variety of excellent wine can be found along the route. On the loam soils of the Upper Haardt grows

Left, where the hills are not too steep the vintners now employ machines to do the harvesting. **Above**, the smiling face of the Wine Queen. A scene from one of many wine festivals.

are normally used as dessert wines. Excellent wines of this variety include the Deidesheimer Herrgottsacker, the Forster Schnepfenflug, the Dürkheimer Nonnengarten and the Herxheimer Honigsack.

Light and lively wines are grown on the chalky soil of the Unter Haardt. It would be possible to establish a list of Germany's best wines just from the wines of the Palatinate. It was here that the Romans first started to cultivate their wines in Germania. Some even believe that wine grew wild in the forests of the Rhine plain long before the Romans ever arrived. In all probability, however, these are nothing more than nationalistic sentiments.

Today, wine for the people of the Palatinate remains an integral part of local culture. As well as playing an important role in everyday life, it contributes to the jollity of their festivals. The fact that the wine goblets in the Palatinate take a full half litre is indicative of the great thirst that the locals work up.

Brezeln from Speyer, curd cheese from Lustadt or the local rye bread with butter and white cheese all go very well with the wine. The new wine is best drunk with sweet chestnuts. In the Palatinate food and drink have a common cause - they hold body and soul together.

Rhine Hessen: Rhine Hessen covers the areas on the west bank of the Rhine in the wine

bles. The Romans were well aware of the fecundity of the land along this stretch of the Rhine. White cabbage grows especially well. In Worms, corned pork chops served with cabbage is one of the specialities served up in the local inns.

As is the case with the Palatinate, the meals one gets in Rhine Hessen are good and fortifying. Cheese plays an important role here, including cheese made from curd which is best eaten when mature, as well as cottage cheese mixed with finely chopped onions. While in France it is red wine that is usually drunk with cheese, here in Rhine Hessen, it is the fine white wine. If the visitor is a fan of cheese, he will soon become a connoisseur of wines, and

triangle between Bingen, Worms and Mainz. Here too, there are wine festivals in every wine growing village, where nobody ever does without copious rations of wine, bread, and sausage - just about the staple diet in this part of the world. Cheese from Mainz is also popular and it is often served together with *Musik* - the local expression for a mixture of vinegar, onions and oil. The ham from Mainz is renowned and goes particularly well with the asparagus from Ingelheim.

Around Ingelheim and Heidesheim the abundance of locally grown vegetables ensures a rich variation in the local cuisine. It is unthinkable to have meat without any vegeta-

if he already knows about the wines, he will undoubtedly soon become well-acquainted with the cheese.

Again, in Rhine Hessen, the cultivation of wine started with the Romans. The Germanic tribes did as best they could to continue this heritage and Charlemagne, who liked a glass or two, without ever drinking too much, drew up the first comprehensive rules for the management of vineyards. The Riesling grape appears to have originated in this part of Germany. The first time it was mentioned was on an invoice of a Rüsselsheimer wine cellar issued in 1435. Fifty years later we find it mentioned once again in invoices from Worms.

In stark contrast to the dry Rieslings, the famous Liebfrauenmilch is exceptionally sweet and not to everybody's taste. This wine was first grown on the loam and sand covered vineyards surrounding the collegiate Church of Our Dear Lady (Liebfrauenstiftskirche) in Worms.

But it is the Riesling grape which reigns supreme in Rhine Hessen. Whether grown on the volcanic soils around Nierstein, the quartz shales around Bingen or the chalky loam and gravel soils in the hinterland, it possesses an incomparable flavour. It is less sharp than the Riesling of the Palatinate. The connoisseur of German wines will certainly recognise the most famous vineyards in which it is produced:

The production and consumption of beer is also enshrined in the drinking culture of Rhine Hessen. The oldest beer in Germany is on display at the museum in Alzey. It dates from the year 350 AD, the time of the Emperor Constantine. Today the *Aktienbier* from Mainz and the *Eichelbaumbräu* from Worms both enjoy widespread acclaim - even beyond the borders of Rhine Hessen.

The Rhinegau: The Rhinegau begins at the town of Hochheim at the confluence of the River Main. It stretches for 50 kilometres past Eltville, Erbach, Hattenheim, Oestrich and Geisenheim right up to beyond Rüdesheim, where, at the town of Lorch, beneath steeply-ascending vineyards, it finally joins the region

Tafelstein and Steinberg in Dienheim, Modern and Teufelskopf in Ludwigshöhe, Glock and Orbel in Nackenheim and Sackträger and Vogelsang in Oppenheim. There is also a milder, spicier red wine which is cultivated in Ingelheim. Lovers of good brandy will also find what they are looking for in Rhine Hessen. In Bingen, wine of the Scharlachberg is distilled in to a high quality brandy that bears comparison with the very best Cognac.

Left, ladies parade with their goblets. **Above**, a cosy atmosphere is enjoyed by all in a wine cellar.

of the Middle Rhine. "Johnson's Guide", the most comprehensive of all books on wine, states: "Characteristics which contribute to the unquestionable quality of the wines of the Rhinegau are its uniformity and stability. One could say that this is the tidiest and best-organised of all German wine growing areas".

An exceptionally mild climate and exactly the right soil lend the grapes optimum conditions. There is nowhere else in Europe where Riesling grapes can grow as well as in the Rhinegau. In good years they produce wines of world renown. Who hasn't heard of the "Goethewein", the Schloß Johannisberger or the Winkeler Hasensprung. The "Rauenthaler" is also known as Fürstenwein - the wine of princes. Wine has been cultivated on the western slopes of the Taunus since the 8th century. Primarily it was the monks from the abbeys of Eberbach and Johannisberg who, over the centuries, nurtured the vines and created the quality which today gives them such a high reputation.

It was no complete accident that the *Trockenbeerauslese* was "discovered" in theses parts. The story goes that in the late 18th century, when the abbey at Johannisberg still belonged to Fulda, the emissary responsible for obtaining the permit to start the harvest was held up by robbers and could only return to the abbey at the end of November. The grapes had already withered away to raisins, and had already been subjected to the frost. Nevertheless, much to the surprise of the keeper of the wine cellar, the harvest brought forth an exceptionally good wine, *Eiswein*, which was hitherto unknown.

Wine has always had a major role to play in the history of the Rhinegau, and the places which contain the best vineyards now link up to form a wine route par excellence: Eltville, Erbach, Geisenheim, Hattenheim, Hallgarten, Kiedrich, Lorch, Mittelheim, Oestrich, Rauenthal, Rüdesheim with its world famous Drosselgasse and finally Winkel where Johann Wolfgang von Goethe enjoyed his Rhinegau Wine in the Brentanohaus.

Burgundy grapes, which produce a pleasant full-bodied wine, are cultivated on the phyllite shales around Aßmannhausen.

The high quality of the region's wines has undoubtedly contributed to the local cuisine, for the food must always be worthy of the wine. Wiesbaden, the capital of Rhine Hessen, has a reputation as being one of the strongholds of the German gourmet scene. It is said that those with a sweet tooth often go there solely because of the pineapple gâteau. Certainly, other specialities apart, the confectioners of Wiesbaden alone are enough to warrant a trip to the city. But the basic cuisine of the Rhinegau, again dominated by good wholesome dishes, is also worthy of attention: chops or pickled bones with sauerkraut, the unavoidable sausages, pancakes with bacon, and curd cheese with onions.

The Ahr Valley and the Middle Rhine are the northernmost wine growing ares in Germany. The Ahr has its source at the spa town of Blankenheim in the Eifel and it isn't long

before it reaches its confluence with the Rhine near Sinzig. Wine has been grown here since the 10th century. While at first there were only white varieties, for the last 150 years it has been the Burgundies which have gradually taken over.

Grown on the clay shales of the steep valley sides, the grapes produce a wine of a full, mellow character. In the lower lying loam areas grows a much lighter Portugese wine. Most of the annual production is drunk locally, which says a lot for the wine of the Ahr Valley, whether it be from Altenahr, Rech, Dernau, Marienthal, Ahrweiler or Lorsdorf.

The region's cuisine is heavily influenced by the culinary delights of the Eifel, the potato once again taking pride of place. Famous are the *Mayener* potatoes; the raw grated potatoes mixed with bacon and ham, and baked in a casserole dish with lard, can be guaranteed to satisfy those with even the largest of appetites. A glass of plum juice from the Eifel is recommended as an accompaniment. Meat roasted on a spit - beef or pork - from the Hunsrück can also be found in numerous inns between Bingen and Koblenz.

The vineyards of the Middle Rhine stretch from the confluence of the River Nahe up to the Siebengebirge near Bonn. Riesling triumphs here as well, while the "Rhöndorfer Domberg" and the "Menzenberger Rot"rank among the best red wines in Germany.

The Lower Rhine: In the northern part of the German Rhine region - the actual Rhineland between Westphalia, Hessen, the Rhine Palatinate, as well as Belgium, Luxembourg and in the Netherlands - there is generally much more beer drunk than wine. Taken as a whole, the region could be said to be the beer centre of the world. It may be worth taking a look at some of the basic differences in the types of beer brewed in the region.

Most beer brewed in the Federal Republic of Germany, such as Pils and light ales, is the so-called bottom-fermented beer, where the yeast sinks to the bottom during fermentation which takes place at the temperature of 4 - 9 degrees celcius. This was not always the case; indeed until the fifteenth century, all beer brewed in Germany was of the top-fermented variety, using a different yeast which rises to the top during fermentation, at the warmer temperature of 15 - 20 degrees. The only area in Germany where the new colder process didn't catch on was in the region of the Lower Rhine, where the consistently mild temperatures would have made brewing far too expensive. After a number of unsuccessful and costly experiments, the brewers of the Lower Rhine therefore reverted to brewing their beer in the old way, and it is this kind of beer which is still very popular in the region. A good example is the *Kölsch* brewed in Cologne. It tastes good and is certainly no less strong than other beer. It goes well with a rye or juniper schnapps from Aachen, a wheat brandy from Ameln, a *Bas* - blackcurrant schnapps - or a *Klarer* with a cube of sugar.

In Düsseldorf, the capital of the state of North Rhine Wesphalia, other beers brewed in the old way are the dark brown ales such as

Düssel or *Altbier*. This is usually served in small *Alt* glasses which the locals call *Stange* (rods). Here too, as everywhere else in the northern Rhineland, one drinks schnapps together with the beer, usually making the excuse that it is very much easier to stand on two feet than one. For newcomers, even German newcomers, the menu cards in Cologne, Düsseldorf and the surrounding regions are bound to create some difficulty. If you have learned that a *Hahn* means chicken, then don't

Above, if the weather holds, the festival is held on the market place.

be too surprised when you order your "halven Hahn" (half chicken) if a rye breadroll with cheese arrives on the table. Many others have suffered the same fate. The people of Cologne like their bread and cheese to be flavoured with cummin.

Nowhere else in Germany are there so many colloquial expressions for food than between Düsseldorf and Cologne. There is *"Flöns mit Öllk"* (black pudding with onions), *"Läwerwoosch mit Ädäppelschlaat"* (liver sausage with potato salad), *"Fresche Brotwoosch mit Zaus"* (grilled sausage with gravy), and *"Reppes on Kappes"* (corned pork chops on white cabbage). A Rhenish speciality are the *Riefkooche,* raw potatoes grated and peeled, mixed with salt and onions and baked in hot oil or lard. Such dishes are generally enough, even for those with a big appetite. The Rhenish stewed picked beef - *Sauerbraten* - has become world famous. Beef that has been allowed to hang for a while is then immersed for several days in vinegar, along with onions, carrots, celery and bay leaves. It is gently roasted and arrives on the table in a sweet and sour sauce.

Even though the sea is still quite some distance away, the people of Bonn and Cologne have a particular penchant for mussels, which are cooked together with onion rings in a strongly flavoured broth. Asparagus with ham or veal is a great seasonal favourite in Düsseldorf, as well as knuckle of pork with Neuss sauerkraut followed up by a desert of fragrant peaches from Wasserberg.

A huge variety of sweets is also available in the Rhineland. Cologne has its almonds coated in sugar, Düsseldorf its cherry gâteau and Bonn its *Zuntz* coffee, which gets its flavour through being finely candied during the roasting process. Biscuits are also very popular. There are the famous *Aachener Printen*, the Rhenish *Spekulatius* and the almond *Spekulatius* from Cleves. Sweet delights also figure strongly in the cuisine of the Lower Rhine. Here, in order to get a complete sample of what's on offer, it is a good idea to wander from restaurant to café - and from café to restaurant.

But the Lower Rhine is also the cheeseboard of the Rhineland. There are delicious Goudas and Edamers - and cottage cheese, known locally as *"Klatschkäse"*, which goes particularly well on a piece of good wholesome black bread from the Bergisches Land.

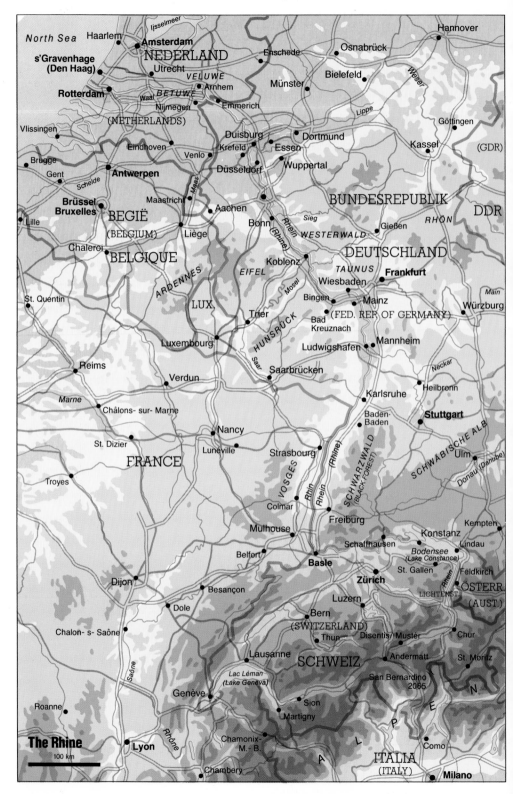

The Rhine

100 km

A RHINE JOURNEY THROUGH FIVE COUNTRIES

The best way of getting to know the Rhine has always been to travel in a luxury steamer from Basle to Rotterdam (or vice-versa). Four or five days of unadulterated Rhine! You can experience - in every sense - the romantic aspect of the river (from Mainz/ Wiesbaden to Cologne) on a sunny summer's day from the deck of a modern ship of the Rhine.

Varied indeed are the types of landscape through which the Rhine flows on its 1300-kilometre journey from its source to the sea. The Vorder- and Hinterrhein, the principal and lesser headstreams of the Rhine, rise high up in the Swiss mountains, far from all traces of civilization; still encompassed by this idyll, the two unite as the Alpenrhein before flowing into Lake Constance, to be surrounded by a cultivated landscape of exceptional charm. And then, near Schaffhausen on the Rhine proper, the river plunges into the abyss - the most powerful waterfall in Europe: what a spectacle! At Basle begins the Upper Rhine, the Rhine as an industrial river - and as such it continues to the sea. The start of the Middle Rhine section is marked by Mainz on the left bank and Wiesbaden on the right; here, the traveller has arrived at the Romantic Rhine, which will hold him in thrall until he reaches Cologne.

Then the river banks slowly become bleaker, flatter. The Lower Rhine begins near Krefeld, the textile town, and Duisburg, on the right bank, with Europe's largest inland port. Eastwards from here lies the Ruhr District - an industrial region full of cultural interest. Further north still, the banks are clothed by meadows, cut by dykes, dotted by windmills; welcoming brick houses nestle on either side of the majestically broad river. Across the Dutch border, the Rhine suddenly changes its name. As the Waal or the Lek its branches splay out, flowing through Rotterdam until at last every arm, every finger arrives at the North Sea.

So climb aboard; join us for a journey along the banks of the Rhine. Visit its fine cities: Basle, Strasbourg, Mannheim, Wiesbaden, Cologne, Bonn, Düsseldorf, Duisburg, Rotterdam. But we shall also show you the picturesque corners near its source in Switzerland, by Lake Constance, across the border in France and Holland as well as in Germany. You will see the many facets of the changing scenery, read tales of joy and sorrow of days gone by, of the castles and the knights who owned them. You will meet the Rhinelanders of today, will celebrate with them their Shrovetide Carnival. Put on your walking shoes to wander with us over the mountains, through valleys and meadows - and through the ever-changing history of this mighty river. Catch your breath and relax with a chilled glass of wine and a typical snack from the region; observe, as you do so, the art and culture of times past. Or take to your bicycle as a means of transport: cycling beside the Rhine is a very special pleasure!

Preceding pages: mountain pastures near the source of the Rhine, a close-up view of the Rhine Falls at Schaffhausen, a Rhine panorama with Oberwesel Castle in the foreground, river freight on the Lower Rhine. **Following pages**: a mountain man from Switzerland.

FED BY TWIN SOURCES

Fed by twin sources, the Rhine begins its 1300-kilometre journey to the North Sea high up in the Swiss mountains. The principal headstream, the 70-kilometre long **Vorderrhein**, rises 2345 metres above sea level in **Lake Thoma**, on the north-east flank of the Badus in the St. Gotthard Massif. From here it rushes through the narrow Tavetsch Valley, reaching the first habitation some twenty kilometres further on in **Disentis**. The village is dominated by the oldest Benedictine monastery in Switzerland, surrounded by churches and chapels worth visiting on account of their fine altars and paintings.

History was made in **Trun**, which lies a few kilometres further downstream. It was in 1424 that the Swiss confederates formed a defensive association here, the "Grauer Bund" ("Grey League"), which was later to become the foundation stone of the Canton of Grisons (Graubünden).

The pilgrimage **Church of St. Mary of Light** possesses an enchanting series of 17th-century paintings; the Parish Church of **St. Martin** is famed for its elaborately carved high altar.

Near the town of **Ilanz**, the Vorderrhein is joined by the glacial waters of the Valserrhein before reaching the confluence with its lesser headstream - the **Hinterrhein** - near Reichenau.

The source of the Hinterrhein lies some 57 kilometres further upstream in the Zapport glacier, in the heart of the Adula Mountains. Only six kilometres further on it has become a sizeable mountain torrent, a potential danger in times of flooding. On a number of occasions the melting snow waters have washed away the **Alte Landbrugg**, the "old causeway" which since 1692 has formed the approach to the San Bernardino Pass. The turbulent young river reaches the village of **Zillis** by means of the Rofla Gorge. The parish church boasts a coffered ceiling with 153 segments and a unique series of paintings dating from the 12th century. **The source of the Rhine.**

A few kilometres farther on we reach the **Via Mala**, where the river provides for the first time a magnificent opportunity to study its capacity for shaping the landscape through which it flows. The spectacle of cascading waters rushing downwards between two vertical walls of rock is truly dramatic. At the foot of the pass lies the hamlet of **Thusis**, affording panoramic views across the Domleschg Valley. The wooden chalets have been destroyed by fire more than a dozen times over the centuries, with the result that few old buildings remain.

Numerous fortresses and castles with heroic names like **Baldenstein, Ortenstein** and **Ehrenfels** form a chain accompanying the Hinterrhein on the last kilometres of its journey to the confluence with the Vorderrhein. They bear witness to the strategic importance of this transalpine road. **Räzüns**, too, owes its existence to the route leading to the San Bernardino Pass. It is worth breaking one's journey to visit the **Chapel of St. George**, famous for its frescoes and a view of the Rhine's horseshoe bends,

The young river cuts its way through the Swiss mountains

guarded by a castle which has stood sentinel for hundreds of years.

The river, now known as the **Alpenrhein**, continues on its way past Reichenau - less turbulent now, flowing through an increasingly broad valley enclosed by high mountain ridges. Here, for the first time, the bordering hillsides are decked with vines - the plants whose destiny is inextricably linked to that of the Rhine, and to which it largely owes its reputation for evoking a mood of romance in men.

Chur, with a population of 34 000, is the first sizeable town along the course of the Rhine. The capital of the Canton of Grisons possesses many important historical buildings, for its origins reach back to pre-Roman times. It has always been the cultural and religious centre of the region. In 1526, in an act of religious tolerance unusual for the time, the Bishop's Palace was awarded the status of an independent political community when the citizens of the town espoused the Protestant cause. This situation actually prevailed until 1852. Of interest is the

extensive collection of magnificent exhibits in the Treasury of the **Cathedral of Our Lady** (12th-13th century), the **Church of St. Martin** - some parts of which date from the 8th century - , the **Monastery Church of St. Lucius** and the 16th-century **Town Hall**.

After Chur the river bends towards the north, wending its way between the Glarus Alps and the Rätikon Ridge. Here the bed of the Alpenrhein has become silted up with deposits. It has to be held in check by embankments which afford protection against flooding, but which lend the river the appearance of a canal. For a short stretch it flows through the canton of **St. Gallen**, passing the spa town of **Bad Ragaz**, where organized cures were the order of the day as early as 1242.

The Rhine then forms the western frontier of the Principality of **Liechtenstein**. With an area of only 160 km2, the principality has its own constitution but maintains close economic and foreign-policy links with Switzerland. Neither customs nor immigration checks await the visitor at the border; the currency in this autonomous state is the Swiss Franc. The country is ruled from **Vaduz**, its tranquil capital, overshadowed by **Castle Hohen-Liechtenstein**, the residence of the royal family.

Further on, the Rhine demonstrates again its function as a boundary. The Austrian province of Vorarlberg advances as far as its eastern bank, whilst the Swiss canton of St. Gallen borders the river in the west. The little Austrian town of **Feldkirch** retains an almost medieval air thanks to the well-preserved remains of its fortified castle, the **Schattenburg** (12th century, museum), and the leafy pergolas in the town centre. The **Parish Church of St. Nicholas**, built in 1478, houses two notable treasures: a reredos dated 1521 and a wrought-iron Gothic pulpit. Feldkirch, founded by the Earls of Montfort in 1190, was sold to the Hapsburgs in 1375.

The neighbouring village of **Rankweil** is home to one of the oldest churches in the country, the **Church of St. Peter**, whose origins go back as far as 830

Vaduz Castle in Liechtenstein

A.D.. It was later rebuilt in the Baroque style. **Hohenems** was once the seat of the Imperial Counts - a fact to which the imposing Parish Church, with its magnificent 16th-century altar, bears witness. No less famous is the **Library** in the Renaissance palace, in which were found during the 18th century two manuscripts of the celebrated Middle High German epic, the Nibelungenlied.

Dornbirn, the centre of the Austrian textile industry and the largest town in the Vorarlberg, has a natural history museum which is worthy of special attention. It is also an ideal base for excursions into the nearby Forest of Bregenz - to **Schwarzenberg**, **Au** and **Hittisau**.

On the Swiss side, the lovingly preserved cultural heritage of the **Appenzell District**, especially the picturesque mountain villages of **Urnäsch** and **Gais**, invite the visitor to make a detour. **Appenzell**, the main town of the half-canton, is a famous high-altitude resort, its main street enlivened by the brightly coloured façades of the houses. If the weather is good, visitors should take one of the four cable cars to the summit of the Säntis (2501 m), or enjoy the panoramic view across the Rhine valley from the Hoher Kasten. The town of **St. Margrethen** nestles in a bend in the Rhine. It can look back over a long history - as evidenced in the wonderful late Gothic frescoes in the **Church of St. Margrethe**.

The little town of **Rheineck** is justifiably proud of its patrician houses, such as the "Löwenhof" and the "Custerhof". Only a few kilometres farther north, near the town of **Rohrschach**, the "Old Rhine" disperses into Lake Constance. Heavy sedimentary deposits have made it necessary in recent times for most of the river water to be diverted into Lake Constance via a man-made canal which branches off from the main river near St. Margrethen. Every year, the deposits push the "Old Rhine" delta 20 metres further into the lake. Geologists have calculated that, as a result, there are only 12,000 years left for mankind to enjoy the attractions of one of the most beautiful stretches of inland water in Europe.

Nuns take an early morning stroll. **Following pages: the entrance to the harbour at Lindau.**

ON AND AROUND LAKE CONSTANCE

The abrasive energy of the Ice-Age glaciers and movements of the earth's crust produced a hollow where the Alpenrhein exited from the mountain region. During the millenia which have since passed, countless northward-flowing rivers have filled this basin, creating Lake Constance. The neighbouring countries - the Federal Republic of Germany (305 km2), Switzerland (173 km2) and Austria (60km2) have agreed to share this second-largest stretch of inland water in Europe. It is first mentioned in seventh-century records, taking its German name (Bodensee) from Bodoma, the royal palace erected on its northern shores. Its present-day boundaries were officially laid down after World War I.

The lakeshore sights are strung out like pearls along the 256-kilometre perimeter, between the Obersee, the main part of the lake, which attains a maximum length of 63.5 km and a breadth of 14 km, and its twin lesser arms, the Überlinger See and the Untersee.

Lake Constance lies in the midst of countryside which has been cultivated by man since ancient times. On the Austrian shore, **Bregenz** (27,000 inhabitants) has grown up on the site of the Roman fort Brigantium, where the Rhine flows into the lake. It still retains its picturesque character in the old Upper Town. Nearby is the **Pfänder** mountain (1063 m), the "balcony overlooking the lake", from whose summit one can enjoy magnificent panoramic views across the lake. Bregenz, has become famous since 1946 as the home of the Bregenz Music Festival, during which performances are staged on the lake itself. For many it also marks the beginning of the 6.7-kilometre tunnel which forms part of the Rhine Valley motorway.

Only a few kilometres away lies **Lindau** (25,000 inhabitants), the most southerly town in West Germany. It, too, can look back on a long and turbulent history, recalled today in the

Mangturm fortified tower, the Brigands' Tower, the Gothic frescoes depicting the Passion in **St. Peter's Church**, and the Lion of Bavaria monument by the port. The **Old Town** lies on an island, and is linked to the mainland by a road bridge and rail causeway. The town's economic prosperity is based on a wide range of industries and intensive fruit farming. The **Convent**, dating from the 9th century, is well-worth a visit. Between 1402 and 1805 Lindau was a Free Imperial City; since then it has been part of the state of Bavaria.

Friedrichshafen (53,000 inhabitants), lies in a bay on the northern shores of the lake. Visitors with a technical bent particularly enjoy a visit to the museum and research establishment here, since the town was formerly the centre of airship production. One can also cross by rail or car ferry to **Romanshorn**, on the Swiss shore. Friedrichshafen is the venue for the annual Lake Constance International Fair. **Meersburg** (5,000 inhabitants), which rejoices in an idyllic setting on a rise

overlooking the lake, enchants romantics with a castle - dating from the 7th century - as well as a number of lovingly restored half-timbered houses. The **Old Castle** (12th century) dominating the medieval town centre. Thanks to the mild climate typical of the region, the steep lakeshore slopes outside the town are ideal for viticulture.

Numerous traces of the Stone-Age habitation of the area can be found in **Unteruhldingen**, which lies on the Überlinger See, the northern of the two secondary arms of the lake. Two reconstructed villages on piles (lakeshore and marsh settlements) from the late neolithic and early Bronze Age periods bear witness to the region's early history. Neighbouring **Birnau** has the loveliest Baroque Church for miles around. **Überlingen**, the main town on this northern arm of the lake, boasts an altar of supreme craftsmanship and a Town Hall with a long and important history.

As the largest and most important town on the lake in the 15th century,

Constance (Konstanz - 78,000 inhabitants) was the setting for the 16th Ecumenical Council, which not only elected Martin V. as Pope - the only one to be chosen on German soil - but also had the religious reformer Johannes Hus burned at the stake. The Old Town is worth visiting for its historic houses with overhanging gables, for the frescoes of the "Upper Harbour House", the "Sacristan's House" ("Haus zur Kunkel") and the five-storey "Tall House" dating from 1294.

Highlights of any trip to Lake Constance are the islands of **Mainau**, with its riot of tropical vegetation, and **Reichenau**, its big sister, famous for its three medieval churches. Those who visit the lake for health reasons will visit **Wasserburg**, a Bavarian resort with a charming old town centre. It stands on a former island which became attached to the mainland in 1720.

Radolfzell lies on the Zellersee, the northern basin of the Untersee - the lower arm of the lake. A popular resort, the town offers a wide range of leisure activities. **Mettau**, on a peninsula, is famous for its remedial sports facilities and Kneipp cures. Patients can recover from their exertions in the Old Town centre or in the bird sanctuary.

The Swiss shore can easily be reached from Radolfzell via Konstanz. The first port of call is **Kreuzlingen**. If you turn to the right you will find the Napoleon Museum in **Arenenberg**, opposite Reichenau near Ermatingen. To the left is a succession of charming little towns: **Münsterlingen**, **Romanshorn**, **Arbon**, **Rorschach** and **Altenrhein**, on the delta of the old course of the Rhine.

Visitors to Lake Constance should not restrict their enjoyment of the lake to the view from the shore. Approximately 40 ships of the **White Fleet** provide regular services and excursions. Hikers and cyclists can take advantage of the "Sail and explore" scheme. Car ferries link Konstanz with Meersburg and Friedrichshafen with Romanshorn. The latest addition to the service is the paddle steamer "Hohentwiel", a mobile museum ship.

Count Zeppelin hailed from Friedrichshafen on Lake Constance

THE HIGH RHINE ABOVE BASLE

The High Rhine is rich in jewels of urban architecture. The parade begins with **Stein am Rhein**, historically the site of one of the bridges across the river. First mentioned in 1001, Stein is regarded as one of the best-preserved medieval towns in Switzerland. The right-bank district is worth a visit, in particular for its fine old houses adorned with oriel windows and frescoes, surrounding the idyllic market square with its magnificent Town Hall (1539). The former **Benedictine Abbey of St. George** has an early Romanesque pillared basilica and an Abbot's House by the river with wall paintings by Ambrosius Holbein. Today the complex forms a museum.

Towering regally above the town is **Hohenklingen Castle** (12th century), perched on the wooded slopes of the Klingenberg. From the restaurant situated within the former fortress the visitor can enjoy a fine view across the Old Town, the Rhine dotted with white pleasure steamers, and - on the far bank - the remains of a Roman fort.

Schaffhausen (34,000 inhabitants) runs Stein a close second in the beauty stakes. Oriel windows and elaborately painted façades, in evidence in the well-preserved Old Town, testify to the earlier prosperity of this capital of the Swiss canton bearing the same name. The frescoes on the **Hus zum Ritter**, the "Knight's House", are amongst the most important late Renaissance paintings in Switzerland.

The town's emblem is the keep of the **Munot Belvedere**, rising up to the east of the town; it is a defensive structure built between 1564 and 1585 in accordance with the principles laid down in Dürer's treatise on fortifications. Offering splendid panoramic views, the castle is the arena for numerous festivals during the summer months. Also worth visiting are the former **Benedictine Abbey of All Saints** - now a museum - and the Cistercian **Abbey Church**.

Preceding pages: the Basle Fastnact , a street scene at dawn.

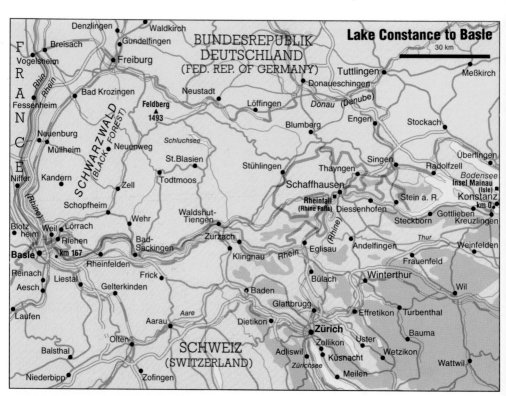

142

Schaffhausen owes its great prosperity to the famous **Rhine Falls**, the most powerful waterfall in Central Europe. All goods had to be unloaded here. River traffic provided the main impetus for the town's economy from the 11th century, whereby a distinction was made between the upper river navigation above the rapids and the lower river navigation below the Falls. Near Neuhausen, approximately four kilometres southwest of Schaffhausen, the waters of the Upper Rhine - 150 metres wide at this point - plunge a height of 22 metres (19 metres at the main section) over a Jurassic limestone sill. Four limestone cliffs rise out of the foaming torrent, dividing the cataract into several branches.

The best vantage point for surveying the Rhine Falls is **Wörth Castle**, on the right bank, which contains a restaurant. From here it is possible to take a boat trip to the limestone cliff in the middle of the Falls. Although this looks an extremely hazardous undertaking, it is, in fact, absolutely safe.

Schaffhausen is a popular tourist destination at all seasons; a short way downstream, however, the little towns of **Waldshut** - with its gabled houses with overhanging roofs - and **Tiengen** - where the Counts of Sulz built their castle in the 16th century - attract visitors mainly in summer. The inhabitants of Waldshut celebrate their **Chilby Festival** on the third Sunday in August; the residents of Tiengen celebrate the **Schwyzer Day** on the first Sunday in July. Both festivals owe their origins to the warlike quarrels which took place with the Swiss during the Middle Ages.

The symbol of **Tiengen**, the former centre of the Klettgau region, is the **Storks' Tower** (15th century), still adorned by its original wooden roof. A visit should also be made to the Baroque church, whose stately tower was designed by Peter Thumb (1753), and to the unadorned castle of the Landgrave of Sulz (1499). The principal sights of Waldshut can be seen lining the Kaiserstrasse between the twin town gates (13th century): magnificently

A bridge over the Rhine in Basle.

decorated guild houses and commercial premises - not to mention the **Town Hall**.

The countryside surrounding the medieval town of **Laufenburg** makes it one of the most attractive sections of the High Rhine. An old stone bridge joins the Swiss town of Laufenburg on the south bank of the river with the German town of the same name on the north. As the Fastnacht pre-Lenten carnival gets under way, the inhabitants of both places are roused from their slumbers by ear-splitting "Chatter Music".

Bad Säckingen (15,000 inhabitants) boasts a unique historical sight. The bridge over the Rhine, over 400 years old, is 220 metres long - and thus the longest roofed wooden bridge in Europe. From it there is an attractive view of the town and the **Church of St. Fridolin**, one of the most magnificent Baroque churches on the Rhine. Bad Säckingen itself is famous as the setting of Viktor von Scheffel's narrative poem "The Trumpeter of Säckingen". Keeping alive the bard's memory is the **Viktor Scheffel House**, where he lived from

1850-51, as well as **Schönau Castle** - also known as the "Trumpeter's Castle" - on the opposite bank. It is the scene of Scheffel's poem, and has been turned into a museum. Apart from exhibits from the High Rhine region, the castle contains the most comprehensive collection of trumpets in Europe.

The first hydraulic power station in Europe (1868) and the associated industrial complex provide **Rheinfelden** (28,000 inhabitants), in the German state of Baden, with a livelihood. On the opposite river bank lies the pleasant Swiss spa town Rheinfelden.

In the three-country triangle where the Rhine makes a right-angle turn northwards, lies **Basle** (182,000 inhabitants) - the second-largest town in Switzerland. Six bridges link Greater Basle, on the left bank of the river, with Lesser Basle, on the right. The latter is primarily an industrial area, whilst Greater Basle retains narrow medieval streets and fine old houses.

Basle's favourable geographical location made the town a trading centre early in its history. A succession of proud monuments bear witness to the fact. Dominating the Old Town on the left bank of the Rhine is the **Romanesque-Gothic Cathedral** (predominantly 12th century), with its masonry of red sandstone from the Vosges and its brightly-coloured roof. The double cloisters, built on Romanesque foundations, are particularly charming. Behind the cathedral is the so-called Pfalz, a terrace some 20 metres above the Rhine, which affords attractive views across the river to the Black Forest. It is also a good vantage point for surveying the **Cathedral Ferry**, which requires no motor as it is propelled by the current.

Basle's other important buildings include the **Town Hall** (1504-1521) on the Market Square. Elaborately painted, it was built in the late Gothic style typical of Burgundy. The **Spalen Gate** (1370) is considered to be the best example of a medieval city gate in the country. Art lovers will take great pleasure in the **Fine Arts Museum**, which houses the most important collection of paintings in Switzerland.

Left, half-timbered houses at Stein am Rhein in Switzerland. **Right**, reflections in a tuba.

Basle to Strasbourg

20 km

N

Rheinau
Achern
Wiwersheim
Schiltighm.
Strasbourg
km 293
Handschuhhm.
Lingolsheim
Kehl
Ergershm.
Marlen
Motsheim
Illkirch
Graffenstaden
Offenburg
Fegersheim
Rhin
Rhein
Obernai
Ichenheim
Gengenbach
Erstein
Ottenheim
Barr
Gerstheim
Lahr
Benfeld
Obenheim
Diebolsheim
Kappel- Grafenhausen
Schloß Rust
(Castle) Ettenheim
Sassenheim
Rheinhausen
Schweighausen
Sélestat
Schoenau
Herbolshm.
Kenzingen
Wyhl
Marckolsheim
Sasbach
Teningen
FRANCE
Stadt
Vogtsburg
Emmendingen
Waldkirch
KAISERSTUHL
Kunheim
BUNDESREPUBLIK
Colmar
Gundelfgn.
Breisach
DEUTSCHLAND
Neuf- Brisach
Vogelsheim
Freiburg
Ste. Croix-
en- Plaine
(FED. REP. OF GERMANY)
(Rhine)
Fessenheim
Bad Krozingen
Grißheim
Ensisheim
Buggingen
SCHWARZWALD
(BLACK FOREST)
Chalampe
Müllheim
Wittenheim
Neuenburg
Heubronn
Kingershm.
Rhin
Rhein
Illzach
Mulhouse
Bad Bellingen
Adelsberg
Rixheim
Riedisheim
Kandern
Niffer
Rheinweiler
Krembs
Idsteiner Klotz
Schopfheim
Sierentz
Efringen-
Kirchen
Rosenau
Lörrach
Weil
Huningue
Riehen
Ransbach-
le- Bas
St. Louis
km 167
Rheinfelden
Möhlin
Allschwil
Grenzach-
Rheinfelden
Folgensbourg
Basle
Birsfelden
Wyhlen
Münchenstein
Pratteln
Férrette
Reinach
SCHWEIZ
(SWITZERLAND)

THE UPPER RHINE ABOVE STRASBOURG

Three countries meet at the Upper Rhine, and yet - geographically as well as culturally - the region between Basle and Strasbourg, framed by the Black Forest on one side and the Vosges on the other, forms a varied whole. The descendants of the Alemanni, whether of Swiss, Alsatian or German origins, speak one language and live in countryside which bears the same marks of long civilization. The most important cities in the area are Basle, Freiburg and Strasbourg. The traveller following the course of the Rhine should also not miss, however, the towns of Mulhouse, Colmar and Breisach.

Mulhouse, the second-largest town in Alsace (120,000 inhabitants), is situated where the hilly countryside of the Sundgau meets the Rhine plain. For many years it cultivated its links with Switzerland, becoming a part of France only in 1798 in the wake of the French Revolution. A room in the Town Hall (a fine Renaissance building constructed in 1552) recalls Mulhouse's ties to the Confederacy, of which the town was a member between 1515 and 1798. Apart from this, however, Mulhouse has few sights evoking memories of times past.

The **Automobile Museum** is worth a visit. Enthusiasts will revel in the sight of 600 veteran cars from all the corners of the earth, including more than 100 Bugattis. Those who have a preference for the Iron Way should visit the suburb of Dornach. Locomotives and carriages dating from as long ago as 1844 stand beside ultra-modern contemporary models in the **Railway Museum**.

Smaller than Mulhouse, but better endowed with historic buildings, is **Colmar** (67,000 inhabitants). It is the third-largest town in Alsace and lies where the Münster Valley carves its way through the Vosges. The past is omnipresent in Colmar, which first appears in records as Columbarium in 823 A.D. The imposing **Merchants' House**, dating from 1480, and countless fine patrician residences, call to mind the town's economic Golden Age. In 1226 Colmar was created a Free Imperial City by Emperor Frederick II; it was conquered by France between 1672-73. Amongst the townhouses, mention should be made of the **Pfister House** (1537), which has a charming wooden gallery and wall paintings by Bockstorffer, as well as the **Adolf House** (1350) - the oldest private house in the town. The **Head House** (1609) has a collection of approximately 100 face masks. It is also worth visiting the house at **30 Rue des Tanneurs**. It was the home of Fréderic-Auguste Bartholdi, the sculptor of the Lion of Belfort as well as the Statue of Liberty which dominates New York harbour. Today a museum, the house contains some fine pieces of furniture and numerous mementoes of the famous Alsatian craftsman.

A stroll through the **Tanners' District** will take the visitor past a number of lovely old timbered houses. Another attractive walk is through the picturesque historic quarter on the banks of the Lauch, which has earned the nickname "**La Petite Venise**" (Little Venice), and which is one of the town's most characteristic sights. No visitor to Colmar should miss the **Unterlinden Museum**, in the former Dominican Convent (13th-18th centuries), which houses the world-famous **Isenheim Altar.** The high altar reredos, painted on a carved altar shrine between 1512 and 1515 by Matthias Grünewald, is generally considered to be one of the greatest and most moving examples of German art.

Colmar has a number of other sights worth visiting: the early Gothic **Church of the Dominicans** (13th century), one of the most perfect examples of the architecture characteristic of the mendicant order and the home of the celebrated painting "The Madonna of the Rose Bower", by the Colmar-born artist Martin Schongauer (1473). **St. Martin's Cathedral** (1230-1370) boasts some fine stone carvings as well as the Old Guardroom (1575), with a Renaissance portal and elaborately decorated oriel window.

Preceding pages: above the roofs of Strasbourg, fancy headgear. **Below**, viticulture in the terraced landscape of Breisgau.

Witnesses of many centuries of past history, romantic narrow streets and corners are abundant in **Freiburg im Breisgau** (180,000 inhabitants), the seat of the second-oldest university in Germany. The unofficial capital of the Black Forest lies some 30 kilometres east of the Rhine. The Old Town, razed to the ground during World War II, has been meticulously restored to its former beauty. The attractive character of the centre is underlined by the so-called Bächle, the streams which run in gullies through the streets and alleys. In the old days the Bächle provided water to extinguish fires. Today they lend the town a welcome feeling of freshness and tranquillity. The third point in favour of the centre of Freiburg is the ban of motor traffic from the heart of the town.

The principal attraction in the town was mercifully spared by the bombing raids: the magnificent **Cathedral** (13-16th centuries), which is more than 850 years old, and forms the focal point of Cathedral Square. The Gothic masterpiece is a miracle of harmony, surmounted by a 115-metre tower topped by a carved stone cock.

The Swiss historian Carl J. Bruckhardt described it as "the loveliest tower in Christendom". The best way of comprehending the uniqueness of this architectural work of art is to climb the steps up to the tower platform. The way leads up past the **Hosanna Bell** (1258), which weighs 100 hundredweight. There is a good view from the top; to the south of the Cathedral Square, the late Gothic **Red Kaufhaus**, completed in 1532 and extensively restored in 1953, attracts attention. To the left stands the **House on the Lovely Corner**, built in 1761 by Christian Wenzinger as a personal memorial. To the north lies the **Corn Exchange** (originally 15th century), which has been restored in the original style; on the east side stands the former **Guard House** (1733).

Inside the cathedral, the visitor can gaze in wonder at such items of artistic merit such as the **Altarpiece** (1512-1516), painted by Hans Baldung Grien, which dominates the chancel. Stained

Oldtimers in the Automobile Museum in Mulhouse.

glass dating from the 14th century can be seen in the side aisles; in the **University Chapel** stands an Altarpiece by Hans Holbein the Younger.

The Herrenstrasse leads from the Cathedral Square to the **Swabian Gate** (originally 15th century), the focal point of the old merchants' quarter known as Oberlinden. Here there are many magnificent noblemen's homes. Of particular charm is the group formed by the **Fountain of St. Mary**, a 250-year old lime tree and the **Bear**, the oldest inn in Germany. It has been serving meals to the public since 1311.

The collection of the **Augustine Museum** should also be visited; it is housed in a former monastery of the Augustinian hermits in Salzstrasse, together with artistic and historico-cultural exhibits from the town and the hill region of Baden. Nor should you miss the **Island**, also known as the **Snail Quarter** (*Schneckenvorstadt*) - a self-contained district of old houses owned by artisans and guildsmen -, the restored **Old Town Hall** (originally 16th cen-

tury) and the Gothic **St. Martin's Church** on the Town Hall Square, as well as the **Old University** (17th-18th century) in Bertholdstrasse.

After our detour to Freiburg we return to the Rhine. And here, picturesquely perched on the summit of a basalt cliff rising steeply out of the river valley, stands **Breisach** - a former Imperial fortress town, later a continual bone of contention between Austria and France, and today the gateway to Alsace. The town is famous principally for the **Church of St. Stephen** and the **Central Wine Cellars** of the Baden Vintners' Association - the largest wine-producing concern in Europe.

The town suffered 80 percent destruction during World War II, but has since been restored. The Romanesque church with Gothic additions stands at the highest point; its twin towers and prominent chancel dominate the town skyline. Inside the church there is a magnificent carved **Altarpiece** by the unknown master HL (1523-1626), a late Gothic choir screen and wall paintings

Below left, fountain in the market place in Schaffhausen. Below right, down from the hills. Right, the Rhine Falls at Schaffhausen.

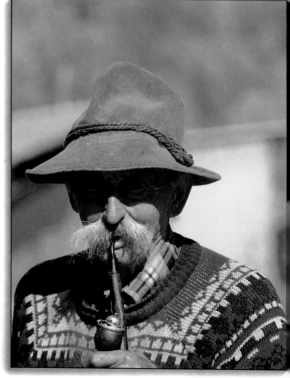

by the artist Martin Schongauer, who died in Breisach in ca. 1490. A few dates indicate the town's turbulent history: 1275 - Imperial City; 1648-1697 and 1703-1713 - occupied by France; 1793 - destroyed by the French; since 1805 - part of the state of Baden. Breisach lies on the west of the **Kaiserstuhl**, a volcanic hill which rises like an island above the Upper Rhine Plain. Here grow the famous Kaiserstuhl vines. Unfortunately the original appearance of the countryside, characterized by narrow vineyard terraces with pathways cut deep into the soft loess layer, was largely destroyed by a large-scale land reparcelling scheme in the 1970s.

The little wine-growing communities, however, have preserved their charm, inviting the visitor to enjoy a pleasant break with a glass of wine to accompany the typical dishes of the region. **Ihringen**, **Endingen** and **Burkheim** are just three examples of such villages. On one's northward journey, in fact, there are numerous opportunities to make a detour into the wine and fruit-growing regions to the left or right of the river. Along the Baden side runs the **Badische Weinstrasse**, the "wine road"; the equivalent, on the French bank, is the Route du Vin d'Alsace.

Strasbourg (257,000 inhabitants), the European Community town at the confluence of the Ill and the Rhine, manages to combine cosmopolitan flair with charm. Its well-preserved **Old Town** lies on an island between two branches of the Ill. The capital of Alsace is also the cultural and economic hub of the region. During the 16th century Strasbourg was one of the wealthiest free cities in the continent; today, it combines German and French elements. Until 1681 it was part of the German Empire. It was then conquered in peacetime by Louis XIV. As the capital the imperial province of Alsace-Lorraine it became part of Germany again in 1870-71. The city has been French since 1918.

The city's dominant landmark and the most important monument to its German period is the **Cathedral**, rising above the Old Town lying cradled be-

The steep gables of Strasbourg's Old City.

tween the twin arms of the Ill. The oldest Early Romanesque sections still in existence - the foundations and part of the crypt - date from the 11th century. The choir and transept were built in the main Romanesque period, i.e. during the 12th and the early part of the 13th century. The Gothic style became dominant around 1250; it was during this period that the lofty nave and side aisles were built. The North Tower, 142 metres high, was started in 1339 but not completed until 1439.

The West Front is an imposing sight with its elaborately carved portal and the famous Gothic rose window. Inside the cathedral can be found beautiful stained glass and further examples of the stonemason's art, such as the so-called **Angel Pillar** (1230-40) on the southern side of the transept. Noteworthy too is the remarkable **Astronomic Clock**; its casing, 18 metres high, was completed between 1570 and 1574. The mechanism was added 270 years later.

To the north, opposite the cathedral tower, stands the **Kammerzell House**.

The elaborately carved edifice is a restaurant today. The three-storey timbered building, constructed in 1589 on a stone ground floor dating from the Gothic period (1467), is one of the finest private houses in Strasbourg. Opposite stands another jewel, the **Stag's Apothecary**. The timbered construction was built in 1567, but predecessors of the chemist's establishment have stood on this site since 1268.

On the south side of the cathedral, and open to the public, is the **Rohan Palace** (1728-1742), the former residence of the cardinal bishops of the Rohan family. The palais contains a museum of artefacts, an art gallery and an archaeological collection. **The Musée de l'Oeuvre de Notre-Dame** (14th-16th centuries) is devoted to the story of the the construction of the cathedral.

Further important monuments in Strasbourg include the **Old Town Hall** (1582-1585) on the Place Kléber, and the beautifully restored **Tanners' House** (1651) at the heart of the picturesque tanners' quarter.

Left, taking in the sights. **Right**, the west portal of Strasbourg Minster.

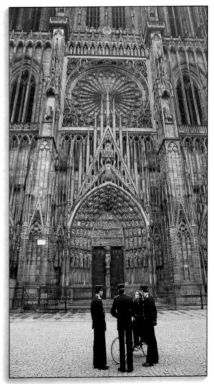

FROM KEHL TO LUDWIGSHAFEN

Almost 250 metres long, the **Europe Bridge**, constructed in 1960, links Strasbourg on the left bank of the Rhine with **Kehl** (30,000 inhabitants), the principal town of South Baden, on the right. During the 17th century Kehl served as Strasbourg's vital bridgehead on the opposite side of the river. And so a little fishing village by the mighty river became an important freshwater port which played a crucial role in Franco-German history.

In contrast to many of the venerable towns along the course of the Rhine - such as **Rastatt** with its castle (1700-1707) built by Margrave Ludwig Wilhelm, now housing a historical museum - the town of **Karlsruhe** (270,000 inhabitants), on the right bank of the river, can look back on only a short history. It was not until 1717 that Karl Wilhelm von Durlach had a new residence built here, christening it with the name "Carls Ruhe" - "Carl's Rest". Under the influence of the Baroque master architect Friedrich Weinbrenner an administrative town and garrison were subsequently created, giving expression to Baroque town planning principles in the roads radiating out from the castle. Classicistic façades gaze down on the market place, dominated by a sandstone pyramid containing the mortal remains of Karlsruhe's founding father. The museums are particularly worth visiting, especially the **Children's Museum** in the Orangery, the **Baden Regional Museum** (containing Margrave Ludwig Wilhelm of Baden's trophy collection), and the **Fine Arts Museum**.

The Rhine Valley now displays its charms once more, especially along the left bank, where the famous **German Wine Road** begins at the foot of the Haardt mountain massif marking the eastern section of the Palatinate Forest. Thanks to its particularly mild climate the region is one of intensive fruit farming and viticulture. With its typical French-style houses, **Landau** cannot disguise its affinities with the neigh-

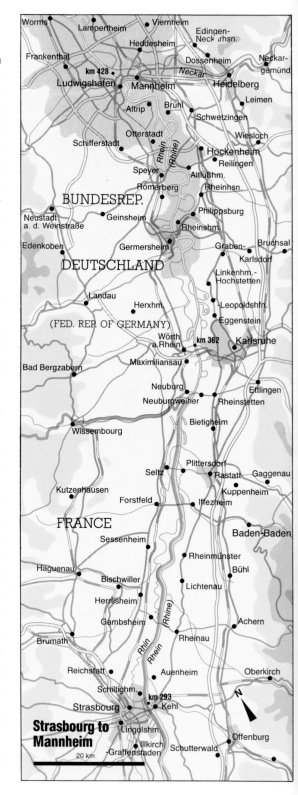

Strasbourg to Mannheim

20 km

bouring country across the river. It bears witness to the many long years during which this region on the left river bank was the prize in the tug-of-war between France and Germany. The town was admittedly founded in 1262 by a German count, but it was ceded to France in 1648 in the aftermath of the Thirty Years War. It was then replanned according to the wishes of Louis XIV. In 1814 the town was taken again by Bavaria; after World War I it became French again; only since 1935 has it permanently formed part of German territory.

Only a short distance away, in the heart of the Palatinate near Annweiler, romantic **Trifels Castle** stands perched high up amongst the red sandstone cliffs of the Haardt. In the Middle Ages it was a notorious "prison", veiled in dark secrets. Within these walls, the legendary Richard the Lionheart was held captive in 1193 by Emperor Heinrich VI. But under the Hohenstaufens the castle was also used from time to time as a place of safekeeping for their sacred symbols of power: the Imperial Jewels - crown,

sceptre and orb. It is unfortunate that the restoration of the castle, undertaken in the spirit of the romantic fantasies of the 19th century, has preserved so little of this medieval heritage.

Let us return to the Wine Road, which leads us - although we have wandered some 30 km away from the course of the Rhine - to **Neustadt**. Its attribute, "an der Weinstrasse", indicates unmistakeably that this is the wine capital of the Palatinate. The town's main architectural landmark is the Gothic **Collegiate Church** with its contrasting towers; the real focal point, however, is wine. Countless wine bars, wine merchants and wine producers lend the town its character, which comes to the fore especially in the colourful autumn wine festivals, with the election of the Wine Queen and the biggest vintners' procession in Germany.

Around Neustadt are scattered picturesque wine-growing villages such as **Diedesfeld** and - above all - **Hambach**. The grape's conviviality may make one forget that an important chapter in Ger-

man history was written in the **Kästenburg castle** overlooking the town. On May 27th 1842 a mob of 20,000 patriots demanded, following the example of the French Revolution, "Unity, Justice and Liberty" for the Free States as well. The **Hambach Festival** was thus a powerful declaration of democracy in Germany, leading to parliamentary resolutions limiting freedom of the press and freedom of assembly; it also resulted in a series of persecutions of political leaders, and is regarded as one of the key events in the build-up culminating in the the bourgeois revolution of 1848.

For tourists, **Deidesheim** represents the heart of the region through which the Wine Road passes as it lies nestled between sunny vine-clad terraces marking the foothill approaches to the Haardt massif. The market place is dominated by the **Church of St. Ulrich**, a Gothic masterpiece dating from the 15th century. The **Town Hall** is 100 years younger, and it later acquired a fine flight of stairs. Much earlier, as long ago as the 12th century, the juice of the grape was poured out for customers at the **Gasthaus " Zur Kanne"**; today the inn remains the best place to enjoy one of the fine local vintages.

The road along the Haardt arrives next in **Bad Dürkheim**, a town of some size which combines viticulture with resort amenities. For some 150 years the town has enjoyed a reputation as a medicinal spa; The salt springs were exploited as early as the end of the 16th century. The **Sausage Fair** is held every autumn on the outskirts of the town; it is a folkloric festival with culinary accents whose origins can be traced back to 1417 A.D..

Far removed from this autumnal merry-making is **Limburg Abbey**, whose powerful ruins with their well preserved Gothic tower and staircase overlook the town from an eminence. The original building, founded in around 1025 by Konrad II and subsequently extended on numerous occasions, was conceived in the pure Romanesque style in keeping with the spirit of the times. It became the principal residence of the **The Palace in Karlsruhe.**

160

Salii and the principal place of safe keeping of the Imperial Jewels. The complex, however, has been in ruins since the 16th century - destroyed, plundered and finally used as a stone quarry. A similar sad fate befell neighbouring **Castle Hardenburg**, a fortress dating from the 13th century which was transformed into an extensive castle complex in the 16th century. It was blown up by the French in 1692; what remained was razed to the ground during the French Revolution, when the entire region belonged to France.

The cathedral town of **Speyer** (44,000 inhabitants) lures the traveller Rhinewards again. One of the bastions of Romanesque architecture, the town is the site of the largest Imperial cathedral on the Rhine. The Celts built a settlement known as Novo Magius here, but the origins of Speyer's present name clearly lie in the Franconian "Spira". Konrad II laid the foundation stone of the **Cathedral** - which still dominates the town today - in 1030, marking the beginning of Speyer's glittering ascent to its later position as Imperial City and Free Imperial City.

The vaulted nave of the church was not only innovative as regards its architectural design; even today it is second in size only to Cologne Cathedral, which was not completed until the end of the 19th century. The crypt contains one of the most impressive collections of medieval tombs to be found anywhere. Eight emperors and kings, three empresses and two Imperial chancellors have found their final resting place here. Small wonder, then, that the town itself should also have been a focal point in the political life of the day. Fifty times the Imperial Diet met within its walls, including the famous occasion in 1529 when the rights of the Lutheran citizens were annulled. When the representatives of the new church left the council meeting in protest, their new name was born: "Protestants".

Speyer's decline came unexpectedly at Whitsun 1689, when French troops stormed the town and virtually razed it to the ground, scattering the Imperial

Camera shy.

Tombs and their remains to the wind. Fortunately, the soldiers did not find everything. It was not until 1900 that the intact sarcophagi of Konrad II, Heinrich III and Heinrich IV were rediscovered, and the burial objects placed on public display in the town museum. What little remained of Speyer's once-proud fortifications after the French invasion was demolished in 1792. Of the original 70 towers only one can still be seen - the **Altpörtel**, the "old gate" at the end of Maximilianstrasse: a slender, well-proportioned building with a steep roof.

Speyer is particularly proud of its **Wine Museum**, which contains elaborately carved wooden barrels, drinking utensils and what claims to be the oldest wine in the world. Dating from Roman times, the dried-out darkish lump is still in its original bottle. Also of interest are the **Jewish Baths**, dating from about 1130 A.D., and the Church of the Holy Trinity and the **Town Hall** - both built in the 18th century.

We must now cross to the other side of the river again, for which visitor would want to miss the opportunity of seeing **Heidelberg** - even if it does lie a short distance away on the Neckar, which some 20 kilometres further on flows into the Rhine. Heidelberg's incomparable position, with the Old Town bordering the river on the floor of the narrow valley, framed by steep wooded slopes and dominated by the imposing ruins of the castle, is surely a prime reason why the town has long enjoyed a reputation as the epitome of German Romanticism. The town's traditional role as a centre of learning, stretching back to 1386, is doubtless also of paramount importance. The University Library contains the **Great Heidelberg Songbook**, the most important medieval manuscript still in existence.

Most visitors, however, make the **Castle** their first port of call; from the terrace there is a magnificent view of the town and the **Old Bridge** across the Neckar. The extensive building complex began to take shape at the beginning of the 13th century. Initially it was primarily a fortress, flanked by numer-

The sun sets behind Mainz Cathedral.

162

ous towers. Over the centuries the electoral princes added new wings, or tore down or modified the existing ones. During the 17th century, the skirmishes of war also left deep scars.

The most prominent buildings are the Gothic **Church of the Holy Ghost**, **Friedrich's Wing** and **Rupert's Wing**. Pride of place, however, goes to the **Otto-Heinrich Wing**, an italianate building constructed in 1557. In spite of being struck by lightning in 1764, this section of the castle is as famous as the repository of the enormous **Heidelberg Vat**, a wooden barrel with a capacity of 221,726 litres. It was guarded by Perkeo, a dwarf from South Tyrol (represented by a wooden figurine in the cellar). He reputedly owed his name to his habit of responding to a request for a glass of wine with the words "Perche no?" - "Why not?" Legend also has it that he even emptied the barrel himself!

Our route back to the Rhine takes us past **Schwetzingen**, as renowned for its **Baroque Castle** containing a Rococo theatre (home of the Schwetzingen Festival) as for its asparagus fields on the slopes above the river. Court life at Schwetzingen blossomed for a second time under Elector Carl Theodor.

From Schwetzingen it is only a stone's throw to the most important river port on the Upper Rhine: **Mannheim** (300,000 inhabitants). A modest fishing village is mentioned as existing here as early as 766 A.D.. During the Middle Ages the town prospered by exacting customs duties on inland navigation. It owes its present-day countenance to the town planning measures adopted in the 17th century. The principal feature is the chessboard layout of the streets surrounding the mighty Baroque **Electoral Palace**, now the university. Fine Art Nouveau buildings are clustered around Friedrichsplatz in rare unity of style.

The opposite bank of the Rhine has been taken over by the industrial town of **Ludwigshafen**, whose economic expansion is mostly due to the founding of the BASF chemical company in 1865. Today the majority of the population is employed there.

A view of Speyer.

FROM MANNHEIM TO MAINZ

Soon after Mannheim, the state of Hessen pushes its boundary forward as far as the right bank of the Rhine, which from this point becomes progressively more heavily used by freight barges. In stark contrast is the **Kühkopf**, the largest nature park in Hessen and, with an area of 2,400 hectares, the largest meadowland conservation ground in Europe. The park, created in 1829 when the river was straightened, lies near Stockstadt. It extends for some distance into the marshes on the right bank. This miniature natural paradise at the heart of a densely populated industrial area is characterized by flooded meadows and groves of silver willows. It is also home to a colony of grey herons and a variety of diving and swimming waterfowl.

On the opposite bank, which is still part of the state of Rhineland-Palatinate, lies **Worms** (74,000 inhabitants), a former Imperial city which is still the

focal point for the region. Inhabited for more than 6,000 years, Worms is one of the oldest and historically most important cities in Germany. Under the Romans it was known as Civitas Vangionum; between 413 and 436 A.D. it was chosen by the rulers of Burgundy as the capital of their territory; 200 years later, Queen Brunhild built her residence here. Under the Carolingians, Worms was the site of the Imperial Palace. The Concordat of Worms of 1122 marked the end of the quarrel over the investiture. Worms's irresistible rise under the Salian and Hohenstaufen emperors made it one of the most important cities in medieval times. It was the setting for many Imperial Diets, until the Swedes reduced the town to rubble during the Thirty Years' War.

In spite of being destroyed on a number of occasions, this bastion of the Romanesque has retained many elements which bear witness to its Golden Age. Pride of place is taken by the **Cathedral**, constructed during the 11th and 12th centuries, a masterpiece of Upper-Rhineland

Preceeding pages: traditional hats. Below, a glass of new wine goes well with the meal.

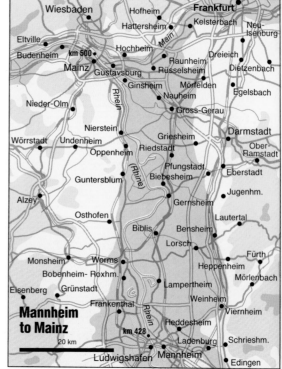

Romanesque architecture, built above the walls of the Roman forum and dedicated in 1181. The decoration of the portals, the crypt of the Salian emperors, the **Baroque High Altar** by Balthasar Neumann, and the multitude of Romanesque and Gothic sculptures and paintings are only a few of the the cathedral's incomparable treasures.

The nearby **Collegiate Church of St. Andrew** is a pillared basilica dating from the 11th century. Not far away stands the **Church of St. Magnus**, the foundation stone of which was laid in the 9th century. It has served the local Protestant community as a church since 1521, the year in which Martin Luther was called before the Diet of Worms. His refusal to retract his "insane doctrines" led to the schism in the Christian church. The **Edict of Worms** had Luther sent into exile and ordered the destruction of his theses. An impressive memorial, composed of twelve figures, celebrates the great reformer and his place in history. St. Andrew's Gate, erected as late as 1906, leads to the **Holy Sand**, the oldest Jewish cemetery in Europe. Like Jews' Alley, the Jewish Baths and the synagogue it is a reminder that a Jewish community lived within the city walls of Worms as long ago as the 11th century. North of the Raschid Gate, surrounded by vineyards, lies the **Church of Our Lady**, a jewel of High Gothic architecture. In the shade of its venerable walls flourish the grapes which produce Liebfrauenmilch - the "Milk of Our Lady", whose reputation has hopefully not suffered too gravely in the wake of the wine scandals of the past few years. The name itself first appears in an English travel journal dated 1687; it has long also been used to describe other sweet grape varieties grown elsewhere in the near and not-so-near vicinity. The Baroque **Church of the Holy Trinity** (1709-1725) stands in the midst of the "Liebfrauenmilch" vineyards.

Situated more than 20 kilometres from the Rhine, **Alzey** always lay in the shadow of the powerful Imperial city of Worms, although its origins also stretch far back into the mists of time. In 400

A modern bridge spans the Rhine.

B.C. the Celts erected a fortified settlement on a ford across the Selz; the Romans later extended it into a fort. It is claimed that the minstrel in the Song of the Nibelungen entitled "The Folk of Alzey" actually lived here; there is, however, no concrete proof of the fact, even if the well on the Fish Market recalls his name. The houses of this picturesque district town are overshadowed by the **Elector's Castle**; building of the latter commenced in 1126 and led to countless alterations and extensions during the course of its history. The last major project was in 1902, when the architects realized here their idea of what a medieval castle looked like.

The crypt of the **Church of St. Nicholas** has a skilfully executed tombstone dating from 1430. Over 1000 years previously, during the reign of the Emperor Constantine I, the beer mash was prepared which today can be still be seen in the **Municipal Museum**: the oldest beer in the world.

The favourable climate of the Rhine valley has resulted in a wine-growing tradition which in the region between Worms, Alzey and Mainz stretches back over 2,000 years. Bastions of Rhineland viticulture are the little town of **Oppenheim** - the warmest place in Germany, which lay directly on the Rhine until the river was straightened in the 19th century - and neighbouring **Niederstein**. The **Sirona Baths** can be seen near the historic town of **Adelshöfen** (16th-17th century); in Roman times they were known for their fountain and hot springs. As elsewhere in wine-growing regions, the vintners' festivals here are also a part of ancient historic traditions. Hardly a weekend passes between June and October without some festival being celebrated in one of the wine-growing villages of Rhinehessen.

All roads in the region have always led to **Mainz** (186,000 inhabitants), the former residence of the princes of the Church situated opposite the point where the Main flows into the Rhine - a town where, during the Middle Ages, sacred and secular power were united. Past glories of the city are enshrined in the

BASF on the Rhine. A painting by Robert Stieler.

Cathedral, which celebrated its 1000th anniversary in 1975. The Bishop of Mainz in those early days, Willigis, was also an Elector and Chancellor of the "Holy Roman Empire of Germany". On the eve of the dedication of the new cathedral the bishop's seat was burnt down; the massive church which can be seen today, and which has sometimes been described as a mountain of a cathedral, was finally dedicated in 1036 under Willigis's successor Bardo. Its external appearance has changed several times since then as a result of fire, plundering and reconstruction. Thus the characteristic tower in the form of a staircase was built in the 18th century after lightning had destroyed the Gothic spire. The interior is a journey through the history of art. The gamut runs from 12th-century Gothic windows and early 13th-century sculptures, via Renaissance tombs to Baroque choir stalls.

The city centre still lies today in the immediate neighbourhood of this important church. Mainz has preserved its original countenance, however, only in

Augustinerstrasse and the narrow alleys in the vicinity, where churches, timbered buildings and classicistic buildings crowd together. Dominating the scene is **St. Stephen's Church**, whose windows contain contemporary stained-glass panels by the artist Marc Chagall.

The glittering display of princely pomp and circumstance is most clearly reflected in the residences of the rulers: the Elector's **Palace Schönborn** and the **Osteiner Hof**. It can also be seen in the Headquarters of the Knights of St. John, the **New Arsenal**, and especially in the **Electoral Palace**, which today houses the Roman German Museum.

Johannes Gutenberg, Mainz's most famous son, is honoured in a museum bearing his name; the **World Museum of Printing**. It was Gutenberg who, in the middle of the 15th century, revolutionized the printing of books by the introduction of movable metal type, thus also helping to establish the reputation of Mainz University, one of the oldest in the land.

Mannheim container port.

FROM MAINZ
TO KOBLENZ

How does the poem go? - "To the Rhine, to the Rhine, do not go to the Rhine, my son - that is my advice to you." But what did he do, then, the Rhineland poet Karl Simrock - born in 1802 in Bonn and buried there in 1876, famous as a professor of Old German? He moved over to Menzenberg and built his "Parsifal House", where he pruned his vines and spread chalk on his asparagus bed in between translating Wolfram's "Parsifal" into New High German, and praising his red Menzensberger wine.

Preceding pages: The Rhine meanders round the Loreley rocks. **Left,** an autumn view of the Rhine.

And if there were ever a single person who stayed away from the Rhine because of Simrock's verses, then surely it must have been because he had not read the next couplet: "For there your life will become too easy, your spirits too cheerful." For Simrock, the countryside bordering the Rhine was "the loveliest land in Germany", both picturesque and romantic. Thus he entitled the book he published in 1840 "The Picturesque and Romantic Rhineland". Which brings us back again to Mainz.

The actual name is of Celtic origin; they worshipped a god of Light by the name of Mogon. The earliest traces, however, are Roman. Moguntiarum was the Roman capital of Upper Germany. The oldest finds here date from 38 B.C., and for that reason Mainz has counted itself since 1962 amongst the 2,000-year-old cities in the land - 2,000 years of existence in one of the most sensitive geographical positions in the country. "That is the place", wrote Anna Segher, the most famous novelist in East Germany, in her novel The Seventh Cross, "where - so they say - the shots fired in the last war stirred up those of the previous one." She knew what she was saying: she was born in Mainz in 1900.

In the Second World War, too, Mainz suffered a great deal - as always. It was reduced to a heap of rubble, for which reason the citizens often echoed the song of Ernst Neger, the singing roofer. Many people take it for just another Shrovetide carnival ditty: "Don't worry, silly goose, all will soon be well again."

Jean Paul, the poet, came to see the Fastnacht, the carnival, as well. He felt himself "transported to heaven". Travel writer Johann Ignatz Weitzel wrote as long ago as 1825: "Yes, I am pleased to be in this area again - as always. The Rhinelanders are a cheerful bunch; they take pleasure in life and know how to enjoy it." He found in addition that "their character resembles that of the French" - an observation which found little favour ten years after the Congress of Vienna. And yet these Rhinelanders had been very close to becoming French: in 1793 the writer Georg Forster, a supporter of the Revolution, had actually submitted a formal application in Paris to the effect that Mainz and the whole of the left bank of the Rhine should be annexed as part of the Republic - the French one, of course. The deed brought him approval in France and banishment at home. There they preferred to attribute their celebrated joie-de-vivre to their wine; indeed, in the city centre, to

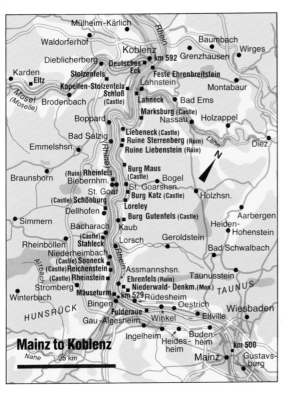

Mainz to Koblenz

the east of the Ministry of Justice, stands the third-century **Roman Column** of senator Davitius Victor - with grapes and vine-leaves on the side.

The citizens of Mainz retained their links to wine even after the Romans had left. St. Bonifatius, the patron saint of Germany and the country's first bishop, chose Mainz as his **Bishopric** in 742 A.D. The town grew, becoming the capital of the League of Rhenish Cities in 1254. It gained in significance, even when the cathedral burned down in 1080. It was rebuilt and together with Speyer and Worms is today considered one of the finest Romanesque churches on the Rhine.

As if striving to counterbalance the weight of medieval Christian tradition the city of Mainz has long been a centre of the mass media. He we refer not to the fact that the the city is now home to Germany's second national television station, but to the idea of one Johannes Gensfleisch vom Hofe zum Gutenberg. It was he was who thought of using a wine press to make books, producing a volume completely "without the help of reed, stylus or quill pen, but merely by means of the wonderful unity, proportion and harmony of stamps and type." Henceforth everyone could read the Bible and form his own opinion of it. The Middle Ages were over.

At least seven towns maintain, like Mainz, that they were the birthplace of modern printing. Certain it is that Gutenberg worked away on his moveable letters in Strasbourg as well; he lived there for many years because of quarrels with the guilds in his home town. Mainz, however, claims fame as the first town where printing was actually carried out; furthermore, one of Gutenberg's famous 200 42-line Bibles dating from the period between 1452 and 1455 is actually on view in the **Gutenberg Museum**. The inventor himself was hardly able to profit from his ingenious discovery; his companion and financier Fust took over the business as soon as it became profitable. The fame and glory, however, remain Gutenberg's: fifty years after his invention, **Urban panorama - Mainz.**

more than 8 million books had been printed - and not just Bibles in Latin. Less than 20 years later, in nearby Worms, the Augustinian monk Martin Luther stood before the Diet and stuck courageously to his dictum that he would say nothing but the truth, "even if you execute me twenty times over".

The means of spreading Luther's truths abroad had been discovered in Mainz: the truth, Veritas, which lies in wine, had always been known in these parts. Moreover, from 1850 the youthful Christian Adalbert Kupferberg had added to the "truth" of German wines the temperament of their neighbours in the Champagne region across the border. He founded his cellars for the production of sparkling wine in vaulted premises bearing traces of Roman and medieval occupation: "Kupferberg Gold", from Golden Mainz.

Every stroll through Mainz rapidly develops into a journey back through the millenia, from the **Roman Stones** of the old aqueduct (first century) to the cluster of Baroque administrative buildings serving the local government of the capital of the German state of Rhineland Palatinate. In between is the **Bell Tree**, lovingly known by the initiated as the "Officials' Alarm Clock". One passes the **Wooden Tower** (14th century) - where the robber chief Schinderhannes was executed in 1802-3 - and the Gutenberg Memorial. And anyone who has lost his way need only look down at the ground in Ludwigstrasse; there he will find a brass rail set in the pavement, indicating that he is standing at a latitude of 50° North.

Opposite Mainz lies **Wiesbaden** (280,000 inhabitants), the state capital of Hessen. It has been situated on the Rhine since 1926; in that year its boundaries were extended to take in Biebrich and the town now boasts a magnificent waterfront promenade along the river. The hot water which issues from the ground here made Wiesbaden famous in the past, and determines its character even in present times; every day, almost two million litres bubble out of 26 springs. It has

been proved that some of them were used by the Romans: the Schützenhof springs, the Adler spring and the Kochbrunnen, producing on their own almost half a million litres per day, gushing forth at a temperature of 66°C from a depth of 2,000 metres. The Romans also gave the town its first name: Aquae matticae, after the Mattici tribe. When the Limes, the Roman wall protecting the Empire against the feared Germani, was breached, the Romans lost their spa and the resort its name. The water, however, remained: the scholar Einhard, the biographer of Charlemagne, mentions the town in 829 A.D. as the castrum quod moderna tempore Wisibada vocatur - "the fortified settlement which is now known as Wisibada" - the "Bath in the Meadows".

Its proximity to Golden Mainz, however, did not suit the town on the opposite river bank; one of the rulers of the former, Siegfried III, the Archbishop and Count von Eppstein, had Wiesbaden, the spa, destroyed because he could not conquer it. It happened in 1242; from that time onwards, the town existed only as a subsidiary residence of the Nassau dynasty. It was, however, large enough to be subjected to all the feuds during the ensuing years, and to serve as an intermediate goal in every war. The only constant factor throughout its turbulent history was the water. And so, after 1810, the year in which the Kurhaus - the **Pump House** - was built, Wiesbaden rose to fame as a world spa.

Goethe lived in the "healing spa" in 1814 and 1815, noting: "Earth, heaven and the people are different; all are of a cheerful disposition and I feel better from day to day."

The town is very much a child of the 19th century - and a pretty one at that. From the Byzantine-inspired **Greek Chapel** (Russian Orthodox), begun in 1849, on the slopes of the Neroberg, via various other churches to the **Castle** (1841), the New Town Hall (1888) and the State Theatre (1894-1902), the town was adorned with public buildings. The last of them were built in the Wilhelminian era, which is why the town also

The towers and spires of the Marktkirche in Wiesbaden.

boasts a monument to Wilhelm I. Admittedly the noble façades of **Wilhelmstrasse** date back to the reign of one of the Dukes of Nassau rather than to the Hohenzollern emperor. And when, in 1907, the original Kurhaus was extended, the town's earliest beginnings were remembered with gratitude; Aquis Mattiacis is engraved on the portico in front of the domed pump room.

"The Rhine Valley brought me forth - that highly favoured and benign region, harsh neither in its climate nor in the quality of its soil, rich in cities and villages, peopled by a merry folk - it must be among the sweetest regions of the habitable globe. Here, sheltered from rough winds by the mountains of the Rhine district and happily exposed to the southern sun, flourish those famous communities whose very names make a wine-bibbers heart rejoice - Rauenthal, Johannisberg, Rüdesheim - and here too is that favoured town in which, some forty years ago, I first saw the light of day." - Thus Felix Krull, a character from a novel and the eponymous hero of

Thomas Mann's novel, describes himself in his inimitably loquacious manner. Felix Krull may be a figment of the imagination, but his native region is real enough - and its eulogy can hardly be treated as one of Felix's customary confidence tricks.

Here the **Rhenish Uplands** lean across towards the river like a sloping lectern. The river flows along a westerly course between Mainz and Bingen, offering the massif's slate-covered slopes to the sun's rays. "Johnson's Guide", the Golden Book for wines and the regions where they are grown, notes tersely of the Rhinegau: "Best wine-growing area on the Rhine...". For British connoisseurs, once they had discovered the area, the **Rheingau Riesling** became the epitome of white Rhine wine par excellence - a role it has maintained until this day. They called the wine "Hock", which was the nearest approximation to Hochheim they could manage to pronounce.

Hochheim actually lies on the Main; furthermore, it is separated from the rest

of the Rhinegau region by Wiesbaden. After that, however, can be assembled the evocative parade of names of which Felix Krull already mentioned the most illustrious. First of all we encounter that "favoured town" of his childhood: **Eltville** (16,000 inhabitants), then as now "renowned for its sparkling wines". The affinity with bubbly drinks might lead one to surmise that "Eltville" has more than just a French ring about it; the name, however, comes from the Latin: alta villa was the settlement's name in the olden days, a possible reminder of the Romans' understanding of the art of wine-making. Of note in the town: the Gothic **Parish Church** dating from the 14th century. The 15th-century **Keep** was once part of an archbishop's castle.

Attractive villages follow each other here in rapid succession: **Oestrich**, with the oldest Catholic parish church in the Rhinegau, dating from the 12th century, also has as a landmark a 16th-century wooden crane. What is possibly the oldest stone cottage in the country - the **Grey House** - can be seen in **Winkel**. In the same village stands the **Brentano House** (1751), with a collection of works by Goethe and various Romantic poets. **Hattenheim**, together with the Cistercian monastery (12th-14th century) four kilometres away at **Eberbach**, is celebrated for its medieval buildings. It was here, and not in a studio, that most of "The Name of the Rose" was filmed. The village is, however, even more famed for its wine. With their own fleet of ships and their own cellars on the banks of the Rhine, the monks were not liable for taxes and were able to distribute their wine and spread their own fame far and wide throughout the region. This fame has remained intact, as have most of the buildings - the heathen period of French occupation notwithstanding. At times, Eberbach served as a stable for sheep and as a lunatic asylum. Today, the wheel has turned more or less full circle, for the erstwhile monastery is now the seat of the Hessen State Land Administration.

Enthroned in massive splendour on the summit above the vineyards is

Wooden casks are becoming increasingly rare.

Johannisberg - it, too, a former monastery, then a castle in the 18th century. Later it was a gift, presented first by Napoleon and then by the Austrian Emperor, as a token of gratitude to Clemens Prinz von Metternich. Each year, any Johannisberger wine which escapes the famous yellow and red shiny bottles is transformed into sparkling wine and adds a touch of feudal glitter to many a bourgeois dining table as "Fürst von Metternich".

The next town is **Geisenheim** (12,000 inhabitants), the seat of the **Rhinegau Cathedral** (a Catholic parish church founded in the 8th century), and of the National Research Station for wine and fruit growing and horticulture. Projects here include experiments with new grape varieties. Then comes **Rüdesheim** (10,000 inhabitants), where Riesling wines celebrate triumphs of a sort at afternoon festivities in the **Drosselgasse**. It is worth paying a visit to the **Rhinegau Museum** to learn about the history of the Rhine. Ruins of three of the four fortresses which once stood sentinel over

the "trade route" - the Front, Middle and Lower Castles - can still be seen. There is nothing left of the fourth castle. Noteworthy, too, is the 15th-century late Gothic **Parish Church**, as well as countless merchants' and noblemen's residences dating from the 16th-18th centuries. High above the town, accessible by cable railway, is the Niederwald Statue, the **Germania**, the German National Monument, a truly colossal vision of bronze and manipulated history.

She is 10.60 metres tall to the crown of her head - and 12.35 metres to the Imperial crown she holds aloft in her right hand. Including the pedestal, the entire monument is 37.60 dizzy metres high. The old lady still receives hordes of visitors: about two million every year. She began her watch over the Rhine in 1883; in order to cast the statue, Kaiser Wilhelm permitted the melting down of old Prussian cannon totalling 550 hundredweight. Everybody profited: the monumental sculptors got the metal they needed, the gunsmiths got new orders, and the Emperor got better cannon. Were

Morning mist unveils the Rhinegau hills.

it not for the fact that it rained so hard on the day of the statue's dedication, today's visitors would have found here nothing except the wine. Anarchists had planted a bomb, hoping to catch the iron lady herself as well as the visiting Kaiser and his entourage. The fuse was already lit, but as it was so wet it went out again. Both the monument and the emperor were saved; the emperor until 1888, the monument until this day. The only victims of the attack were the conspirators themselves; they were executed in Halle.

The Rhinegau continues round the next bend. Here lies **Assmannshausen** (1,200 inhabitants) where, on the slopes of the Hollerberg, a pleasantly mild red wine grows - the only one in the area on the right bank of the Rhine. On the left bank, by contrast, between Mainz and Bingen, is **Ingelheim** (19,000 inhabitants) - site of the former **Imperial Palace of Charlemagne**, and a town with a frequently-cited epithet: the Red Wine Town. The wine has always been celebrated; legend has it that it was the reason for Ingelheim's being annexed by Lothar the German. Of the Imperial Palace, however, few traces remain. Long past, too, is the age when affairs of national importance were enacted in Ingelheim. One of the last of these was the Ingelheim Royal Congress on 30 December 1105, when the alliance of the bishops of Mainz, Worms and Cologne succeeded in overthrowing the emperor of the time, Heinrich IV - and not only by decree. The most famous of all Ingelheim residents, Sebastian Münster, the 16th-century cosmographer, reports the incident thus: "They removed the crown from his head, and pulled him from his throne, and robbed him of all imperial insignia."

Bingen (24,000 inhabitants) enjoys a pretty situation at the mouth of the Nahe, opposite **Bingerbrück**, and dominated by a medieval-style castle built in the 19th century. **Burg Klopp** (13th century), standing on the foundations of a Roman fort, was constructed by the rulers of the time at a critical defensive point. Today it houses administrative offices. Most of the buildings still

The confluence of the Rhine and the Nahe at Bingen.

standing date from the 19th century. The citizens of Bingen have thought up a couplet to describe its position: "If you are out of breath, you must be in the Town Hall." And yet even more than the castle, and more than the medieval **Drusus Bridge** across the Nahe - which reminds us of the Romans, leaving us with the unsolved question as to whether they were really the ones to build the first wooden bridge across the Nahe at this point - more than all that, Bingen's principal attraction in the eyes of travellers is the **Mouse Tower**, where the Rhine turns to wend its way through the mountains above the **Bingen Hole**. It is the town's principal landmark.

The tower itself (13th-14th century) owes its name not, of course, to the four-legged rodents - at least accoring to enlightened accounts - but to the Maut, the customs duty, which was levied here. Others claim that the origin lies in the verb mausen, which means to spy; that, indeed, was the function of the tower. Simrock then brings forth the musketeers' weapons, which could have

left their names here: the tower was the arsenal of the Ehrenfels family - not a trace of customs duties or spying! With so many explanations, perhaps we may yet feel inclined to believe Sebastian Münster's none-too-endearing tale of Bishop Hatto of Mainz (see page 70).

Bingen Hole marks the beginning of the "Rhine Romanticism" phenomenon, which at the beginning of the nineteenth century was more invention than discovery. Two English inventions - steel engraving and steam-powered boats - were primarily responsible in those days for the sudden rise in popularity of the Rhine - a factor only describable in English as The Boom. Paradoxically enough, this was the era of accelerating industrial development; the two factors, technology-based economic progress and backwards-facing nostalgic sentimentality, met head-on. In 1817 the first steamship, the "Caledonia", sailed down the Rhine. In 1825 the "Rijn" was the first steam-powered vessel to successfully negotiate Bingen Hole, which in 1830-32 was widened for the new river

traffic with the aid of explosives. Later came the railway lines along both banks. And yet, as the original character and the long-standing Romanticism of the Rhine Valley fell increasingly victim to progress, so they increased the enthusiasm with which they pressed forward with their technical innovations. The tunnel entrances were adorned with battlements like romantic castles. The castles themselves were rebuilt, mostly by the Prussian nobility, for after the Congress of Vienna the Rhineland fell into their hands - quite contrary to their wishes, at first: they would have preferred Saxony. And so they set about the task of tidying up the Rhineland in the style of times past.

In 1825, **Rheinstein Castle** was the first monument to be subjected to this new vocation: it was built by Prince Friedrich Ludwig of Prussia. Reichenstein Castle is a robber baron's nest a short distance upstream; it was renovated in 1834 by General von Barfuss. In the same year, the little town of Nieder-heimbach sold the ruins of **Sooneck Castle** to the sons of Friedrich Wilhelm III of Prussia; the rebuilding work was interrupted here several times, but in 1862 the completed project was finally dedicated under Wilhelm, who from 1871 was to be the Emperor of Germany. It was the aim of the Hohenzollerns to use the castle as a hunting lodge in season; in the end, the Prussian emperor actually managed to visit Sooneck on two occasions.

Any properties which were not taken over by the old nobility, fell prey to the new: this was the era of the barons of industry. One of them, Hugo Stinnes, had sections of the Heimburg, also known as **Hoheneck Castle**, transformed into his private residence.

Anybody anxious not to lose cargo or vessel in the rapids of the Bingen Hole had to have his goods transferred here, preferably into small boats or carts. This procedure was usually undertaken in **Lorch** (9,000 inhabitants). During the 14th century, two cranes were available for the task - assuming one did not finally opt for the land route, the well-

A coal barge on the river.

182

trodden "traders' path" up through the Wisper Valley and across to Rüdesheim. Its favourable situation made the little town the object of envy even in the early days. For this reason, **Nollig Castle** (14th century) - originally a part of the town fortifications - was progressively transformed into a real fortress in the late Middle Ages.

A few kilometres farther on lies **Kaub** (1,500 inhabitants), with a medieval city wall with its parapet walk and the remains of **Gutenfels Castle** (13th century). This fortress, too, was rebuilt in the late 19th century; it had also been captured late in its history. It was not plundered until 1805, upon orders given by Napoleon.

But if Napoleon springs to mind at all in Kaub, however, then it is in a very different context: in flight. For here one thinks of "Prinz Blücher von Wahlstadt, Field Marshal Forwards March", as the hero of the war of liberation was described at the time on a monument on the left bank, on the "French" side. This is the place where Blücher crossed the Rhine on New Year's Eve 1813. So they say - and so all school children are taught. He was, however, not completely alone - and at the beginning there was neither ice nor snow. Instead, he sat in his headquarters in the inn "Zur Stadt Mannheim", whilst outside his infantry - and especially the Russian pioneers - were building their bridge which was finally completed at 10 o'clock on New Year's Day. The cavalry, the hussars and the artillery could continue to chase the French, who had improvised a defence from their base at Bacharach as best they could. Blücher crossed over the Rhine and headed purposefully towards his place in history. The boatmen, however, and the vintners and the traders, who had all been forced to assist in the undertaking, were now left to repair the damage. For whilst the pioneers were building the bridge at four o'clock in the morning, part of it broke free and they had had to anchor it a second time. And what did they use to supply the emergency materials? They plundered the town, as Kaufmann, the boatman,

records in his diary: "Not a single gate or door was left standing in the stalls and houses. There was not a single shutter left at the windows, nor was an axe to be found anywhere in the entire village." World history had trampled roughshod over the residents' window shutters. And the only monument is the one to Blücher; he stands there with a fluttering greatcoat and monitory finger.

The most beautiful jewel in the entire district stands neither on the right nor on the left of the river, but in fact right in the middle. We refer to **Pfalzgrafenstein Castle**, with its countless towers and oriel windows and little slate-grey roofs. It was once a customs tower, like the Mouse Tower; as early as the 14th century, it became a public bone of contention, causing one Pope to curse: only because of the "accursed taxes" - according to Johannes XXII - had the castle been started in the first place.

"Below the Rhinegau, where the river banks lose their smiling countenance, where mountain and rock adopt a more defiant mien with their eccentrically-perched castles, where a wilder, more serious-natured magnificence arises - there, like a spine-chilling myth of days gone by, lies the ancient, sinister town of Bacharach."

Thus it is that Heinrich Heine starts his tale "The Rabbi of Bacharach". Not every visitor will share the writer's opinion; nor is Bacharach quite as ancient as Heine maintains a little further on. Bacchi ara: altar of the god Bacchus - that is an attractive but erroneous derivation of the name. Not everything along the course of the Rhine has its origins in the Roman occupation. As for the mood, this can be traced back to the dark spirit overshadowing the concept of the novelle, which picks up an ancient local legend: the murder of the boy Werner, by Jews - at least, according to rumour. This, in the 13th century, was reason enough for a pogrom. The Gothic ruin of the blood-red **Chapel of St. Werner** overshadows the village even today. Everything, however, is still dominated by **Stahleck Castle** (12th century), which now serves as a youth centre.

A steep descent through the vineyards.

Bacharach (2,500 inhabitants), is well-known as a pretty little wine-growing village. It possesses well preserved ramparts, timbered houses dating from the 14th to the 19th centuries, and a late Romanesque Protestant church built in the 13th century. The Catholic **Parish Church of St. Nicholas** is about 300 years old.

The magnificent 10th-century **Schönburg** boasts a Kolping Christian Community House and a hotel. It is the star attraction amongst the numerous sights of **Oberwesel** (4,500 inhabitants). This time it was neither the Prussian gentry nor the money aristocracy of the Old World who restored what Victor Hugo once described as the "most glorious pile of stones in Europe" to its former magnificence. It was an American, born with the name Rhinelander, who earned himself merit in the homeland of his ancestors.

Oberwesel is surrounded by a circular wall interspersed with 16 (originally 21) watch-towers which were built in the 13th and 14th centuries. The **Ochsen-turm** - the "Ox Tower" - dates from the 14th-15th century. The Parish Church of Our Lady contains, amongst other treasures, a fine Baroque organ and a high altar of the same period.

"By Bacharach on the Rhine/lives an enchantress..." Thus she appears for the first time in print, in a poem by Clemens Brentano - the **Loreley** on the Rhine, the beautiful siren last sighted on the rock which bears her name, and which has been her dwelling-place ever since. If it is really true that the spot has represented a special hazard for passing ships across all the years, then surely it must have been the currents around the rocks caused by the deep hollows in the river bed which were once the haunts of the sought-after salmon.

Instead of the salmon the tourists come today, and as they reach the 554-km marker post along the river they sing Silcher's "Loreley" with the famous lyrics by Heine. The French sing the poet's own translation ("Henri Heine"), the Americans that of Mark Twain ("I cannot divine what it meaneth"); the

The facades of Boppard viewed from the river.

Japanese sing in German, feeling not in the least flattered that the name on the 132-metre rock is also written in Japanese. Everything in the vicinity is devoted to the magical woman. **St. Goarshausen** (1,700 inhabitants) calls itself the "Loreley Town", and opposite, in the town of **St. Goar** (3,500 inhabitants) - named after the hermit from Aquitaine - visitors are proudly shown the house where the Loreley was born. The problem is, of course, that she was never actually born.

Our Rhine journey continues past little towns and magnificent castles: **Katz** and **Maus** (14th century), two neighbouring feudal residences: the "Maus" (Mouse) castle was named after the "Katz" (Cat) fortress, whose name derives from that of the owning family, the Katzenelnbogen. Then we pass the castles of two once-warring brothers: **Sterrenberg** and **Liebenstein** (12th century and later) - only an arrow's shot apart, which proved to be their downfall even after they had buried the hatchet. They planned to wake each other by firing an arrow through the window, but one brother opened the window just at the wrong time and was killed.

Further on, then, to **Boppard** (18,000 inhabitants), a lovely slate-grey town with medieval ramparts, the Catholic **Church of St. Severus** (12th-13th century) and the Gothic **Carmelite Church** (14th century). Then we see **Stolzenfels Castle** (13th century) before us - restored by Crown Prince (later King) Friedrich Wilhelm IV. Finally we pass **Braubach** before arriving at **Marksburg** (13th century) - the only fortress on the Rhine which did not have to be rebuilt. It alone survived the turbulent times and seems as such the ideal choice to act as headquarters for the German Castle Association.

Directly opposite Stolzenfels, where the River Lahn flows into the Rhine, lies **Lahnstein** (19,000 inhabitants), which is dominated by **Lahneck Castle** (13th century). This spot marked the end of the area of jurisdiction of the bishops of Mainz, who held up their hand here for the last time. The next castle came under

A welcome sign for the thirsty.

the sway of the Archbishop of Trier: **Ehrenbreitstein Fortress**. The river flowing into the Rhine at this point was no mere tributary like the Lahn; it was a major waterway in its own right - the **Moselle**. For this reason the settlement at the confluence was given the name Confluentes; its contemporary name, **Koblenz** (114 000 inhabitants), thus means "those which flow together". Even the Romans saw the necessity of securing the crossing of the Moselle with a castrum apud confluentes; Koblenz has remained a symbol of military might to this day. The Third Corps of the Federal Army is based here.

Once upon a time this symbolic importance was given concrete expression: at the Deutsches Eck ("German Corner"), where the Moselle flows into the Rhine, stood until the end of World War II an equestrian statue of Wilhelm I astride a bronze steed. Then they pulled him down from his high horse. Even today only the pedestal remains.

The lovely Old Town around the Romanesque **Church of St. Castor** (9th-12th centuries), as well as the **Church of St. Florin** (12th-14th centuries) and the old **Church of Our Lady** (12th-15th centuries), have been meticulously restored over the past years. They provide the attractive scenario for a stroll from the Old Castle on the banks of the Moselle - now housing the town archives - to the Electoral Palace on the Rhine. Here, too, prevails the general rule of the Rhineland: whatever did not stem from the hands of the Romans, was mostly the work of a bishop. The one in question here - Clemens Wenceslas - was the last Elector of Trier. He moved, however, from the Moselle to the Rhine and had his **Electoral Palace** built here in Koblenz. It was completed in 1786 - just in time for the Revolution. The French occupied Clemens's town in 1794 and his dream of building a new classicistic New Town next to the old one was never fulfilled.

It was not until 1799 that the French were able to capture **Ehrenbreitstein** as well. The citadel had been built at the end of the 10th century by a certain Erembert or Ehrebrecht, whose aim it was to control the Rhine itself as well as the Moselle from this strategic site. The Church took an interest in the scheme too, so that by 1020 Ehrenbreitstein Fortress was in the possession of Archbishop Poppo of Trier, the ruler of Koblenz at the time. Over the following centuries every product of the warmongers' imagination, every weapon to issue from the armourers' smithies, found its way up the hillside - with the result that in the last resort the fortress could not be taken by force of arms alone. A siege was the only possibility. In 1801 they decided to put an end to the arms race once and for all; the French needed 30,000 pounds of gunpowder to blow up the invincible pile by the Rhine. But then, in 1815, the Prussians allocated 24 million golden guilders for its reconstruction. Ehrenbreitstein survived three more conventional wars: 1865, 1870-71 and 1914-18. After that it was finally recognized that bunkers like that are really only worth preserving for their fine view - and as a war memorial, and a reminder of more violent times.

Aboard a float at a wine festival.

CASTLES FOR ROMANTICS

The passion for building castles really came into fashion in the 12th century. Each and every lord - whether spiritual or temporal - built his own in the lovely Rhine Valley. For this reason there is no other valley in the world containing 31 castles or ruins within a 60-kilometre stretch. Each castle owner was entitled in those days to exact large sums of money as customs duties from all who passed, by land or by water.

Some of the sites proved to be veritable goldmines for their proprietors. For this reason, quarrels sprang up regularly between the noble gentlemen. Castles changed hands; some of them were destroyed or neglected by their new masters, rebuilt or adapted. Ownership was also altered by marriage and by gift, or by natural or violent death. For several centuries the knights were able to live well in or from their castles. But then the King of France, Louis XIV, wanted to put an end to customs duties. In 1689 he instructed his army to "destroy or demolish so that you are in the position of being able to become the supreme masters of the Rhine...". Almost all castles on the Rhine were burnt down during the course of that same year.

Today, visitors from every corner of the globe come to admire the ruins and the rebuilt castles. They travel to the Romantic Rhine, the stretch which starts by Mainz/Wiesbaden and ends near Cologne. The romantic witnesses of times past tell many a story which is part of history.

Let us begin with **Burg Klopp**, on the left bank of the river. It is likely that its origins lay in a Roman watch-tower. It was inhabited successively by the kings of the Franks, the archbishops of Mainz, and the Swedish army of occupation. In 1639 the castle was taken by Duke Bernhard of Weimar; it was destroyed by the French in 1689. It was subsequently restored, only to be blown up again. The castle was then rebuilt in 1875-79, and houses today the local history museum of the town of Bingen.

Between 1208 and 1220 the Archbishop of Mainz had a castle built overlooking the Rhine. In times of war the treasures of Mainz cathedral were placed in safety within its thick protective walls. Today, as the **Ehrenfels** ruin, the former fortress gazes down from its position on the right bank overlooking its watchtower in the middle of the river. The **Mouse Tower** was also built by the Archbishop at the same time. From this vantage point shots were fired at anyone refusing to pay customs duties. It was later destroyed and then rebuilt in 1855 as a signal tower.

A powerful knight by the name of Gerhard von Bingen was probably the first steward to waylay pilgrims and merchants from his base at **Reichenstein Castle**, on the left bank above Trechingshausen. The castle was destroyed and rebuilt several times; after it was razed to the ground by the French in 1689, it was finally reconstructed in about 1900.

Also on the left bank, near Niederrheimbach, we find two castles: **Sooneck Castle** and the **Heimburg**. Both were built in the 12th-13th centuries. Either the knights who owned them became bored, or they fell on hard times; both feudal lords subsequently became robber barons. The Rhenish League of Cities under Arnold Walpode had Sooneck Castle destroyed.

After its restoration, the Hapsburg King Rudolf issued orders that the robber baron's haunt be burnt down again. It was rebuilt yet again in 1344-55, only to be destroyed once more in 1689, by the French. Crown Prince Wilhelm of Prussia had Sooneck Castle reconstructed in 1834. The **Heimburg** was built in 1295 by the Archbishop of Mainz; it, too, was destroyed by the French in 1689. **Nollig Castle** also lies on the left bank, 125 metres above the Rhine valley near Lorch. After a colourful history its circular towers and keep were restored in 1939. **Fürstenberg Castle**, on the left bank near Rheindiebach, was built by the Archbishop of Cologne in about 1200. It was captured by King Gustavus Adolphus of Sweden during the Thirty Years War, and subsequently fell to the French in 1689.

Also on the left bank, near Bacharach, stands the magnificent **Stahleck Castle**, today a youth hostel. Here it was that the secret marriage of the lovely Agnes von Stahleck with the Guelph lord Henry took place during the 13th century.

Like a stone ship floating in the middle of the river near Kaub, **Pfalzgrafenstein Castle** - dating from the 13th century - enjoys an ideal site from which to exact customs duties. Here King Friedrich Wilhelm II crossed the river with his army; on New Year's Eve 1813, Blücher did the same, commanding his soldiers to build a bridge across the Rhine. Surveying the scene from a vantage point on the bank stands **Gutenfels Castle**, which was badly damaged during the Thirty Years War.

The most beautiful castle amongst those built by von Schönburg on the left bank of the Rhine during the 11th century is undoubtedly **Schönburg**, near Oberwesel. Swedish troops captured it in 1639; in 1689 it was destroyed by the French army. Then, in the 19th century, the ruin was purchased and rebuilt by an American by the name of Rhinelander. In the meantime an international youth encounter centre has established its headquarters there.

In 1393 Count Johann III von Katzenelnbogen had **Katz Castle** built on the right bank as a customs post. It belonged to the Princes of Hessen for many years, was blown up by the French in 1805, and then rebuilt at the end of the 19th century. Katz Castle, above St. Goarshausen, is a holiday centre today.

One of the most impregnable fortresses in the central Rhine Valley stands on the left bank near St. Goar. **Rheinfels Castle** was built in 1245 by Count Dietrich II von Katzenelnbogen. It, too, succumbed to the explosive charges of the French during the 18th century. Prince Wilhelm of Prussia purchased the ruin in 1845.

Count von Katzenelnbogen called it simply "Mouse"; the correct name is **Thurnberg Castle**, situated on the right bank above Wellmich. The nickname, however, is the one by which it is known today. Mouse Castle's history can be

"Katz" Castle...

summarized thus: built in 1355, destroyed in 1806 and rebuilt between 1900 and 1906. Such was the enmity between them that they had a high wall built between their two properties, **Sterrenberg Castle** and **Liebenstein Castle**. In popular parlance even their fortresses were known as the "Hostile Brothers".

Perched high above Braubach on the right bank of the river stands the **Marksburg**, perfectly preserved since the Middle Ages. It is uncertain exactly when the castle was built. Certain it is, however, that it was taken by the Counts of Katzenelnbogen in the 13th century; subsequently it came into the possession of the Princes of Hessen, and then became Prussian. In 1899 Wilhelm II donated the castle to the Association for the Preservation of German Castles.

From **Stolzenfels Castle**, situated on the left bank, there is a breathtaking view across chapel rooftops down to the Rhine Valley below. The Romans built a fort here long ago. In 1242 the Archbishop of Trier began with renovation work. Once again it was the French who destroyed the entire castle complex in 1689. Opposite Koblenz, on the right bank of the Rhine, towers the massive hulk of **Ehrenbreitstein Citadel**. It is surmised that a castle stood here as early as 630 A.D.. The present fortress, the foundations of which were laid in the 10th century, was extended in the 15th century. The French blew up the citadel in around 1800; the Prussians rebuilt it between 1815 and 1832.

Lahneck Castle, on the right bank near Lahnstein, was built to exact customs duties in the 13th century. It fell victim to the French army in 1689, but was reconstructed in 1860.

Of the former **Hammerstein Castle** (right bank) - a building which dates back to the 10th century - all that remains today is a romantically beautiful but slightly sinister ruin.

Rheineck, on the left river bank near Bad Breisig, shared the fate of many Rhine castles. During the course of its history it was destroyed and rebuilt several times. The castle was originally

...and a view from the steamer.

built in the 11th century and captured in 1151 by King Konrad III, only to be destroyed by him a few years later. The Archbishop of Cologne had the complex rebuilt in about 1165; Rudolf von Hapsburg, however, ensured that it was transformed into a ruin again in 1282. The reconstruction this time was the work of the Elector of Cologne, providing the French with the chance of demolishing it once more in 1689. Our thanks are due to Moritz von Bethmann-Hollweg for the present reconstruction, undertaken in 1831.

Arenfels Castle (on the right bank above Bad Honningen) was built by Count von Isenburg in 1260. After a succession of owners and its rebuilding in a castle-like form, the French came along to raze it to the ground yet again. Count Westerholt-Gysenberg purchased the ruin and commissioned its restoration by Ernst Friedrich Zwirner, the master builder of Cologne Cathedral.

A knight by the name of Werner von Dadenberg is chronicled as residing in **Dattenberg Castle** (right bank) in 1242.

The complex belonged to an archbishop of Cologne; later it was the property of the Nassau-Weilbergs, and then of the Prussian royal family. Here, too, the French showed their capacity for destruction in 1689. Today Dattenberg Castle, between Leubsdorf and Linz, is used by schools for short excursions to the country.

Also near Linz, on the right bank of the river, stands **Ockenfels Castle**. Various knights lived here over the course of the centuries. The complex, which lay in ruins for many years, was only restored in 1925-27.

Ivy-clad and welcoming, the **Rolandsbogen** looks down on the river Rhine below. It is all that remains today of Rolandseck Castle. When Heinrich IV posed a threat to Archbishop Friedrich I, the latter had the castle built. It later suffered damage when attacked by Heinrich IV. In the middle of the 12th century, Archbishop Arnold I had it rebuilt; it was destroyed again in 1300, and restored and extended in 1328. Karl the Bold took the castle in 1474. Before the Burgundian troops left it, however, they set fire to it, so that only the window arch remained. Even that fell one day into the Rhine below, giving the ruin its name. Ferdinand Freiligrath, the poet, organised its reconstruction.

Visible from afar on the right bank stand the majestic remains of a castle: the **Drachenfels Ruin**. The fortress was built between 1101 and 1132 by the Archbishop of Cologne, Friedrich I. Archbishop Arnold I extended the complex, which was subsequently captured by King Gustavus Adolphus of Sweden during the Thirty Years War. Archbishop Ferdinand contributed the first phases of its destruction in 1642; the French finished the job and all that remains today is a romantic ruin near Königswinter.

The **Godesburg** (on the left bank above Bad Godesburg) was begun in 1210 by the Archbishop of Cologne. It was extended on a number of occasions by various owners. The Archbishop of Cologne took sanctuary within its walls in 1583 when he espoused the Protestant cause during the Reformation.

Left, the Ochsenturm near Oberwesel. Right, a view of Rheinstein Castle.

WELCOME ABOARD

At about 7 p.m. we embark upon our ship: "Welcome aboard!" In four days and nights we shall travel along the river almost 800 kilometres from Basle to Rotterdam. The M.S. "Britannia" is one of the large luxury liners owned by the Cologne-Düsseldorf Rhine Steamship Company, usually abbreviated to the KD. It was founded in 1826 as the Prussian Rhineland Steamship Company. Today the KD owns some 25 ships, 17 of which are employed in the provision of day trips on the Rhine, the Main and the Moselle. The eight bigger liners are used exclusively for cruises lasting several days.

Journeys with the KD can be booked through any main travel agent. The currency in use during the journey through four countries is the D-Mark. There is a bureau de change on board, as well as a souvenir shop, a bar, restaurant, reading and television room, observation lounge, sun deck, and on some ships a sauna and a heated outdoor swimming pool. When travelling downstream the liner maintains an average of 14 knots - roughly 26 kilometres per hour. Progress on the upstream trip from Rotterdam to Basle is slower, achieving an average speed of only 16 k.p.h.

Our Rhine cruise begins in **Basle**. The embarkation point is on the Elsässer Rheinweg. Passengers may board in the early evening, taking up residence in their cabins and glancing for the first time out of the window at the river, whose seaward tendency is marked here by a temperamental rocking of the waves. Later, as the river bed becomes wider, the Rhine will struggle more slowly forwards. Near Basle, in the **Three-Land Triangle**, where the borders of Switzerland, France and Germany meet at the river, stands a monument to the "Trinity".

It is well worth taking a stroll through Basle before embarking on the long journey down river; past the brightly-painted Town Hall in Burgundian Late Gothic style (16th century), and round the market place. From here a romantic stairway leads to the Spalenberg quarter, to the Spalentor Gate of 1370. Then back to the "Britannia"; the crew is awaiting our return - as is a magnificent buffet. An international clientèle assembles: our fellow-guests are from Denmark, France, the Netherlands, Switzerland, Great Britain, Australia, New Zealand, South Africa, Singapore, the United States and West Germany.

At approximately 4 a.m. the passengers, the bunks, the cabin, start to vibrate; the entire ship drones as the noise becomes progressively louder. A glance out of the window; the monster is moving, casting off from the quai, turning in the swirling current before setting purposefully off in the direction of Strasbourg. Not a single sleeping passenger is aware of the customs formalities at the Swiss-French border. In the first grey dawn the customs officer comes aboard from his launch, dressed in a green uniform and carrying a black briefcase. With a single leap he lands on deck. He will disappear into the mist again as quietly as he arrived.

We arrive in **Strasbourg** the following afternoon. The city is over 2,000 years old, like Mainz - but we have not got that far yet. The "Britannia" sails down a canal to Strasbourg, for the Rhine is not navigable for a ship of this size at this point. In the meantime we have passed through several locks, an experience for landlubbers of every nation: precise navigation into a lock chamber, the closing of the iron gates behind us, the slow sinking of the water level in the lock chamber - deeper and deeper the slimy damp walls slide past the cabin windows, overgrown with bright green moss. How much further can the ship actually sink? Finally it comes to a halt. The quiet and isolation in this damp shaft are rather frightening. And now the gates in front of us open, and we can continue on our journey. The locks are a necessity in order to negotiate the change in depth - 258 metres - which occurs between Basle and Rotterdam.

A bus awaits us in Strasbourg for an interesting sightseeing tour of the city.

We take in the principal sights at breakneck speed; streets, squares and buildings. The crowning glory is naturally the visit to the Gothic **Cathedral**. That evening we have enough time to explore the capital of Alsace under our own steam. We walk to "Petite France" (well-signposted and easy to find), the old tanners' district with its medieval alleys, picturesque timbered houses and the covered bridges across the Ill.

The "Britannia" sets sail from the River Port at approximately 3 a.m. Breakfast is served from 7 a.m.; the menu is extensive. An early start is recommended for those who wish to travel by coach from Speyer to Heidelberg. Most passengers are early risers anxious not to miss the chance to see the world-famous university city and its castle. **Heidelberg**, it must be admitted, does not actually lie on the Rhine. It is on the Neckar, which flows into the Rhine near Mannheim.

We set off. We are offered a sightseeing tour (in a variety of languages, of course), taking in the castle and - in its cellar - the largest wine vat in the world, with a reputed capacity of exactly 221,726 litres. Everyone is amazed: "Ahhh" issues involuntarily from our polyglot lips. We all enjoy the lovely view from the castle terrace.

That afternoon we tie up at Rüdesheim. A coach takes us to beautiful **Eberbach Monastery**. The medieval complex is in an excellent state of preservation; today it is a state-run wine producing concern where, after a multilingual tour through courtyards and impeccably restored buildings, we take part in a wine tasting in a shadowy cellar illuminated by flickering candles. According to the vintner, the innumerable old wine barrels, black with age, are just part of the scenario for the tourists - as are the candles.

Our faces are slightly flushed as we emerge into the fresh air again. It is still drizzling slightly; we drive through the vineyards back to the river, to our floating hotel. Contrasting alternatives are now open to us; we can remain aboard the "Britannia", changing our damp socks and drinking Rüdesheim coffee in the comfortable observation lounge, or we can visit Siegfried's mechanical musical instrument museum before strolling through the streets of the celebrated town - including the famous Drosselgasse, with its colourful bars. After an excellent eight-course dinner on board, a dance rounds off the day.

Today, our third on the "Britannia", the atmosphere becomes romantic. For one whole day we experience at first hand the Romance of the Rhine. The river meanders through the **Rhinegau**; over 20 million bottles of wine are produced here every year for pampered palates the world over.

Our route takes us past the **Binger Loch**, once a dangerous section of the river marked by the Mouse Tower in the middle of the stream. An endless succession of defiant fortresses, fairy-tale castles and mysterious rocks can be observed from our ship's eye vantage point. Rheinstein, Sooneck, Stahleck, Kaub. As we approach the **Loreley rock** the ship's loudspeakers begin to blare forth - inevitably enough - "I cannot divine what it meaneth..." We scan the rocks anxiously for a glimpse of the beautiful long-haired maiden - but no sign of her, apart from "her" song over the loudspeakers. Our cruise carries on: Castle Cat and Mouse, Liebenstein and Sterrenberg, the Marksburg, Stolzenfels.

In **Koblenz** the Moselle flows into the Rhine from the left-hand side. The **Deutsches Eck**, a bleak memorial, towers at the water's edge. The Ehrenbreitstein Citadel opposite can be reached by chair-lift in summer. The park promenades along the banks of the Rhine are 18 km long. In August, between Koblenz and Braubach, the "**Rhine in Flames**" festival is an impressive summer firework display. But the romance is not over yet; after Rheineck Castle and the Drachenfels come many other famous spots and excursion destinations: Andernach, Bad Breisig, Bad Hönningen, Bad Honnef, Rhöndorf and Bad Godesberg.

That afternoon our ship ties up in **Cologne**; sightseeing tour. We are introduced at a dizzy pace to the city of churches, art and eau-de-cologne. The last port of call is a short stroll through the **Old Town** near the river, a visit to the Roman-Germanic Museum or the contemporary exhibits in the modern Wallraf-Richartz Museum and the Ludwig Collection between the **Cathedral** and the river.

Our peaceful trip continues to **Düsseldorf**. A sightseeing trip by night, across the Düssel, across the "Kö" - the elegant Königsallee - past old alleys with countless taverns: the "longest bar in the world". Anybody who hankers after beer and city life after dinner can note that our sailing time will not be until 3.30 a.m.. Late that morning our crew takes its leave of us before bringing us minutes later to our destination. After Düsseldorf we pass **Krefeld** to the left and **Duisburg** - with the largest river port in the world, and the **Ruhr District** spreading beyond that, to the right. Now the Rhine assumes a different countenance: no longer does it flow through a narrow, romantic valley, but rather through a broad, expansive countryside with green meadows and cattle. Houses and villages are dotted here and there, nestling behind the dykes.

Soon after the Dutch border we find that the Rhine is suddenly rechristened the Waal. We go up on deck and sniff the air. Can we smell the sea, or is it our imagination?

At long last, **Rotterdam** comes into view: vast harbour basins, imposing ships. We moor alongside the Maas Boulevard in the course of the afternoon. Our ship slowly empties. On the quay-side we spot a truck with fresh flowers, clean linen, fresh-baked rolls. Now we, too, must leave; our taxi, ordered from on board, is waiting for us. We drive through the bustling city to the main station; others head for the airport. A glimpse at the timetable, a hastily-drunk coffee, and we leap onto the train. The steel monster careers through the countryside bathed in the enchantment of the evening sunlight. We shall be in Frankfurt by midnight.

It was a lovely trip. Our thanks to the KD, to the crew for the pleasures of the Rhine. No thanks to the weather-makers; it wasn't worth talking about.

THE RHINE ON FOOT

The walker can make rapid, easy progress along the flat, mostly well-maintained footpaths which run along the banks of the Rhine. There are no steep inclines, so that the weight of the rucksack packed with essentials will remain tolerable all day. The characteristic charms of the river along its upper section are more restrained, more even. Valley woodlands, the constantly flowing, somewhat monotonous current and the obstinate chugging of the diesel engines of passing ships provide a scenario of constantly repeated impressions.

From Rastatt to Worms: The undoubted highlights of this walking trip through Baden are the towns of Rastatt, Karlsruhe, Speyer, Mannheim and Worms. This is the Route of the Residences, starting with those of the state of Baden and continuing with those of the early medieval German Empire. **Rastatt Castle** contains a permanent exhibition which provides interested visitors with a clear insight into the era of the Bourgeois Revolution of 1848-49. Rastatt was also the scene of the last throes of the 1838 revolution.

One has merely to follow the course of the River Murg from **Rastatt** in order to reach the Rhine. As the west river bank is French as far as Lauterburg, and there is a complicated network of interlinked waterways on the east side, the walker will need a 1:50 000 map which shows the dykeside paths and secondary tracks as well as bridges.

Karlsruhe offers overnight accommodation in all categories. The castle is worth visiting as is the town's landmark, the pyramid on the market place.

The next day's destination is **Germersheim**, with its cosy taverns. The following stage, as far as Speyer, is only a short one, and so the Rhine walker will have time to explore at leisure.

The towers of **Speyer** announce from the distance the presence of the **Imperial Cathedral** dating from the 11th and 12th centuries. One thousand years

Preceding pages: a boat trip on the river - an experience not to be missed, young and old on the sundeck near the Loreley. *Below*, a rare encounter.

202

ago the town had the same number of inhabitants as it does today. **The Palatinate Museum** near the cathedral is worth visiting; the exhibits give an impression of the cultural and historical development of the town on the Rhine. The **Wine Museum** is an integral part of the display and arouses thirst and hunger for the specialities of the region.

As we continue our journey towards Mannheim, **Schwetzingen Castle** encourages us to pause for a while. Is one of the concerts which form part of the summer festival on the programme? Then **Heidelberg**, with its popular Old Town, tempts us to make a detour.

Another journey into the past awaits us in the **Residence of the Elector Palatine in Mannheim**. After the destruction in the wake of the French War, the Elector Karl Philipp moved the electoral residence from Heidelberg to Mannheim. The youthful town henceforth expanded rapidly to become the cultural centre of South-West Germany.

A stroll along the promenade.

Famous painters and sculptors followed the architects. In music, the "Mannheim School" set a new tone through the works of Johann Stamitz and especially those of Wolfgang Amadeus Mozart. It is worth interrupting one's Rhine journey to attend a concert in the **Rose Garden**. Stay on the right bank of the river after completing your detour to the castle, the television tower and the Neckar confluence; the west bank is the exclusive domain of BASF. The island of Friesenheim, on the other hand, is a popular destination for its fish restaurant "Dehus", not far from the bridge to **Sandhofen**. Passing through the fishing village and continuing along the west bank of the Rhine, one soon reaches the city of **Worms**.

The oldest Imperial City in Germany was the arena for 100 Imperial Diets. The list of historical events which took place here is long; it includes the Edict of Worms, which sent Martin Luther into exile in 1521.

Along the Romantic Rhine: The journey on foot from **Rüdesheim** to **Bonn** is considerably longer and much more strenuous. Only short stretches of the

journey directly by the river are unaffected by the proximity of busy trunk roads. Following the topography of the region, most Rhine Mountain Footpaths - marked by a prominent capital R - wind their serpentine way on both sides of the river, often meandering down into side valleys before climbing to the next vantage point.

Hasenbach - Feuerbach - Wellmicher Bachtal: such are the names of some of the minor valleys cutting through the mountains bordering the Rhine. Many well-known river views gain a new dimension when seen from the perspective of the walker: **Kaub**, the **Pfalz**, **Gutenfels Castle**. From up here they look both picturesque and forbidding. One calls to mind again Blücher's Rhine crossing near Kaub on New Year's Eve 1813-14. One forgets all the prejudices aroused by the over-poeticized, over-lyricized Rhine. From this angle, the Rhine is, quite simply, impressive. No visitor can fail to be captivated by the very sight of the mist-filled valley in the early morning light, as the sound of the chugging engine of a barge rises from the depths below, or by the all-round view across the river as it meanders between its steep banks. The view from the **Loreley** is not the most impressive; others, such as that from the valley slope near **Dörscheid**, are more natural.

Soon after **Boppard** the dramatic tension which has characterized the riverscape since Bingen, begins to ease off. The height of the accompanying mountains becomes less pronounced, the countryside gentler. After the pilgrimage town of **Kamp-Bornhofen** we soon reach the confluence of the Lahn and the town of **Lahnstein**, an amalgam of two distinct districts. A pleasant spot for a rest before the Koblenz Basin is in the shadow of **Lahneck Castle**. Since every village between Rüdesheim and Bonn caters for travellers, the walker can plan his trip in stages according to his energy and inclination. It is advisable, however, to secure the next night's accommodation by telephone not later than noon each day. **Koblenz** is the home of two German monuments often glossed

over by patriots but nonetheless impossible to ignore: **Ehrenbreitstein Citadel** and the **Deutsches Eck**. The view from each takes in the other whilst down below the **Moselle** flows into the Rhine, and the observer ponders the futile question as to whether the Wilhelminian monument should once more stand at the confluence.

Beyond Koblenz, the capacity of the Rhine to afford a unique experience changes once again. It is not so much that there is a lack of physical beauty, with the exception of the **Neuwied Basin**, a low-lying industrial region that has developed as a result of the pumice stone processing plants there. But our eyes discern nothing really sensational until we reach Andernach. If we follow the old tow-path alongside the river - or the riverbank paths which follow the course of the river, then the Rhine landscape slides past us as if on a revolving stage: the **Siebengebirge** (picturesque and crowned by castles), the **Drachenfels** (an opera-worthy ruin), and - dotted between - **Unkel**, **Bad**

Honnef, **Rhöndorf** and **Königswinter**. Façades as from a picture-book; Rhine villages which, thanks to the presence of the river, have spread regularly up the slopes and which therefore invariably proffer a pleasant countenance characterized by terraces, jetties and avenues. Before we reach Bonn the names assume a political significance. **Rhöndorf** was the home of Konrad Adenauer.

The **Petersberg**, on which the new guest house of the Federal Republic now stands, is remembered as the seat of the allied High Commission after the war. From **Mehlem** onwards it is worth continuing on one's way along the riverside paths through the towns. Neat and tidy, cared for by gardeners, the promenades hug the Rhine. It is easy walking, with no traffic to distress the pedestrian along the west bank. Hotels and restaurants such as the Dreesen promise gourmet pleasures and recall simultaneously political summits and their consequences. This path through German history runs directly beside the river as far as the Bundeshaus.

The first rays of sun.

CYCLING ALONG THE RHINE

To follow the course of a river is always an attractive prospect for a cyclist, for here there will be much to see in rapid succession without the necessity of coping with steep mountainous inclines. Along some stretches of the Rhine there are even good grounds for maintaining that the bicycle is the only sensible means of transport. The distances involved are too large to cover on foot, and the most attractive tracks are barred to motor traffic.

Even those who claim to be not particularly fit can easily reach the vicinity of the source of the Rhine in the **St. Gotthard Massif**. In Switzerland trains travel to the most unlikely destinations, and bicycles can be taken along, too, without any difficulty. Travel by rail to the Oberalp Pass at an altitude of 2044 metres and start your Rhine tour here by following the road downhill along the valley until you have passed **Chur**.

This is the starting point for one of the most attractive cycling tours you can imagine: flat tracks run along the Rhine banks. There is little or no motor traffic (and, considering the perfect conditions, very few cyclists too). Along a 50-kilometre stretch, almost as far as **Lake Constance**, the cyclist can enjoy the spectacular mountain panorama without having to exert himself unduly.

The **High Rhine** - i.e., the stretch between Konstanz and Basle - also deserves the epithet "romantic". The route is admittedly not completely unproblematic for the cyclist. There are not always roads - or even tracks - along the river bank; sometimes you will find yourself having to push your bicycle up onto the heights in order to avoid a narrow gorge, the river gushing below. It is not a route, therefore, for those who back away in the face of the slightest incline. A good map is indispensable in order to avoid making unnecessary detours or - even more annoying - finding oneself on a riverside track which suddenly comes to a dead end.

Cycling along a dyke.

206

The roofed wooden bridges - river crossings within the little towns - are very attractive; they serve simultaneously as pleasant border stations between Switzerland and Germany. The longest, and perhaps the most famous, is the one at **Säckingen**. As it is closed to cars, it is a rare treat for cyclists to freewheel across to the other bank in the twilight of the old wooden structure, rumbling gently across the planks which make up the floor.

Frontiers are basically open for cyclists as they are for walkers, as long as they "transport no goods with them". During the course of our cycling tour along the Rhine, following quiet roads with little traffic, we shall frequently cross these friendly borders, often marked only by a sign.

In **Basle** the river becomes the Upper Rhine, taking as it does so a right-hand turn towards the north. On the western - the French - bank, those cyclists devoted to achieving a high mileage will find themselves in paradise. Lonely roads hug the lower boundary of the embankment which in some places runs along the **Grand Canal d'Alsace**, and in others along the course of the Rhine itself. If you wish actually to see the river or the canal you must climb to the top of the embankment. These roads are definitely not for the inexperienced cyclist. One may start to wonder whether one really is still in the middle of densely-populated Central Europe.

On the other side, on the German bank, you will find typical roads linking one village with the next; in some places, the paths run directly next to the river. Take care, however: often the good, peaceful roads may be the very ones which lead to some peninsula formed by the old course of the river. Or the cyclist may suddenly find himself standing at the edge of a gravel quarry; the track has petered out, and he will have to retrace his route over many kilometres.

May we anticipate the description of the course of the Rhine in this book and cycle on ahead of the others? From the Franco-German border near **Lauter-**

Summer paradise on the river: breakfst with the swans.

bourg almost as far as **Mannheim** the west bank of the Rhine offers ideal paths for cyclists. They mostly do not afford a direct view of the river, for the embankments, the majority of which have well maintained asphalt tracks along their summit, also enclose the riverside woodlands. Within the flood plain of the Old Rhine these have been designated nature conservancy zones. Sometimes you will cycle through a dark-green fairy-tale forest in which frogs croak, strange birds twitter and only the occasional hoot of a ship's siren in the vicinity betrays the proximity of the major waterway.

However, he who wishes to enjoy the wine-and-Rhine countryside without throwing himself into the bustle of the Central Rhine, is advised to try the **Rhine Hessen** section - the stretch between **Worms** and **Bingen**. The mountains are just beginning, but river, towns, roads and vineyards still have sufficient space without the need to crowd each other out. Along this stretch you should make a point of leaving the riverside path in order to cycle uphill along one of the asphalted vineyard roads. From the luxuriant heights beyond Oppenheim you can see the Odenwald; the sun shimmers over the broad plain of the Hessen marshes.

The Romantic, the "German" Rhine proper begins in **Mainz**. Along the narrow valley there is little room between the steep cliffs and the river. And so one can cycle over to the other bank: away from the traffic, completely undisturbed and with a completely uninterrupted view - of ships and castles, rapids and islands. When the cycle track comes to an end one continues along the road, until a new river-bank track begins.

You will meet here hikers and cyclists from all over the world. It is really not at all lonely; in fact it is rather noisy: cars and railways, boats and possibly even a maiden singing in the evening sun on her lofty clifftop.

When he reaches the **Lower Rhine** the cyclist will find excellent tracks once more. Between **Düsseldorf** and **Emmerich** there are embankment paths **First comes all the hard work...**

along much of the river's course; here the cyclist can devote his full attention to the luxuriant meadows and the busy river traffic without the slightest risk of losing his sense of direction.

Things become complicated, alas, in **Holland**. Not because the paths along the river are missing, but because it is no longer clear which is the real course of the Rhine. The river splits itself up into a spider's web of natural sections of the river, old river courses and artificially constructed canals. The choices if one wishes to follow the Rhine as far as the sea along good embankment tracks are indeed numerous.

The Dutch have a fitting respect for the wind. Often it blows in from the sea, and when progress against it becomes too tiring, the cyclist should not struggle against the elements for too long but take up his bike and board a train heading for the sea (**Hoek van Holland** is a railway station.) Then, with the wind in his back, he can continue his Rhine journey in the other direction. Cyclists are recommended to use ferries for crossings whenever possible; there are still a great number of them on the Rhine. There is no sense of haste and restlessness as on the ramps of the major bridges; the pace, by contrast, is leisurely. The crush of motorized vehicles is kept within bounds, and if you are lucky you will discover one of the little ferries intended only for pedestrians and cyclists. In Basle they are boats moored by a chain, which use a rudder and the strength of the current as their only means of propulsion.

Before the ferry leaves, the cyclist usually has time to get his breath back after the exertions of the trip - there is usually an inn or a snack bar nearby, offering an icecream or something to drink. When the ferry ties up, the cyclist can find a place to stand near the railing, putting the handful of coins the crossing will cost into the old-fashioned cash box slung around the ferryman's neck. He can then relax completely to experience the short trip across the river with all his senses; he feels, hears, sees and smells it: the Rhine.

...and then you can relax.

FROM KOBLENZ
TO COLOGNE

Beyond Koblenz the river becomes wider, passing through a region known as the Neuwieder Basin. Nothing remains today of the first bridge over the Rhine which Julius Caesar crossed in 55 B.C.; its site lies at Urnütz, between Weissenthurm and **Neuwied** (60,000 inhabitants). The name of the town hints at the existence of an old Wied, a palace which, indeed, can be found a little further on. The **Castle** in its beautiful park was constructed between 1706 and 1756 in the style of Versailles. It is also worth looking at the meeting hall of the Heernhuter Brethren (1783-1785), the Mennonite Church (1768) and the remains of **Altenwied Castle** (12th century) in the Altwied district.

The foundations of Neuwied were laid in 1648, at the end of the Thirty Years War. In order to attract new burghers to this freshly-formed community during those hard times, the Count of Wied offered a variety of incentives to ensure compliance with the new building regulations: not only access to the fertile soils of the valley terrace, which was in his possession, but also freedom from socage after 1653, freedom of religious practice, and the right to build on the land completely free of charge. As a result the community to this day has the somewhat rigid appearance of a planned town. In the historic district of **Enders** can be seen the remains of old timbered houses as well as the old town wall, the original town hall and a chapel of rest dating back to 1662. The scene is dominated by the ominous silhouette of the Mülheim-Kärlich nuclear power station, occupying a prominent position on the left bank of the Rhine; it was decommissioned after a court enquiry in 1988.

The river is constrained again by cliff-like banks by the **Andernach Gap**. Here, too, is Romanticism, where Ernst Moritz Arndt (1769-1860) discovered the loveliest view, that "splendid rocky gateway, which looks as if it has been carved directly out of the mountain",

with hilly summits, ruined castles and the town of Andernach on the horizon.

Andernach (28,000 inhabitants), built on the site of the Roman fort of Antunnacum and serving as a royal capital under Charlemagne, was always a much-coveted base thanks to its favourable situation on the northern edge of the Basin. One of its defensive battles has even found its way in to local folklore; the saga of the baker boys who, as they were delivering the morning rolls, discovered the town's enemies from Linz before their very gates. They had no weapons, so they improvised in the defence of their home and their friends by casting beehives over the city wall. Not in their wildest dreams would the local citizens have thought of summoning such effective reinforcements. The bees, of course, are no more, so the only proof available to sceptics can be found in the weathered sculptures of the **Baker Boys** on the Rhine Gate.

The medieval town wall is still in good condition, and some of the majestic gateways, including the **Round**

Preceding pages: oriel windows in Koblenz.

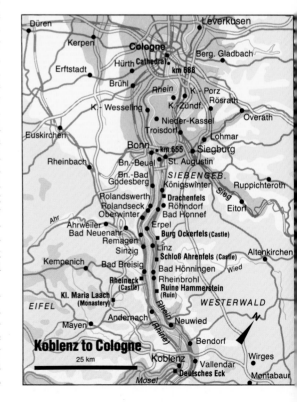

212

The "Deutsche Eck" in Koblenz - the confluence of the Moselle and the Rhine.

Tower of 1448, with walls which are five metres thick, have remained impervious to the vagaries of history. Intact, too, is Andernach's "Cathedral" - as the late Romanesque **Church of Our Lady** (13th century) is affectionately known. The town's most prominent landmark, however, is a monument to the town's early industry. Clearly visible on the riverbank footpath leading to the Namedy quarter is the **Old Rhine Crane**, dating from the 16th century. It is pivoted and was operated by human labour using two large driving wheels inside. The crane was still in use as late as 1911, being employed to help with the unloading of the barges, or to heave pumice or millstones on board - a symbol of the changing industrial landscape. Also worth visiting are the **Town Hall** (16th century) and the **Lutheran Parish Church** (14th-15th century).

Like Andernach, the town of **Weissenthurm** - situated on the left bank - is also a good starting point for an excursion to **Maria Laach**, the Benedictine Abbey on the Laacher See. Founded in 1093,

the community's landmark is the six-towered **Abbey Church** which is periodically depicted adorning the cover of a book. The monks who live there are knowledgeable guides to the popular tourist destination, set in the characteristically bleak landscape of the Eifel.

The volcanic rocks of the eastern Eifel region have brought both work and prosperity to the inhabitants of the **Brohl Valley** and the Rhine, which have been maintained to this very day. Pumice is still extracted here, and the local tuff was once popular as a construction material. Most important of all was the trass, a loosely cemented and - if finely ground - watertight type of pumice stone when mixed with limestone. Even the Romans knew of its existence; the bulk of it, however, was exported to Holland over the years. There it was used to build sea walls, thereby further increasing the prosperity of **Brohl** (25,000 inhabitants). An amazed visitor wrote in 1786: "In the little village of Brohl, a small cart of trass costs four and a half guilders; once it has reached Holland, it is worth 28 guilders." Such were the trading margins which transformed the water millers of the day into "Trass barons" - as they were often called. Even the transport arrangements were in their favour; all they had to do was to let the ships float downstream on the current; costly towing charges only arose on the upstream journey, when a good dozen horses were required to haul the barges back home.

On the opposite bank, where the valley is still wide enough, lies **Leutesdorf** (2,000 inhabitants), surrounded by vineyards and one of the few Rhine villages not separated from the river by the main road. The little wine-growing community, spared the ravages of through traffic, has many fine timbered houses (16th-17th century) and an important Baroque Parish Church. It is also an ideal location for a respite and a meal and wine. The **Pilgrimage Church of the Holy Cross** dates from the 17th century. Lower down, though, the valley narrows again. Perched on a rocky eminence above a Werth, an island in the Rhine, stand the ruins of **Hammerstein Castle** (11th century). Leutesdorf is first mentioned in 775 as a gift of Charlemagne; it seems, however, doubtful whether **Hammerstein** really dates back in similar fashion to Charles Martel, the "Hammer", and his personal steward Pippin - as the locals maintain.

Beyond dispute, nevertheless, is the Hammerstein feud, an event which took place in 1020 A.D.. The local count, Otto von Hammerstein, had cast his eyes appreciatively in the direction of a certain Irmingard, a fairly close relative of his, whom he then led to the altar. No man of the church was able to countenance this dreadful deed; furthermore, as the Bishop of Mainz was involved in a border dispute with the Count, he took it upon himself to blacken the couple's name with both the emperor and the pope. Again and again, the aggressors laid siege to a castle and the marriage was annulled. But nothing that anybody did could ever separate the two lovers.

Hammerstein has a 12th-century Romanesque parish church as well as the

Left, tired after a long day. **Right**, organising the crowd at a local fair.

Steward's House dating from the 16th century.

Rheineck Castle is perched on a 182-metre cliff above **Bad Breisig** (6,500 inhabitants). Thanks to its three thermal springs the town is allowed to describe itself as a "resort". The mineral spa has attractive public gardens and fine old houses (17th-18th century). The **Parish Church of St. Victor** dates from the 13th century; **St. Mary's Parish Church** was built in the 18th century.

Rheineck Fortress stands on a picturesque promontory high above the Vinxtbach valley. As early as the 12th century it came into the possession of the archbishops of Cologne. In 1832 a member of the Bethmann-Hollweg banking family raised sufficient money to purchase and restore it.

On the right bank can be seen a reconstruction of the first watch-tower marking the **Limes**: a fortress representing the outermost limit of the Roman Empire. The frontier was indicated by a wall and palisades stretching from this point to the Danube. **Rheinbrohl** (4,000

inhabitants) was still part of the Roman Empire, for the Limes Romanus passed below the site of the village. **Bad Honningen** (6,000 inhabitants), however, lay beyond its jurisdiction. It seems likely that a settlement existed here even in Roman times, so that we can imagine the lively exchanges which took place across the boundary ditch. Then, in 1813, the town bubbled forth to a position of prominence ahead of the neighbouring wine-growing or river-bank communities, with the discovery of "prickly air" - not yet identified as carbon dioxide - which issues from the ground at this point. The town soon changed its allegiance from wine to fizzy water; today Bad Honningen, with its carbonated spring known as the **Dreikönigsquelle**, is the resort with the highest production of carbonic acid in Germany.

Rising above a sea of vines, **Arenfels Castle** dominates the scene. It was completed in 1259, but bears today the countenance it acquired after 1849 at the hands of Zwirner, the master architect of Cologne Cathedral. With its stepped

A view of Koblenz.

gables, turrets and crenellations he transformed the old fortress into an utterly romantic setting. Not only is Arenfels beautiful, it is also highly significant - as many steps as there are days in the year, and 365 windows. The castle's last incarnation was as a restaurant; today it is not even that.

The confluence of the Ahr and the Rhine, where the larger river is forced to turn towards the east, marks the point where the Rhine Romanticism gives way to **Ahr Romanticism**. From here walkers and poets like Gottfried Kinkel (1815-1882) headed up the Ahr valley, past Neuenahr and Altenahr as far as Blankenheim, to the river's source 89 kilometres away in the Eifel Massif. Even today the Ahr, one of the Rhine's vinous tributaries, is famous for its late Burgundies; he who has indulged to excess should heed the words of the ancients, as Kinkel has passed them on to us: "The monks and the ecclesiastical gentlemen of the Ahr Valley discovered long ago the rule that one should drink white wine as an antidote to the over-

imbibing of the red. The cure is well-proven." Should this remedy prove inefficacious, there is always the mineral water from the world famous **Apollinaris Spring**, which gushes forth in the Ahr Valley near Neuenahr.

The mouth of the Ahr near **Bad Kripp** is the last natural river confluence on the left bank of the Rhine. Its course may change from one flood to the next as it continuously pushes silt and gravel into the bigger river. The alluvial soil which has been deposited here is known as the Golden Mile. The town behind it, a short distance upstream, is called **Sinzig** (14,000 inhabitants), from the Latin "Sentiacum". The town is thus mentioned in 762 A.D.; that was only its Roman name. Many years previously, before the dawn of the Christian era, the region was settled by the Celts, who recognised the advantages of its location on the upper edge of the Golden Mile, above the point where the flood waters of the Rhine were likely to present a threat. Situated on higher ground like the town itself is the Hohenstaufen **Souvenirs.**

Church of St. Peter, thought to have been dedicated in 1241. The local history museum is housed in the Castle, built in the 19th century on the ramparts of a 14th-century moated castle.

Opposite the mouth of the Ahr lies **Linz** (6,000 inhabitants), the "colourful town on the Rhine" - as its citizens fondly call it. Between the twin town gates, the Rheintor and the Neutor - remains of the town fortifications, which were demolished in 1861 - lovingly restored timbered houses from various centuries cluster round the late Romanesque **Church of St. Martin**. In the early days the city wall had been the object of great pride, regarded as an expression of civic self-confidence. The Archbishop of Cologne, whose summer residence was situated here, saw the town as a bastion of power. In 1365, in order to nip in the bud any tendency to cockiness on the part of the inhabitants of Linz, he had a **Castle** erected in the centre of the town as a permanent reminder that the real authority in the town was his. As a counterbalance, the burghers of Linz promptly had a town hall built. It still stands in the centre of town: still known as the **Town Hall**, and is the oldest still in daily occupation in the Rhineland-Palatinate. In recent years the Elector's castle has been adapted to cater to visitors. It contains a restaurant where medieval-style dishes are served, as well as a torture chamber and - in the roof - a discothèque named "Castello".

An extensive view across the Rhine and the Ahr can be enjoyed from the **Kaiserberg** (178 metres), with its neo-Gothic pilgrimage church. Everything of substance in the Linz area is based on basalt: the towers within the town limits, the railway embankment and the well-being of the entire community. Here, as on the opposite bank, the inhabitants live from the legacy of the site's prehistoric igneous heritage. Nothing remains of the nearby **Dattenberg** today except the name itself; once a mountain of basalt, it is now nothing but a deep hole in the ground.

An attractive example of the pillared rock formation can be seen at the **Erpeler**

Roofs with a view.

Ley, a precipitous cliff rising 140 metres above the Rhine and the pretty little village of **Erpel**, which lies just beyond **Remagen**. The sinister ruins of the **Ludendorff Bridge** (1916-1918) stand sentinel in front of it - two pillars to the left and two to the right. War veterans from the United States still make the pilgrimage to see the railway bridge which was initially defended to the bitter end; then the order was given that it should be blown up. It should have sunk to the bottom of the river on March 7th 1945; the charges were already laid, the order had been given and the fuse was lit. And yet - as if by a miracle - the bridge remained standing for ten whole days. Large numbers of allied troops were able to cross over onto the right bank, and in May of that year the Second World War finally came to an end. On the left bank there is a **Museum of Peace**, recalling the crossing of the river. Furthermore, any visitor who is so inclined can purchase the bridge itself here, finger-sized splinters of it, cast in resin, as a war souvenir.

Remagen (14,000 inhabitants), christened Rigomagus in ancient times, has an attractive riverside promenade next to which lie little-known Roman remains such as the choir of the Basilica of Peter and Paul facing the Roman gateway, the **Pfarrhoftor**, with decorated relief sculptures whose significance is still not completely clear. To quote Gottfried Kinkel for a moment, however, "the majority of our readers will be less attracted by these relics of antiquity than by the fine modern building standing on a hillside just outside the town on the site of the no-longer-existent **Church of St. Apollinaris**, and worth visiting for the fine view across the Rhine Valley."

The scene today is not very different from that in 1849: the neo-Gothic pilgrimage church built by Zwirner, the master of Cologne Cathedral, reveals his handiwork clearly in the finials. Constructed in 1839-1857, the exterior is as harmonious as the interior, which is extensively decorated with frescoes of the Nazarenes in the Romantic manner.

The Riesling harvest.

The building resembles nothing as much as an exquisite treasure chest - and as such, indeed, it was planned. It is a repository for the head of St. Apollinaris, which - according to legend - was to be brought to Cologne in 1146 along with the bones of the Three Wise Men. But the ship came to a halt near Remagen, and all attempts to sail on were to no avail until Rainald von Dassel, the Archbishop of Cologne, decided to abandon a part of his holy cargo. He chose the relics of an unknown saint, Apollinaris, and was thus responsible for the latter's rise to fame.

Hard by the last hill of any note on the left bank of the Rhine, on the slopes of the late volcanic Rodderberg, stands the **Rolandsbogen** - the epitome of Rhine Romanticism. It is an artistically stylized 19th-century ruin. Other buildings constructed between Remagen and Oberwinter during the same period, including Marienfels Castle and Ernich House were designed to live in or as an expression of status. The arch, however, was of purely sentimental value.

In the past, the Archbishop of Cologne had built the **Rolandseck Fortress** as a bastion of the Electorate of Cologne. It was attacked on various occasions and partly destroyed, the last occasion being during the Thirty Years War. After that the castle fell into disrepair, and as the walls became increasingly overgrown with ivy, so the legends attached to the ancient stones flourished too. Below the castle, in a convent on Nonnenwerth Island, lived Hildegard. She was in love with Roland, but had entered the convent on hearing an erroneous report of his death. But he was alive and well, and all that poor Hildegard could now do was gaze up at the castle. Roland was so moved that he remained there for the rest of his life.

In the 19th century the Rolandsbogen became a place of secular pilgrimage. When, in 1839, a winter storm blew what remained of the archway into the valley below shortly after Christmas, a cry of horror echoed through the Rhineland. Ferdinand Freiligrath (1810-1876), a famous poet at the time,

Timber designs.

launched an appeal in verse. In 1840 the celebrated Zwirner himself, who in any case had been working in Remagen since 1839, took on the task of rebuilding the arch from the ruins of an old castle. And so this popular destination for outings was not lost, described in Jörg Ritzel's song "I came from far to visit the Rhine". And even if one cannot see the convent on the island from the arch, one can still enjoy the view of the Rhine with all seven hills beyond.

A little later, in 1856, the imposing **Railway Station** was constructed for visitors; the future Emperor Wilhelm II wanted a country house with a railway connection. The station still stands today, even if it is no longer a station as such, but a meeting point for prominenti from the arts, from politics and from the big, wide world at large. It is simultaneously an atelier, exhibition hall and concert hall in one. It was really always all those things: not just a place where the train stopped, but rather a meeting place within the main station which had always existed - for Queen Victoria and

Simrock, for Kaiser Wilhelm and Franz Liszt. Just as one could look across from the classicistic terrace of the railway station to Unkel and Bad Honnef on the other side, so could one also look across from the far side to the station. Freiligrath lived in **Unkel** (3,500 inhabitants) when the lofty Rolandsbogen collapsed into the depths of the river. He was able to arrange an advance without resorting to the composition of much poetry. He had created a "Belvedere hard by the Rhine", his "Strolchenburg" on the Rhine promenade. Today it is known as the **Freiligrath House**.

Even today , Unkel is the setting for more festivities than serious work - if you exclude that of gourmets. This pretty village is particularly worth visiting in the autumn, at the season of the wine festivals - those liquid variations on the pious harvest thanksgiving theme, at which hordes of wine-bibbers - even Beethoven himself - were wont to partake. The story goes that he was unable to pay his bill, and that he therefore spent a night in the tower which marks **A sign to the river.**

the southern end of the old town ramparts. Today this same tower, adorned with a pointed roof, is the object of admiration from near and far.

Further downstream, in **Bad Honnef** - for Alexander von Humboldt the "Nice of the Rhineland" - the hill country peters out in a sevenfold flourish. Legend claims that there were once seven giants who helped to cut through the barrier of mountains behind which the Rhine was impounded like a lake. They did so with seven spades, accomplishing the task in a twinkling, and as they finished they banged the seven spades on the ground - presumably seven times, thereby leaving seven mounds of soil lying on the ground: the **Siebengebirge**, the "seven mountains".

"Even today I can taste the names like nuts and berries", wrote Vilma Sturm in 1959: "Drachenfels, Wolkenburg, Lohrberg, Löwenburg, Nonnenstromberg - with an altitude of 461 metres the highest of the seven - Ölberg, Petersberg". If you count the mountains yourself you will in fact invariably end up with a total of seven, if only because you always stop counting when you reach number seven. In truth, however, this northern border of the **Rhenish Uplands** has more than 40 peaks and summits, many of which have individual names - even if no one can remember them as they can those of their seven better-known brothers: Geisberg, Schallenberg, Kuckstein, Ennert, Stenzelberg... In reality the origins were quite different from the story: the word seven comes from the Siefen, the little streams which characterize the region; the **Drachenfels** (321 metres) is not the home of a dragon, but named after the trachyte which even the Romans quarried from its slopes.

At the time when Alexander von Humboldt described the Siebengebirge region as one of the loveliest in the world, the stone for which the district was famous was still quarried here: trachyte, andesite, latite and basalt were the proper names for what the stonemasons extracted here - mullions, mantelpieces, window-sills, cobblestones,

A storm gathers.

kerbstones, stones large and small, embankment cladding and ballast for the new railway.

Before the quarrying began the summit of the **Wolkenburg**, as its name indicates, appeared to be lost in the clouds. Of the **Finkenberg** in Beuel today nothing but the name remains; of the mountain there is no sign. The demolition would have continued were it not for the fact that the local residents of this romantic region banded together as early as 1869, forming an association whose aim was the conservation and improvement of the Siebengebirge. To their efforts was added an official designation supplied by the Council of Europe in 1971; since then, the Siebengebirge has been considered particularly worth preserving. It is a paradise for walkers, who can find rest and recreation in the oldest national park in Germany.

"One of the loveliest and sunniest spots" - if one is to believe Ernst Moritz Arndt - is **Bad Honnef** (21,000 inhabitants), sheltered from the winds and blessed with a mild climate. Thanks to its "Drachenquelle" spring it is also a spa favoured by those suffering from heart disease or rheumatic problems. Konrad Adenauer, the first Chancellor of the Federal Republic, once lived in the nearby district of **Rhöndorf**. Adenauer's house, high up on the hillside, has been preserved as it was before he died. It is a memorial to the post-war period and contains a large collection of personal memorabilia - including the famous shepherd's check hat - recalling the elderly rose-growing gentleman who once lived there.

A footpath leads from Rhöndorf through the vineyards to the **Drachenfels**, the symbol of the Siebengebirge. It is one of the principal attractions of the Rhineland and in summer often referred to as the "highest mountain in Holland". A path and a rack-and-pinion railway lead down the other side into much-visited **Königswinter** (3,500 inhabitants). One way lies through the "nightingale valley" of popular song, past the **Drachenburg**. The latter was **A cloudy day.**

also built in 1882-84 by a man with both money and an aristocratic family tree. He chose, however, not to build on the site of an old castle but rather to start from scratch. The style was completely that of times gone by - or at least, what his contemporaries imagined it to be: a bacchanalian riot of kitsch and candelabras. Cultural events have been held here since 1972.

Above **Oberkassel** the disused opencast basalt quarries can be clearly discerned even from the river. Here glowing lava solidified into pillars as if instantaneously. It was here, too, that the skeletons of a human couple, buried some 16,000 years previously, were discovered at the foot of the Rabenley in 1914. They are not only the oldest human remains to be found in the Rhineland, but are also the oldest which can be categorized as Homo sapiens, as opposed to Neandertal Man.

And finally, around St. Laurentius, near **Oberdollendorf**, prettily situated on a hillside, the farmers have cultivated for 1000 years the most northerly vineyards in Germany. Above the village lies the **Petersberg**, the picturesque site of the old and the new guest house of the Federal government. Before the First World War a hotel stood here, and before that - centuries earlier - an Augustinian monastery. It was soon taken over by the Cistercians, but only for three years: in 1192 they moved into the neighbouring **Heisterbach Valley** where they built their beautiful monastery. Today only the ruined choir still stands in picturesque splendour. The church itself was sacrificed to Reason after the French invasion. In 1809 it was sold for demolition, and the stones were then taken downriver for use as revetment for the Rhine-Meuse canal.

This is also the place where the famous story-book tale of the "Monk of Heisterbach" had its humble beginnings. A young monk, beset by doubts, retired to the rocky landscape to ponder over his problems. When he finally knocked at the monastery door again, three hundred years had flown by as in a flash, and he was no longer recognized. The

Right and left, the **Drosselgasse** - a popular destination in the Rhinegau.

monk lost at least his doubts in the truth of the saying of old, that one day for the Lord is like a thousand years!

Further downstream, already on flat countryside, and once surrounded by water, lies the Romanesque jewel of **Beuel**, on the opposite side of the river to Bonn. The **Double Church of St. Clement in Schwarzrheindorf** was consecrated in 1151, built after the pattern of the palace chapels of German kings. An octagonal opening links the upper and lower sections of the church, recalling thereby the memory of Charlemagne's royal palace in Aachen. Here the nobles could sit in the upper section and take part in the mass without being sullied by undesirable contact with their servants. The little church is famous for its fine murals.

On the left bank the land has already been flat for some time; now the hills retreat even further and command a view of the long-inhabited plains. The medieval **Godesburg**, with its ruins and the circular tower, occupies a dominant position on its 122-metre hill overlooking **Godesberg**. The archbishops of Cologne had it built in 1210. Politically speaking the spa has belonged to Bonn since 1969; it has, however, been able to preserve its nickname of "spa" on the "right" side of the hyphen; the official name is Bonn-Bad Godesberg, and not - for example - Bad Bonn.

Health alone is a boring subject, and so Godesberg - like Wiesbaden - developed into a town of merrymaking and pleasure at the end of the feudal era. The spa gardens were adorned with casino and theatre, the **Redoute Castle** was begun in 1780 and finished in 1820 as a ballroom providing amusement for heart and soul for the distinguished spa patients. Those who could only boast nobility of intellect celebrated at the foot of Castle Hill in the famous student tavern "Zur Lindenwirtin Aennchen" - the most popular in town since 1646. It was transferred to new premises where it would be less of a traffic hindrance in 1976, but since then it has been the traffic itself which has been the main disturbance.

Konrad Adenauer in his home town of Rhöndorf.

Muffendorf, still relatively unknown although one only has to climb the hill to reach it, has preserved its essentially rural character. In the old heart of the village, the numerous timbered houses surrounding the castle-like **Baroque Kommende** (now the residence of the Belgian ambassador), remain silent in the face of their busy neighbours.

Godesberg, too, suffered less bomb damage than many other towns during World War II. And so the town, like the southern part of Bonn, has become a highly sought-after residential area, especially amongst the Bonn diplomats.

The post-war political situation has brought more change to **Bonn** (287,000 inhabitants) and Godesberg than any previous reform. More than three years after the cessation of hostilities, on September 1st 1948, the Parliamentary Council assembled between the stuffed mammals and preserved birds, next to the fish and amphibians of the still-intact museum of the research biologist Alexander König. On May 8th of the following year the constitution was agreed, and two days later Bonn was declared the temporary capital of the new republic with a total of 200 votes to 176.

Over 2,000 years old, the city had already savoured the taste of power and influence as the residence of the electoral archbishops of Cologne. After that, the **Palace of Clemensruhe**, the 18th-century **Poppelsdorf Castle** and the Residence in the Hofgarten became home to the sciences, for since 1816 they have housed the Friedrich Wilhelm University of the Rhineland.

The political heart of Bonn developed further to the south, in the direction of Godesberg and Plittersdorf. It still lives in a state of uneasy tension in relation to the town's image as a long-established retirement centre as well as an the historical home of the aristocracy. Traces of this awkward equilibrium can be seen everywhere. Bonn, as an administrative town, has the highest percentage of civil service widows - and the highest percentage of dogs - per head of population. Not all aspects of life in Bonn were able

A broad view of the river near Bonn, Drachenfels Castle in the background.

to keep pace with the boom. It is often claimed that a Bonn student will need a good half year longer to complete his studies than elsewhere; he will spend the extra time waiting at the level crossing, for the railway runs right through the centre of the town. But Bonn has nonetheless remained a unity, lying as it does between the **Hofgarten** and the main station (built in 1885 and immortalized 25 years ago by Heinrich Böll's "Face of a Clown"). The official residence of the Chancellor of the Federal Republic is the **Villa Hammerschmidt** on the Adenauer Allee. Here, too, can be found the Schaumburg Palace, the **Federal Chancellery** (completed in 1977), and the Alexander König Zoological Museum. The **Bundeshaus** (at present undergoing rebuilding) and the **Members' House**, on Görrestrasse, have become the town's symbols.

Here, surrounded by busy commercial activity, the roots of Bonn's local history and the buildings dating from the town's Golden Age - the Collegiate Church, the palaces and the Town Hall - can be found packed together within a small area. Bonn became the base for a Roman legion as long ago as 11 B.C.. About 50 years later the camp was fortified, and mentioned by Tacitus as the "castra bonnensis". During the third century two Roman officers named Cassius and Florentius were condemned to death as martyrs because of their Christian faith. Their final resting place was on the spot where today the octagonal crossing tower of the collegiate church, 92 metres high, soars up to heaven. According to legend it was St. Helena, the mother of Constantine the Great, who financed the building of the first church here as a mausoleum for the two martyrs. In approximately 1050 the **Collegiate Church of St. Cassius and St. Florentius** was constructed on the site of the Carolingian basilica. A town landmark, it has remained even today a place of rest and contemplation. The collegiate church, originally built for a monastery, boasts a Romanesque cloister which - even in this stone jungle - encloses a little garden.

A demonstration on the market place in Bonn, with Beethoven in the background.

Not far away stands **Ludwig van Beethoven** (1770-1827), who, since 1845, has occupied a pedestal in front of the Post Office, housed in a former nobleman's residence. Despite the image projection of political personalities, the musical genius is still the best-known native son of Bonn, with the result that the visitor will encounter him several times on a journey across town: in the **Beethoven House** and the **Beethoven Hall**. His birthplace at Bonngasse 20 has been the town's house of remembrance for its great son for over a century now. It contains an archive and a museum, and - in the room in which he was born - a marble bust. Further on, you can now see him again, larger than life, in concrete. Here, too, is his famous determinedly grim expression, which probably has less to do with the Tax Office opposite than with the futuristic concert hall behind: the Beethoven Hall, which was completed in 1959.

The town's focal point has always been the market place, with its baroque **Town Hall** built in 1737 after a design by Michael Leveilly. Its soft pastel-toned façade dominates the town centre. On two crucial visits Charles de Gaulle and John F. Kennedy both spoke from its staircase to the citizens of the town, and hence to the citizens of the republic. During the "Bonn Summer" festival, cultural events take place here. Otherwise there is a daily market.

The town's heyday as an electoral city can also be experienced just outside its boundaries. On the **Kreuzberg** - with the Venusberg, one of the town's twin hills - there stands a little **Pilgrimage Chapel** dating from 1628. In 1746 it was transformed by the Elector Clemens August into an architectural jewel by the addition of a new wing and a staircase by the celebrated Balthasar Neumann. Behind the chapel lie the **Kottenforst** woods, once the royal hunting grounds and planted specifically for that purpose. The fashion of riding to hounds necessitated long open tracts of land, clearings as straight as a die through the forest. It has left its mark on the terrain to this day. Much else has

disappeared, including the summer hunting lodge "Herzogsfreude", built in 1854 and containing 100 rooms. It was pulled down on the orders of the occupying French army.

Two other buildings also dating from the end of this feudal period have, however, remained: **Augustusburg Castle** and the **Falkenlust Hunting Lodge** in **Brühl**, which lies between Bonn and Cologne. For almost half a century, between 1725 and 1768, the most famous artists of the time were involved in the construction of a palace for Elector Clement Augustus. Then the most magnificent royal residence in the Rhineland was finished at last - and Clement Augustus was dead, having expired in 1761. From time to time the Federal Government uses his legacy to invest state banquets with a little feudal pomp. TV audiences are all familiar with the staircase by Balthasar Neumann, said to be the most beautiful in the world.

North of Bonn, before the Rhine traveller reaches the Cologne industrial belt, he passes the **Siegaue**, the delta region marking the confluence of the little tributary with the main river. The land here is so flat that the slight eminence on the upper edge of the channel bank by the meander actually bears the name Bergheim, "mountain home". Opposite, in a rounded arc like the rim of a basin, lie the foothills, the land of the *Kappesboore*, the "Cabbage Growers", as the local peasants are called. Fertile soil and a sheltered situation have contributed to making the plain stretching across to the Rhine, and the neighbouring slopes as far as the woodland on the upper reaches of the Swist valley, a rich area of farmland. Wine was formerly cultivated here; today, fruit and vegetables are grown, *Kappes* und *Schavu*, "White cabbage and Savoy cabbage", as the locals sing in a parody of a song popular on St. Martin's Day.

Somewhere along this stretch of the river, the Rhine Romanticism finally takes its leave. Even so, it is only here that our Rhine journey actually reaches its climax - if indeed such a climax exists: **Cologne** (approx. 1 million in-

The "Ostermann" Memorial in Cologne.

habitants). The Roman capital, et hillije Kölle, "Holy Cologne", is not only the biggest city on the Rhine; it is also one of the most beautiful cities in Germany.

Few contest the fact that this is so; opinions differ, however, as to why this should be the case. Could it be because of the view? Or the magnificent cathedral? Because of the people, especially during the pre-Lenten Carnival? Because of the museums or the post-modern pavement architecture? Or because of the effect of all these elements together? If one considers the matter from a historical point of view, it is certainly surprising. In Spring 1945 there was so little left of the original city that the allied troops added insult to injury by suggesting that it would perhaps be easier to rebuild Cologne somewhere completely different. Only the **Cathedral** still stood proudly amongst the ruins; 157.38 metres high. Even that, too, had not entirely escaped damage. But the city had not been killed stone dead. Hanging outside a house which would normally have overlooked the Rose

Everybody is happy at carnival time.

Monday Carnival procession was, as in previous years, the standard notice with which the local citizens let out their front room for this one day: "Room with a view". Underneath, a wit had scribbled three laconic words: "Bring your own floorboards".

It was not just a case of renewing the floorboards. Around the Gothic cathedral the city was completely rebuilt, often in the style of the old. The **Old City**, for example, surrounding the **Church of St. Martin the Great** and the **Town Hall** (15th-16th centuries), will offer the visitor no reminders of the nights the city was bombed during the war. This is the entertainment and tourist heart of the city; for some years now, the traffic has passed through this area underground. There is now nothing to hinder access to the Rhine through the lovely **Rheingarten** park.

Only since 1888 has the Rhine actually flowed directly through Cologne; until that date, it flowed past the city. Cologne lay on the left bank; across the river was - even in Roman times - the

"Land of the Barbarians" (thus it is written on a tombstone in the museum).

After World War II the old bridges were also rebuilt, and new ones were added; the Rodenkirchen motorway bridge, the South bridge, the Severin bridge and the Deutz bridge, the Hohenzollern bridge, the Zoo bridge, the Mülheim bridge and the northern motorway bridge.

In 1888 Cologne's boundaries were redrawn to include **Deutz**, since time immemorial "the town opposite Cologne". Cologne could now expand on both the right and the left banks of the Rhine; the inner city, if measured according to its medieval boundaries, today occupies just one percent of the total area of the city. It is the part which visitors will want to see as it contains most of the historical sights; here the city's meeting places and attractions are all crowded together.

It was here that in olden times two Roman roads met and crossed. Their present-day names are **Hohe Strasse** and **Schildergasse**. There is the cathedral quarter, begun by one of the archbishops, Konrad von Hochstaden, in 1248 - and finished in 1880 by a Hohenzollern emperor. Directly next door stands the **Roman-Germanic Museum** containing the multiplicity of treasures still being unearthed from the ground in the area; all one has to do, it seems, is to dig. Next door again is the **Wallraf-Richartz Museum**, still the subject of controversy but undoubtedly one of the most significant buildings of the century. It contains two separate museums and is named after two benefactors; the second collection, the **Ludwig Museum**, bears the name of a chocolate manufacturer and patron of the arts. Inside the building is a magnificent concert hall, the **Philharmonie**.

Cologne's **Romanesque Churches** are amongst her architectural jewels. Since their restoration (which was largely completed by 1985), they bear witness again to the city's vanished opulence; in the Middle Ages it was the wealthiest city north of the Alps. Later on the Prince Bishops developed their love of Baroque pomp in Bonn and

elsewhere, tearing down a number of old churches. Cologne, however, a secular city since the famous Battle of Wörringen in 1288, subsequently lapsed into poverty. Today it can only boast one large Baroque church: Our **Lady of the Assumption** in Marzellenstrasse near the cathedral. It stands hidden behind the gleaming façade of a bank.

Cologne, famous as a city of the arts, is also a city renowned for its art of living. It was not long ago that a much-travelled man, who was neither a native of the city nor even a German citizen, claimed that the gastronomy industry was better developed here than in New York. The favourite meeting place remains the **Kölsche Weetschaff**, a tavern which calls to mind the most extensive brewing tradition in the land. With a rough charm which takes some getting used to the *Köbesse*, as the waiters are called here, mostly deposit glasses of beer before guests unasked. So crucial is the role played by the foaming brew in the city's identity that it shares the name given to the local dialect: *Kölsch*.

Below, the Köbes - the local barman - tapping the "Kölsch" ale in Cologne. Right, contrasts.

COLOGNE CATHEDRAL

As the train rolls slowly through Deutz on the right bank of the river, and then over the mighty steel bridge construction, the traveller has a chance to open the window and to make the most of one of the finest urban panoramas in the world: the Rhine promenade with the colourful façades and pointed gables of Cologne's historic centre, and rising above it all the mighty towers of the cathedral. Downstream, supported by a single tower, the unmistakable silhouette of the Severin bridge can be discerned through the steel lattice of the Deutz bridge. In the meantime the most important sacred Gothic edifice, the most ambitious construction project ever planned and executed within Germany, advances inexorably until the train finally comes to a halt scarcely 200 metres from the main portal.

When Archbishop Konrad von Hochstaden put the church's seal of approval on the repeated wish to start building, Cologne was the largest city in Germany. It was also the third-largest in Europe - after Paris and Constantinople - and was also one of the wealthiest. In 1164 the Shrine of the Magi had been transferred to the original cathedral. It was planned that Cologne should be given a more fitting repository for this unique treasure, to which pilgrims travelled from all over the world. The architects took the French cathedrals, in particular Amiens, as their model. They retained, however, the five-chambered nave of the 11th-century basilica. Cologne cathedral was to become the most perfect example of "French" sacred architecture, the culmination of Gothic cathedral building. *Omnium ecclesiarum, quae sunt in Allemania, quasi mater et matrona* - the "Mother of all Churches in Germany" - thus the edifice was described by an English chronicler.

The chancel was completed in 1320, and dedicated in 1322. The transept and the nave, however, remained unfinished. Building work stopped in 1560; it was

The splendid interior of Cologne Cathedral.

only revived at the beginning of the 19th century, when historic consciousness was awakened as the country succumbed to a wave of nationalism and enthusiasm for the Middle Ages, resulting in a Gothic revival throughout Europe.

In 1843 King Friedrich Wilhelm laid the foundation stone marking the beginning of the resumption of construction work. The cathedral was finally finished in 1880, a masterpiece of Romantic conservation of a historic monument. In 1944 the bombing raids devastated the Old Town and the main station nearby. As if by a miracle, however, the cathedral remained intact.

The charm of Cologne Cathedral lies in the unmatched harmony of the individual elements, and the perfect unity of its external appearance. For this reason, any sightseeing tour of the cathedral should begin with a tour of its circumference. The interior is 144 metres long, 44.8 metres wide and 43.5 metres high. The towers, 157 metres high, were the tallest in the world in 1880; one can still climb to a height of 95 metres up the South Tower by means of a staircase with over 509 steps. The interior, with its circular columns and windows embellished with tracery, corresponds to the contemporary idea of weightlessness and the necessity of striving for perfection. The visitor's gaze is drawn automatically past the buttresses to the windows and the vaulting which soars heavenwards.

The Shrine of the Magi is situated in the middle of the chancel. The gold sarcophagus was started in 1184; it was the biggest of its kind in Western medieval Christendom, created by the renowned goldsmith Nicholas de Verdun. The Cross of Gero, a large-scale example of Othonian art, was produced in 969-76 in Cologne. It is the oldest larger-than-life-size wooden representation of the Crucifixion to be produced north of the Alps, and is thus the second treasure to find a permanent place within the chancel. The Baroque frame was added in the 17th century. The Treasury contains the most valuable items belonging to the Cathedral.

Left, Cologne Cathedral nearing completion (19th century). **Right**, Cologne after the Second World War.

FROM COLOGNE TO DUISBURG

North of Cologne the picture changes rapidly; the Lower Rhine begins at the latest at the mouth of the Wupper. This is much more than just a geographical label. From now onwards the river will be accompanied by willows and poplars, and by high water marks.

Leverkusen (162,000 inhabitants) follows Cologne: the metropolis built around a chemical factory. The name is derived from that of Carl Leverkus, a native of Wermelskirchen, who moved his ultramarine plant from the Bergisches Land to the Rhine in order to be near the waterway. Later on the company was taken over by a manufacturer from Wuppertal named Friedrich Bayer, thus acquiring the name by which it is world famous today.

The chemical giant could hardly have chosen a more suitable place to settle: the **Wupper**, 100 kilometres long, is the most industrially exploited of all the Rhine's tributaries. It is also the dirtiest; even Friedrich Engels (1820-1895) complained that the river flowed crimson - not bloodstained from battle, "but solely due to the large number of dyers along its course." The "silver snake" which winds its way through the green surrounding countryside had lost its skin even in Engels's time: Since then it has become more like a black mamba.

On the left bank of the Rhine, not far from Worringen - where in 1288 the citizens of Cologne, the peasants from the uplands and the troops from Brabant fought against the archbishop for their independence - lies **Zons**, with its well-preserved medieval ramparts. The town has the reputation of being a sort of Rothenburg on the Lower Rhine: dark-red brick façades, brightly painted shutters and hordes of visitors every day of the year. Zons was a customs fortress until 1767, situated in a prime defensive position on the flat dyke and dominated by the sails of its windmill.

Even **Neuss** (150,000 inhabitants) was once a Roman town, the site of one of the most important legionary camps on the Rhine, on the road from Xanten to Cologne. Today the magic ring of the Roman name, Novaesium, has been lost apart from a reference in a brand of chocolate: Novesia. And yet Neuss has a richer tradition than Düsseldorf, its great opponent. The archbishop of Cologne and the unloved Saint Anno gave the town its constitution as long ago as the 11th century. Even then, the city scene was dominated by the **Cathedral of St. Quirinus**, housing the relics of a Roman martyr. A few years ago archaeologists also unearthed the site where a pagan-oriental cult was practised.

During the Middle Ages Neuss lay directly on the Rhine. Then the river escaped the clutches of the town, which then lost its dominant trading position - and its profits. Nothing except good intentions ever came of a canal which was to link the Rhine and the Meuse, which Napoleon intended to construct. Thus the town was left with only the River Erft, enriched with the waters from the opencast excavations in the nearby brown coal mining area. Warm

Preceding pages: the Wallraf Richartz Museum in front of the Cathedral.

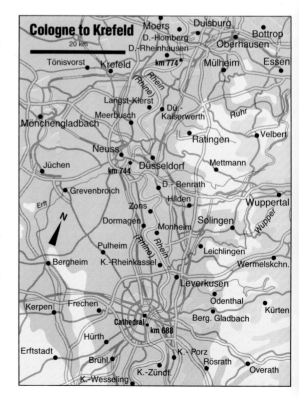

Cologne to Krefeld

and sluggish, it flows here into the Rhine. And whoever sees a lorry bearing the clearly visible logo "NS" can rest assured that the initials stand for a local speciality for which this town in the middle of an agricultural region is famous: Neuss Sauerkraut.

Major political decisions took place on the other side of the river. In 1288, at the battle of Worringen, the domination of the archbishop of Cologne was broken too for the Dukes of Berg. They had fought for access to the Rhine, choosing not Deutz or Mülheim - both too close to Cologne for comfort - but rather a little fishing village further north, on the confluence of the Düssel. Here they settled and built themselves a town: Düsseldorf. In 1380 Berg was elevated to a duchy; in the same year, the ruler moved to Düsseldorf, abandoning his principal residence, Burg on the Wupper.

As the ducal residence until the French conquest, **Düsseldorf** (595,000 inhabitants) experienced the rise of the duchies of Jülich, Cleves and Berg and the earldoms of Mark and Ravensberg. It

also profited from this expansion. "What a world of difference there is between Cologne and this attractive, prosperous Düsseldorf! A well-built city, with fine, solid houses, broad, straight streets and diligent, well-dressed inhabitants. It brings joy to the heart of the traveller!" Thus wrote Georg Forster in 1790. The town merely profited from the fact that the regents, from the house of the Palatinate, had long ago moved elsewhere - first to Mannheim, and later to Munich.

The last electoral prince to reside in Düsseldorf was also the most popular: Johann Wilhelm, known as Jan Wellem. He is still present in "his" city today - mounted on a bronze horse in the Old Town, a masterpiece by the court sculptor Gabriel Grupello dating from 1711. It is said that the metal for the statue was enriched by silver spoons donated by the citizens of Düsseldorf when it transpired, in the middle of casting, that insufficient alloy was available. When the Prussians arrived in 1815, Düsseldorf was considered as a possible regional capital. The fortifications were torn

The colourful facades of Cologne's Old City.

down and rebuilt as a boulevard, which was subsequently dedicated to the new Prussian rulers: the elegant **Königsallee**, today known as the "Kö". Düsseldorf is the seat of the state government of North Rhine Westphalia; with approximately 30,000 jobs available, the latter is the town's principal employer. The university is at last allowed to bear the name of one of the town's most famous sons - Heinrich Heine. South of the Rheinkniebrücke -where the river turns almost back on itself - the **Rhine Tower** soars 234 metres skywards.

To the south, reflecting the magnificence once associated with the Rhine, is the late Baroque **Benrath Castle**. Started in 1756, it was built over a period of 14 years by Nicolas de Pigage. In those days the castle lay quite close to the town; following the course of the Rhine, however, it is 24 kilometres from the Hofgarten because of the river's meanders. To the north of Düsseldorf, in attractive countryside, lies the little town of **Kaiserswerth**, with the massive **Palace of Barbarossa**. Kaisers-

werth originally lay on an island in the middle of the river. In early times the British bishop Swidbert - Suitbertus - had settled here on his mission to convert the inhabitants of the Bergisches Land. Emperor Barbarossa developed the island as one of the strongholds - and cashier's offices - of his kingdom. The section of Marktstrasse running along the river is significantly referred to as the "Golden Ground"; here it was that most of the money changed hands.

Krefeld (223,000 inhabitants) is the next town to the north, round the next bend in the Rhine. The town had become prosperous as the home of spinners, dyers, silk-weavers and tanners - especially after the Reformation, when Maurice of Orange offered sanctuary here to the persecuted from neighbouring lands. During the 18th century Krefeld had earned itself the reputation of being the "cleanest, friendliest, most charming and most prosperous manufacturing town" in Prussia.

Situated on the river are the castle and the town of **Linn**, with a number of in-

Busy street life in Düsseldorf's Altstadt.

teresting museums. Before that is a landscaped park surrounding **Greiffenforst House**, the summer residence of Cornelius de Greiff, a 19th-century textile manufacturer. He built his home in a curious pagoda-like style which seems to recall simultaneously Chinese exoticism and Berlin classicism.

Duisburg (560,000 inhabitants) now accompanies the Rhine for thirty kilometres along its course - the largest freshwater port in the world, with harbours for ore and oil, for coal and scrap metal: 40 basins all told. Here the Ruhr District borders our river. Underground, the coal mines provide passages which cross the Rhine beneath the river bed. Duisburg has also established an international reputation for its organization of rowing regattas and its performances under the rubric "German Opera on the Rhine" (in cooperation with Düsseldorf). There is also the **Wilhelm Lehmbruck Museum** (sculptor, 1881-1919) in Düsseldorfer Strasse and - at the entrance to the harbour - the **Museum of German Inland Navigation**.

In the 12th century Duisburg already had a town charter, and was a significant trading post. Later - as in the case of Neuss - the river changed course, bypassing the town some two kilometres to the west and Duisburg's importance declined. The most important local son from this period - in fact, the most important to date - was Gerhard Mercator (1512-1594), the cartographer, whose consummate skill consisted in his discovery of a method of rolling the surface of the globe to fit inside a cylinder.

In 1780 the Ruhr was made navigable to facilitate the transport of coal. When, in the late 19th century, the Ruhr District spread beyond the confines of the Wupper Valley, and when Duisburg joined forces with Ruhrort in 1905, the **Ruhr District** experienced an economic boom - a fact which can be deduced from the names and emblems visible along the Rhine itself. "No poet can be born here", observed Hans Brandenburg in his poem "Duisburg-the port on the Rhine". To this day, no one has contradicted him.

Left, the port of Duisburg. **Right**, The big wheel at the annual fair in Oberkassel, with a view across to the Rhine Tower.

MAX VON DER GRÜN: THE RUHR BASIN

In times past it was the Imperial Road No. 1, the historic salt and amber road from Aachen to Königsberg, the road along which Napoleon's army marched on the way to Russia. Today it is the Bundesstrasse 1, the National Road no. 1; along its periphery, on the right and the left, are the Ruhr towns - or, more simply, the Ruhr Basin. The B1 is, so to speak, the main artery of the region. Along its length stretched out in olden times the trading towns and the towns of the Hanseatic League. Over the past century, however, they have grown into major industrial cities.

Some men arrived one day. They excavated a mine shaft and later extracted coal. Later still, they erected steel furnaces, which required coke; and last of all they built homes for the workers. And so the industrial landscape was created: an area where today factories and houses stand cheek by jowl, so that it is almost impossible to tell which town one is leaving, and which one is entering. It was thus that the largest clearly defined industrial region in Europe came into being.

The River Ruhr - today one of the cleanest in West Germany, the provider of water for industry and millions of people - also gave the region its name: the Ruhr Basin. Or, simply: the *Revier*- the "Patch" - reviled and admired, praised and cursed. Because the region's industries emit so much dust and dirt, the inhabitants of the area have always been a thirsty bunch. And so it is hardly surprising, but rather a logical development, that breweries should have established themselves in every major town, in recent years making Dortmund - rather than Munich - the principal beer town in Europe. "Work makes you thirsty - and through beer your thirst will become an adventure" is a truism often quoted in the city's pubs.

An industrial landscape of this kind will naturally leave its mark on the residents, on their character and mentality. The immigration process in the district

has been under way for 150 years. The people came from all corners of the country, and later from almost all parts of Europe. This seemingly endless influx turned small towns into larger ones, whilst the major towns with their seemingly endless suburbs coalesced inexorably into each other.

Over the past few years we have been able to observe the same procedure in reverse, for a migration has been taking place. The Ruhr Basin is undergoing a structural crisis unlike any other experienced in its 150-year history; young men are leaving for other parts of the country in order to escape unemployment. The population of the largest cities is decreasing at an alarming rate, and so, too, is the amount of local taxes paid. Many communities are in a sorry financial state. I have spoken to many migrants who found themselves forced to leave the Ruhr Basin. The answers I received from these men - and women - had one common theme: they would all return to the Ruhr at once if they could only find approximately equivalent work for approximately equal pay.

This answer alone is sufficient to indicate that the Ruhr Basin has become home for these people, and that they have put down deeper roots here than they would ever have expected. One cannot just throw off one's home town as one does a soiled shirt.

Nowhere is the beer tapped with more skill than in the Ruhr's inimitable pubs, those uniquely democratic institutions. Here the labourer stands next to the priest, the mayor next to the unemployed worker, the prosperous citizen next to the have-not. There are no class barriers; you simply position yourself by the bar and talk about everything under the sun, about the injustice and opportunities in the world. You do not sit at a table to talk to the same people all the time, but rather you stand at the bar, where you can observe the constant comings and goings. Nothing is more typical of this ritual than a short story which is too real to be imagined:

A foreigner strayed into a pub in the Ruhr Basin. He sat down, as was his wont, at a table, and ordered a beer. He

There are many green oases to be found in the Ruhr Basin.

sat there for one hour; for two hours; for three hours. The other customers were standing one, two and even three deep by the bar. Eventually, after three hours, the foreigner could stand it no longer. He stood up and pulled at the sleeve of the nearest local, asking - not without a certain irritation - "Well, for heaven's sake, why don't you sit down?" The man he addressed turned to face him and answered, somewhat reluctantly, "Why? Well, my good man, because we don't have the time."

Woe betide the landlord who is unpractised in the art of tapping barrels, and whose beer is not properly cooled; his pub will be avoided and he himself will be derided as a bungler and treated with scorn. It is quite safe to speak here of a pub culture, and to roughly equate that with the culture of the "Patch" itself.

The constant influx of new residents from almost every European country has made the citizens of the Ruhr Basin more tolerant, for in the factories and even underground, Germans and foreigners alike perform the same tasks under the same conditions. It is of little relevance what nationality your colleague happens to be; the main thing is that he does what is expected of him and does not play the sleeping partner - one who lets others do his work for him. There is no xenophobia - although, as always, there are exceptions which prove the rule.

The Ruhr Basin has its problems, for the monopoly industries of coal and steel, which have dominated the scene for almost two hundred years, are passing through another period of recession. Their position of supremacy has also resulted in the prevention for many years of the establishment of other industries. The Opel factory in Bochum is a recent acquisition, as is the chemical plant in Marl-Hüls. It was also many years before the Ruhr acquired universities of its own in Bochum and Dortmund. This, too, is an indication of past neglect, in line with the adage: "Where the people work they will have no time to study." It is sometimes no more complicated than that, although later generations may well

New recreation areas are being created in the region.

shake their heads in amazement that their forefathers should have had so little foresight.

And yet the structural crisis today is rooted in other causes, even though they are not of a fundamental nature. The increased awareness of the environment has made people more sensitive in their attitudes to industry and economic principles. They are no longer prepared to accept in silence the dirt and the foul air which have been belched out at them for generations. They believe that there is another way of doing things. Politicians and those responsible for business and industry, for their part, are also seeking new ways of attracting "green" industries to the region or of modernizing existing ones. They aim to prevent the stream of employable young men leaving for other parts of the country.

The workers who spent most of their time in factories and pits where they seldom saw the light of day, became - logically enough - sun-hungry, longing for green open spaces, for flowers, and anxious to own domestic pets. Thus

Garden allotments.

arose the local traditions of pigeon-breeding - with the carrier pigeon as the race horse of the little man - and specialist poultry breeding. Thus arose, too, the multitude of allotments and garden developments which, in recent years, have become vegetable patches instead of flower gardens once more.

Such developments are much more common in the Ruhr Basin than elsewhere. For its owner an allotment becomes a sort of Majorca-on-his-doorstep; he will invite his neighbours to join him on the patio for coffee and home-made cake; later they will grill sausages and tackle a crate of beer. They will, in short, celebrate together, and they will always find a reason for doing so. There is no need to wait for a birthday or an anniversary.

I know people living in my neighbourhood who are hardly ever at home during the summer months. They spend all their time at their allotment, in a do-it-yourself or ready-made wooden chalet which they have made progressively more comfortable over the years. It will

contain an electric stove and a refrigerator, a plumbed-in W.C., television, radio and a fully-furnished living room with a sofa bed on which one can even sleep if need be. And when they have a party, the celebrations will continue until the grey light of dawn - accompanied not by the singing of the nightingale, but by the lark.

In the olden days the allotment owners may well have kept pigs, sheep, rabbits and goats for their own consumption. This custom then died out over the years; looking after so many animals was a time-consuming business, and restricted one's freedom of movement. Today, the pendulum has swung back again; rabbits are kept on allotments once more, as are geese, ducks, goats and chickens. One reason for this trend is undoubtedly the lack of faith in the major industrial food manufacturers, underlined by the rediscovered desire to taste home-produced food. A bird from one's own coop tastes very different from the mass-produced "rubber eagles" in the supermarket.

Many small farmers were forced to give up their smallholdings because they were economically unviable. Some of the quick-thinking ones amongst them took advantage of the trend and converted their farms into riding stables. Nowhere in Germany will you find more establishments of this kind, more horses and more young people who enjoy riding, than here.

Although outsiders may find it hard to believe, the Ruhr Basin has remained an agricultural region. Farms have been able to survive in the countless suburbs of the cities, despite the fact that the agricultural pricing policy laid down in Brussels certainly does not make life easy for small and medium-sized concerns. My neighbour owns a pig fattening farm; he has a permanent stock of 300 swine, from young piglets to sows ready for slaughter.

He also keeps 300 chickens, for he cannot live by fattening pigs alone; he needs a second string to his bow. Sometimes, when the wind is in the wrong quarter, we get a whiff from his **Duisburg possesses the largest inland river port in Europe.**

pig sties. We have got used to it. When, on occasions, the smell becomes too overpowering my wife remarks laconically that she finds it less obnoxious than all the diesel fumes. That's certainly one way of looking at it.

Of course, there are less attractive districts of the Ruhr Basin. But few foreigners are aware that there is still much open countryside. Dortmund, one of the largest cities in Germany if you consider its area, includes 50% green open space within its boundaries. One can cycle for hours along tracks without ever having to resort to busy roads.

Part of the cultural traditions of the area and impossible to ignore is the *Kirmes*, the fair. Here, to put it bluntly, you can still experience that "Here the people are in heaven; here I am a man; here, I can be what I am." Or, in other words, to quote the comment of a young couple I once encountered: "Will you come to the fair with me on Sunday?" - "Yes, I will." - "Will you shoot a rose for me?" - "I'll shoot you a bear." - "I don't like bears. Then I won't go to the fair with you." - "All right, then, I'll shoot you a rose."

According to a UN report, the Ruhr Basin is one of the most culturally interesting regions of Europe. This fact is probably less due to the excellent theatres, which can look back on a proud tradition, than to the many creative groups which seem to spring up from year to year like mushrooms, and which receive little or no state subsidy.

The Ruhr Basin - a long house number, an enormous house inhabited by millions of people with varied interests, who nevertheless have one thing in common: they belong to a community - notwithstanding economic crises or fear of unemployment - a community which stretches from Duisburg to Hamm, and from Marl to Wuppertal. They relax at the weekend in the parks, of which there are many: for example, the Westphalia Park in Dortmund, and the Gruga Park in Essen, which represent here the scores of others. Nor should we forget the "front gardens" of the Ruhr Basin - the Münsterland and the Sauerland...

Pigeon breeders beam with pride.

FROM DUISBURG TO EMMERICH

We are now rapidly approaching the border country. Here, increasingly as one travels northwards, the chimneys and winding towers which have hitherto risen out of the flat countryside are replaced by windmills and trees - and even woodland: the "Leucht" forest, for example, which is a popular walking area on the edge of **Kamp-Lintfort**.

No bridge traverses the Rhine on its journey from Duisburg to Wesel; the "Pont" near **Orsoy**, opposite Walsum, is the only river crossing for motor vehicles. Passing along endless avenues fringed by linden trees, the traveller finally arrives in Rheinberg, which owes little more than its name to the river.

In the days before the Rhine became too warm and too salty, this was a point where, in winter, the ice floes were often driven together, so that finally the current was completely blocked. That is why, in the 17th century, the river changed its course in a sharp bend near **Rheinberg**. What remained was a branch of the main river, which the Prussians then sealed off in the 18th century, so that from then onwards they alone could live by the water's edge.

In Alt-Rheinberg, the old part of the town, the sights are all clustered within a compact area: the 15th-century Town Hall and the buildings of the world-famous bitters firm, which - like its home town - has a Berg, a mountain, in its name, in spite of its geographical position in the plains: **Underberg**.

Far below the town, underneath the river itself, can be found the biggest rock salt mine in Europe: 200 metres of strong sea salt, 200 million years old.

Wesel (57,000 inhabitants) lies where the River Lippe flows into the Lippe Side Canal. For centuries the town was important and sought-after, as a member of the Hanseatic League as well as as a fortified city. During the last war the inhabitants were forced to experience at first hand what it means to be a bridgehead - a role which Wesel has played ever since the time of Julius Caesar. The town was bombed flat, until not even ruins remained as obstacles to the Allied advance.

Also destroyed was the **Church of St. Willibrord**, which dated from the early 16th century, and which was incorrectly but proudly referred to by local citizens as the "Cathedral". It has since been rebuilt and is now once again a monument to the Lower Rhineland late Gothic style. The memory of Peter Minuit (1580 - 1638), the religious refugee who sought sanctuary in Wesel, is held in especial esteem: with gold and goods to the total value of 60 guilders he acquired a plot of land in North America which was to prove of great significance. He bought the island of Manhattan from the Indians for the aforementioned price, and thus became the founder of New York.

The other famous son of Wesel is Konrad Duden (1829-1911), who led a campaign against the many much-loved idiosyncrasies of German spelling by means of a guide to correct usage which today still bears his name. His success at the time was only partial, for his critics

included even the emperor himself: despite the reformed spelling of Thal - valley - which became Tal, and Thränen - tears, which became Tränen, Emperor Wilhelm steadfastly refused to give up his "Thron". His preferred spelling remains in the Duden to this day.

The port at Wesel is one of the oldest on the Rhine. In the centre of the town one can still see the remains of the old ramparts. Other sights include a carved altar dating from 1510, housed in the **Church of St. Martini**, which is scarcely forty years old. In 1835 the classicistic architect Karl Friedrich von Schinkel designed a monument to eleven army officers who had been shot dead. It stands on the Schillwiese.

The land is now so flat that standing before Wesel you can see far away in the West the most famous towers on the Lower Rhine - those of **Xanten** (16,500 inhabitants). The town's most illustrious son probably never lived at all - at least, not in the way that legend claims, and certainly not in Xanten. The hero in question is Siegfried, the idol of the heathen Germani, who has since been at least half converted to Christianity. In the Nibelungen saga his native town is referred to by its Christianized name: Ze Santen, "To the Saints".

The most famous saint is reputedly buried far below the 70-metre-high towers which are the town's landmark: a martyr of the Legion of Thebes by the name of Victor. And Victor, the Victorius One, bears a name with the same origins as the Helper from the Lower Rhine who was feared and much envied at the court at Worms. The Gothic **Cathedral of St. Victor** (13th-16th century) boasts a fine altarpiece of the Virgin by Heinrich Douvermann.

So famous was the town's reputation in the past that Xanten was known in medieval times as "Troy". "Holy Troy", for example, is the name by which it was mentioned on 11th-century coins. Any explanations and derivations offered to throw light on the matter tend to be highly unconvincing. In one case it is even embarrassing, for it was claimed that Xanten was founded by Hagen von

Broad views across the Lower Rhine Plain.

Tronje - the supposed murderer of Siegfried, of all people. In fact, however, the sound of the name "Troy" is a mutation of the settlement's Latin name. After Cologne, "Colonia Ulpia Traiana" was the largest town in the province of Germania Inferior.

Extensive relics from this early habitation have been exposed in the **Xanten Archaeological Park**. They have been reconstructed and, together with the accommodation, harbour facilities, water supply systems, fortifications and Roman arena provide ample tuition in the history of Roman culture.

Our journey continues between poplars, wheat fields and meadows, past extensive stretches of open water to **Rees** (17,000 inhabitants). The town enjoys an attractive setting above the Rhine, the classicistic towers of the **Church of the Ascension** welcoming visitors from afar. We pass by **Kalkar** on the flat, empty horizon, once famous (like the entire Lower Rhine region) for its magnificent carved altarpieces. Today it is home to a "B" type fast-breeder

reactor. And then we reach **Emmerich** (32,000 inhabitants), the frontier station by the 852-kilometre marker along the river, five kilometres before the border. The town was rebuilt from the ruins in its original form. Here the river reaches its maximum width; since the bridge was completed in 1965, it has therefore been able to claim to be the longest suspension bridge in Germany.

Worth seeing in Emmerich are the Gothic **Church of St. Adelgundis** (15th century), and the **Shrine of St. Willibrord** (the earliest example of the goldsmith's art in the Lower Rhine), which can be viewed in the **Church of St. Martini** (11th-15th century).

Somewhere in the broad valley, 13 kilometres between Elten, on the right, and the cliff from which the historic town of **Cleves** (44,000 inhabitants) derives its name, the river flows in a leisurely manner between dykes and windmill sails across the border into the Netherlands. It is now only 16 metres above sea level. This is the home of Lohengrin, the Knight of the Holy Grail; and had no one asked where he came from, he would doubtless have disappeared as secretly as he came. There is no room for Knights of the Swan between bowling clubs.

Apart from the former ducal residence, the **Swans' Castle** (15th-17th century), Cleves offers a number of historical sights: the former **Church of the Minorites** (15th century) - now Catholic - and the **Collegiate Church** (14th-15th century). The right bank here is already in Holland; the village of **Rindern**, on the left, is still on German soil. The altar of the Parish **Church of St. Willibrord** was once dedicated to Mars, the god of war, and to the well-being of the Emperor Tiberius. This was because he defeated the Germani here. Only much later did the stone become a Christian symbol.

And here, too, we find the grave of 17-year-old Johanna Sebus, who tried her best to help in the disaster of 1809 when the river froze and the dykes were breached. The brave girl died in the attempt - until Goethe immortalized her in a moving ballad.

Left, a patrol boat in the port of Duisburg. **Right**, typical Lower Rhine landscape, with poplar trees.

FROM EMMERICH TO ROTTERDAM

Once it has passed the 862-kilometre marker post, the river finally becomes a Dutch inland waterway. One has to accept the fact, for there is no evidence to prove it. And yet, this transition marks the end of the Rhineland; almost as soon as the river crosses the border it abandons its purposeful attitude - and soon after that, its name. Lingering on as the "Kromme Rijn" - the "Twisted Rhine", and later as the "Oude Rijn" - the "Old Rhine", it finally gets lost in the sand near Katwijk.

The Netherlands are not part of the Rhineland, but are a delta region. The waterway splits the land into sections as it alternately divides and rejoins, making its own contribution to the oft-quoted aphorism that God doubtless created the world, but not the Netherlands; they were organized by the Dutch themselves.

In 1966 a white whale suddenly appeared and demonstrated to the news-paper-reading public more clearly than any geography lesson could possibly have done, just how interlaced the waters of the Rhine actually are. "Moby Dick", as the white Beluga whale was christened, swam upriver as far as Duisburg, turned round and almost ended up in the Ijsselmeer. But then he somehow swam back upriver again, reaching Cologne before he tranquilly disappeared from view.

The main branch of the Rhine has been known as the **Waal** since Caesar's time. Let us call the second branch, the "Neder Rijn", the Lek - as it was later christened. And let us not forget that the town of Utrecht, situated far away to the north, also lies on the Rhine. Its Latin name confirms the fact: Traiectum ad Rhenum - "Rhine Crossing".

Nijmegen (148,000 inhabitants), like Arnhem, was rebuilt after World War II. Both are Hanseatic towns with a rich historical tradition. Nijmegen is also famous as the site of a palace wherein resided the Emperors Charlemagne and Barbarossa. Sights in the old town cen-

Preceding pages: loading a cargo vessel in the port of Rotterdam.

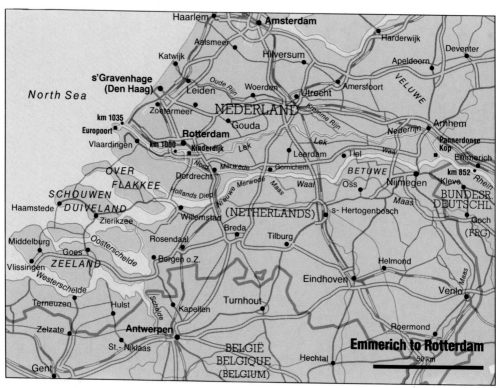

tre include the **Grote Markt** and the **Waag** (1612). The **Town Hall** is also of historical interest.

The old town centre of **Arnhem** (290,000 inhabitants), situated near the Rhine, is worth visiting, as is the **Basilica of St. Walburgis**, dedicated in 1422. So, too, are the remains of the Town Wall, such as the 14th-century Sabelspoort, and the **Groote Kerk**, the "Great Church", dating from the 15th century. North of Arnhem lies the forest and heathland countryside of the **Hoge Veluwe Country Park**, the largest conservation area in the Netherlands (5,500 hectares). Surrounded by this attractive landscape is the district town of **Otterlo**, site of the **Rijksmuseum Kröller-Müller** - one of the jewels of contemporary Dutch culture and housing a collection of more than 250 paintings by Vincent van Gogh (1853-1890).

It may be an exaggeration to maintain that the Dutch actually built their country without assistance, but it is certainly fair to claim that they have altered its countenance no little. Anyone exposed

Making for the open sea.

continuously to the caprices of the elements, as they are, will soon construct defences - dykes and an ultra-modern system of locks and canals to control the water.

The disaster of the floods of 1920 can never be repeated. At the time even the Emperor of Germany, who was fleeing with his wife the Empress, had to don kid gloves to help carry the wooden boards which were being erected in front of Amerongen Castle to keep out the waters. The couple subsequently moved to Doorn, some 10 kilometres distant. Little more was heard of Wilhelm II, except for the rumour that he spent his days chopping wood - for twenty long years. His mausoleum is in Doorn.

At one time the Rhine actually flowed directly through **Utrecht**. Today what remains of its waters splash peacefully through the Grachten, the canals. Utrecht's fame also rested on its association with a second stream - that of the pilgrims who left the town for Santiago in northern Spain. And then one day there were no more pilgrims; after 80

years of religious wars the Netherlands became Calvinist; the Calvinist fervour was translated into diligence in trade, so that if anything at all flowed through the town, it was money from all corners of the globe. The Calvinist legacy is still visible today - and not only in Utrecht. No lace curtains obscure the windows, so that everyone could see that the inhabitants lived a blameless life.

Utrecht's Old Town is surrounded by an ancient moat. It contains the tallest cathedral tower in the Netherlands. **St. Michael's Cathedral**, built in the 13th century on the site of a Romanesque church, was destroyed by a storm in the 17th century. **The Church of St. Peter** was dedicated in the 11th century.

Gorinchem (30,000 inhabitants), once a strategically important defence post, is a pretty town today - complete with a church, the 15th-century St.-Jan belltower and gabled houses dating from the 16th and 17th centuries. **Dordrecht** (108,000 inhabitants) lies on the main river, somewhat nearer the sea. During the heyday of the Hanseatic League it was the port of destination for the goods trade on the Rhine. Tree trunks felled in the Black Forest were tied into rafts and floated downstream as far as here. Since the floods of 1421 Dordrecht has also been a coastal town, for it lies on an arm of the sea known as Hollands Diep. Were it not for the high water level, Dordrecht's **Grote Kerk** (14th century) would still have a tower in the same style as the rest of the building. Unfortunately, when they reached the 70-metre level the foundations gave way; and so only the superstructure for the clock remained.

The last few kilometres are ones with rapidly changing impressions. **Kinderdijk**, whose name refers to a tale of a child in a basket which was stranded on the dyke at high water, charms the visitor with its succession of 19 windmills.

Rotterdam (600,000 inhabitants) has developed over the past 150 years from a herring fishing village to a world port - the largest of all. It retains its position of supremacy in spite of being bombed into the ground by the Germans during

A museum village in Ardenheim in Holland.

the Second World war. The famous sculpture by Ossip Zadkine entitled "The ruined city" (1953) is a memorial to the destruction.

The town's most famous citizen was undoubtedly the humanist scholar Erasmus of Rotterdam (1467-1536). His works can be viewed in the **City Library** on the Nieuwe Markt. The town also possesses a number of interesting museums, such as the **Museum of History** (the 17th-century Schielandhuis), the **Boymans-Van Beuningen Museum** (paintings, sculpture and artefacts), the **Museum of Navigation**, housing an ethnological collection. The **Waalhaven**, with an area of 310 hectares, is the largest man-made harbour basin in the world.

Beyond Rotterdam, the Rhine is prosaically known as the "Nieuwe Waterweg". **Europoort** (1966) is now the last port of call of the Rhine. It is situated near **Hoek van Holland**, where the moles thrust out far into the North Sea. The delta to the south is now protected for all time against further flooding since the high-water catastrophe of 1953, which with its toll of 1,800 victims was the worst in history. The biggest lock gates in the world now guard the common estuaries of the Scheldt, the Meuse and the Rhine. Ten dams have shortened and straightened the total length of Holland's coastline by several hundred kilometres.

Where the Rhine finally loses itself in the open sea, there are still idyllic towns like **Zierikzee** (10,000 inhabitants), lying directly on the five-kilometre-long **Zeelandbrug** which forms part of the Delta Plan. It is a pretty place, with white-painted clapboard houses and black-framed sash windows. The tower of the **Town Hall** (16th century) has a glockenspiel; there is the "Havenplein" and the Grachtenpromenade, and white bascule bridges across the water - today unchanged since the days when the travelling merchants, laden with salt and crimson - the ingredients for an intensive red dye - raked in a goodly portion of the Good Life as well as their own fortunes.

Such vessels are too big for the Rhine.

A LAST PARADISE FOR FLORA AND FAUNA

The Rhine as a biotope for plants and animals? Surely there can be no nature left with all the huge industrial conglomerates and the many built-up areas on either side of the Rhine? But there is. Like islands in the midst of a landscape exploited by man, areas of "unspoiled nature" can still be found dotted along the river: they are the habitats of a great variety of flora and fauna, as well as being a refuge for people suffering from the stresses of modern life.

Industrialization, road building and settlement have taken their toll. While this is less the case along the Alpenrhein, Lake Constance, The High Rhine and the Upper Rhine where more than a third of the bank areas have managed to keep their natural character, along the Middle Rhine on the other hand, only around five percent of the adjacent area can be said to be as it originally was, and along the Lower Rhine only 0.4 percent.

The rectification of the Rhine in the upper section in the nineteenth century, named after Tulla, the initiator of the project, has had serious consequences for the flora and fauna. The measure, undertaken primarily to benefit navigation and protect against flooding, shortened the river between Basle and Worms from 354 to 274 kilometres and forced it into a straight, fixed bed. As a result there was an enormous increase in the velocity of flow and hence also in erosion. The bottom of the river has since dug down around five metres deeper into the ground. The water table has consequently sunk and large sections of the once damp riverbank areas have degenerated into steppe.

Prior to Tulla's straightening of the Rhine, the river sought its way through the Rhine meadows, which were up to six kilometres wide, in a labyrinth of lateral arms, branches and loops. Floods were the order of the day and nourished a luxuriant vegetation which was unparalleled in Central Europe. The

Preceding pages and left: there are only a few places along the Rhine where animals and plants remain undisturbed by man.

region was also a haven for a unique and flourishing animal world.

Surviving tracts of the once extensive riparian forests can still be found today in the 2378-hectare Kühkopf-Knoblauchsaue nature reserve between Gernsheim and Oppenheim, and in the 1600-hectare nature reserve of Taubergießen near Rust. In addition there are a number of smaller wooded areas such as the Rastatter Rheinaue (845 hectares), the Hördter Rheinaue (818 hectares), the Lampertheimer Altrhein (516 hectares) and the Ketscher Rheininsel (490 hectares). All these areas are flooded every spring. They feature the typical riparian forest vegetation, pedunculate oak, ash, field elm,

impenetrable thicket along the banks in combination with such proliferate climbing plants as wild hops and hedge bindweed. In the water itself are various types of reed, as well as the rare yellow flag *(Iris pseudacorus)* and dogwood.

Behind this "protective" biome is the start of the riparian forest proper. The impressive white willows in the area, still frequently subject to floods between the bushes on the bank and the oak and elm woods at a higher level, reach a height of up to 25 metres. When it is drier they give way to denser, more varied forest with a fascinating array of different species. Mighty pedunculate oaks, fluttering and field elms, black poplars and

white willow, white poplar and traveller's joy, and provide a haven for birds such as the cormorant, kingfisher, coot, great crested grebe and great reed warbler, that have now become rare species.

Taubergießen: The most extensive tract of riparian forest in the Upper Rhine area is Taubergießen, with a width of up to four kilometres. Almost all the natural elements of river meadows are represented here. At the water's edge are various shrub willows such as almond willow, osier and purple willow. These are affected neither by floods nor an excess of sand. Where the current is at its slowest, elder bushes form an almost

ashes tower above field and mountain maples, durmast oaks, grey and white poplars and winter limes. At a lower level are grey elders, various types of willow, hawthorn, ivy and traveller's joy. Still further down we find hazel, sloe, hawthorn, honeysuckle, spindle-tree, wild privet and climbing plants such as the extremely rare black byrony *(Tamus communus)*.

On the ground, finally, the shrubs, herbaceous plants and mosses take over with more than 100 different flowering plants forming a brightly-coloured carpet. No other wood biome in Germany can offer such a variety of species. Far above the high-water line the oak and elm wood is replaced by oak and hornbeam woods, which also harbour a wealth of different species. The diversity of the vegetation is paralleled by a rich variety of animal species. 30 percent of all the species of butterfly found in Central Europe are resident in the unique meadow landscape of Taubergießen; no less impressive is the occurrence of over 100 mussel and snail species, almost 1000 types of beetle and over 350 types of hymenopterous insect.

Almost 120 species of bird breed in Taubergießen. Black-cap and lesser white-throat, hedge sparrow, wren, golden oriol, chiff-chaff and willow warbler and many others blend their voices in a rich chorus. The

the east the dam cut off the Rhine and the forest died. It was replaced with ploughland and green fields. The meadows which formed on the gravel and sand banks, high and dry after the completion of the project, developed into the habitat of an extraordinary number of flowers. In some places, the scene is dominated by thousands of orchids.

The Mainzer Sand: The Mainzer Sand is of quite a different character to Taubergießen. This nature reserve, only 33 hectares in area and situated one kilometre south-west of Mainz-Mombach, is part of a larger region of ice-age flood sand and dunes between Ingelheim and Heidelberg. The very special thing about the Mainzer Sand is that ice-age

rare kingfisher wih its azure blue feathers is a feast for the eyes. In the winter the native birds are joined by numerous guests such as the long-tailed duck, the black-throated diver and the cormorant.

The orchid meadows are a special feature of Taubergießen. They actually owe their existence to the deeds of Colonel Tulla already mentioned, who divided the meadowland in two with a dam. To the west of this the riparian forest was preserved, to

steppe flora has been preserved. Over 30 steppe plants thrive in this nature reserve. It is the only place in the Federal Republic where golden drop (Onosma arenarium), chalk plant (Gypsophila fastigiata) and couch grass (Agropyron maritimum) can be found. In the Mainzer Sand there are over 200 species of plant in all, among them many that are on the "red list" of plants threatened with extinction. There are also a number of mosses, lichens and fungi.

With every season the Mainzer Sand presents a different picture. In the autumn the field scabious (Scabiosa canescens), twiggy magwort (Artemisia campestris) and

Left, a line-up of anglers. **Above**, a fine view of Stolzenfels Castle.

fennel dominate the scene: The early spring marks the arrival of annual herbs such as the common whitlow grass *(Erophila verna)*, the rue-leaved saxifrage *(Saxifraga tridactylites)* and the scorpion grass *(Mysotis stricta)*. Then comes the turn of the madwort *(Alyssum gmelinii)*, the common pasque flower and the hairy cinque foil *(Potentilla arenaria)*, followed later still by the devil's milk *(Euphorbia segueriana)*.

In the spring and high summer it is the grasses that are the dominant feature of the Mainzer Sand. In addition to the Baden meadow grass *(Poa badensis)* and silver grass, the rare *Stipa joannis* also occurs here. With its long awns resembling feathers, it is

coming increasingly rare - the Mainzer Sand is one of the few places where it is still to be found. The wood lark is special not because of its appearance, but because of its song; in the Mainzer Sand it breeds in unusually large numbers.

There are many varieties of butterfly, even though the number has already been considerably reduced by the encroachment of civilization. While 82 species were counted at the beginning of the century, by the end of the sixties this had fallen to 65. In spite of this it is still possible to spot some extremely rare species.

In addition, there are least 127 sand wasps building their earth nests in the ground of the

one of the most striking of the steppe plants. Less conspicuous by comparison are the yellowish flowers of the rare golden drop *(Onosma arenarium)* that form a cluster up to 50 centimetres high above a flat leaf rosette. In the late autumn the cluster breaks off above the ground and is whirled away by the wind, giving it the apposite nickname of "steppe runner".

The warm sandy ground is however not only an ideal place for steppe flora of a variety unparalleled in Western Europe, it is also the home of a quite remarkable collection of animals. Here bird-lovers can see the splendid hoopoe, that is unfortunately be-

Mainzer Sand, 163 types of spider spinning their webs and 200 species of bugs lying in wait for their prey, as well as numerous other insect species, making the Mainzer Sand a paradise for entomologists.

Altrhein: Another nature reserve is the favourite of bird-watchers: the Altrhein which is situated between Bienen, Praest and Dornick. It is one of the best preserved backwaters of the Lower Rhine. By contrast with the meadows of the Upper Rhine, which are regularly subject to floods, here there is no longer any link with the Rhine. The fault lies not with man but with the river itself, that once formed numerous meanders on its way to the North Sea. With time the Rhine arms worked their way further and further towards the side of the valley. At some point the detour became too great for the water, and at high water the river once again took the direct route. The old loop of the river was cut off and thus became a backwater or oxbow lake. The Altrhein at Bienen-Praest is known to have lost its link with the Rhine as long ago as the first half of the sixteenth century.

In 1969 an area of 340 hectares was turned into a nature reserve. The surface of the water is almost completely covered with yellow and white water-lilies. This rare plant biotome has been digging its own grave. Dead plant material can no longer completely

undertaking that was supported by the Federal Minister of Food, Agriculture and Forestry, who contributed 1.9 of the total of 2.4 million marks required. In this way extensive areas of the typical vegetation of floating plants and reeds were preserved.

A special feature of this oxbow are the large quantities of fringed water-lily *(Nymphoides peltata)*. The small, yellow-flowered lily has actually profited from the use of the neighbouring meadows by farmers. Grazing cattle going down to the water to drink or cool themselves have in many places bitten and trampled the other water-lilies and reeds and thus cleared the way for the rare plant, which occurs in a greater concentration

decompose in the water because oxygen is in short supply as a consequence of the dense covering of floating leaves. The plant debris thus sinks to the bottom and accelerates the process of sedimentation. Reeds are encroaching from the edge and gradually pushing out the water plants.

In order to bring this process to a halt, in 1982 the town of Rees cleared the mud from part of the oxbow. A total of 170,000 cubic metres of mud were removed, an expensive

Left, the fish stocks in the Rhine always seem to recover. **Above**, a land of poppies and windmills.

here than anywhere else in Europe. There are thus aspects where cattle farming has had a very positive effect. Overall however the uncontrolled access of the animals to the Altrhein has led to a marked reduction in the reeds, resulting in an increase in erosion and the destruction of the breeding grounds of many different types of bird. Conservationists are therefore demanding that fences be put up to restrict the access of the cattle to the water to a few specific places.

But as one can see, a few extremely valuable havens for plants and animals have been preserved on the Rhine. It is to be hoped that they will continue to thrive in the future.

THE ENDANGERED RHINE

In November 1986, a warehouse of the Basle chemical combine Sandoz caught fire. With the water that extinguished it tons of pesticide flowed into the Rhine. Soon, hundreds of thousands of dead fish floated to the surface. The helpless world at large looked on as the full extent of the disaster became clear. After Seveso and Bhopal the chemical industry was in the dock for the third time.

Only a few days beforehand the industry had attempted to polish up its tarnished image with the launch of an advertising campaign. The "dear fish" was assured that it was to his good that the chemical industry had achieved a reduction in the organic pollution of the water of over 90 percent. The "dear Rhine" was informed that "We have been largely responsible for the fact that your oxygen content is a great deal higher today than it was in the fifties."

The water quality of the Rhine is indeed better than it was in the sixties and seventies. At the beginning of the seventies the river was on the point of collapse. For decades it had been treated as the "largest sewer in Europe". In their enthusiastic pursuit of growth, industry and communities uninhibitedly allowed filth and poison to flow into the Rhine. In those days conservation was still a foreign word.

In the meantime the oxygen content has risen again. This is due to the increased use of sewage plants, the decrease in economic activity and the noticeable increase in water management since 1976.

Nevertheless, the most travelled, most densely settled and most industrialized waterway of Europe is today still far from being in a state of ecological balance. Every day tons of poisons flow into the river from industrial concerns, all quite legally. Generous waste discharge permits make it possible. The BASF giant at Ludwigshafen alone discharges 240 million cubic metres of wastewater a year into the Rhine, or 27,000 cubic metres an hour.

Left, a worker in the furnaces. The German steel industry is presently going through a crisis as a result of over-capacity.

The waste-water from the various areas of production is of course purified by the firm in its own plants. However, even the BASF purification plant, which is held up as an example to the whole industry, only copes with a proportion of the chemicals. For this reason the Rhineland-Palatinate Ministry of the Environment has decided to limit the amount of poison that BASF is allowed to discharge into the Rhine to under half a million tons per year.

The amounts of waste-water that other firms are allowed to discharge are much the same. The chemical factory of Bayer in Leverkusen, for example, are permitted to release 78 million cubic metres of waste-

pected to be introduced by the Basle Office for the Prevention of Water Pollution until well into the nineties.

Until then a lot of dirty water will flow down the Rhine. According to the magazine "Der Spiegel" (1/1987), the annual quantities of pollutants in the Rhine as measured at the German-Dutch border are as follows: around a million tons of organic chemicals that do not decompose easily, if at all, 31,000 tons of ammonium, 20,000 tons of phosphorus, 3840 tons of heavy metals and around 3000 tons of chlorinated carbohydrates, of which at least 40 tons are neurotoxins.

Experts estimate that there are around 100,000 different substances contained in

water into the Rhine per year from its purification plant. Everyone knows that this means way over 200,000 tons of poison.

The conditions in Basle are far worse. For the three international firms Sandoz, Hoffmann-La Roche and Ciba-Geigy, regulations are in force which allow concentrations of harmful substances in the waste-water up to six times higher than those permitted in the Federal Republic. The reason for the generosity on the part of the Swiss is the faulty design of the waste-water purification plants in Basle, which are unable to cope with the enormous variety of chemical substances. Remedial measures are not ex-

the water of the Rhine. Only a few thousand of them are known, and only a few hundred can be analysed using the methods currently available. Nobody can say with any certainty what long-term effects this chemical cocktail will have on the ecological system, or indeed on man.

Those responsible for the officially permitted daily poisoning of Europe's most important river are primarily the chemical giants on both sides of the Rhine. Around 20 percent of all chemical firms in the west are within reach of the Rhine. Nowhere else in the world is there such a high concentration of danger potential. The Basle area has the

Swiss chemical giants Hoffmann-La Roche, Ciba-Geigy and Sandoz, and on the Federal Republic side of the border Dynamit Nobel and Aluminium-Hütte. BASF, Hoechst and Bayer leach against the riverbanks between Ludwigshafen and Leverkusen. The Düsseldorf area is the base of the detergent giants Unilever and Henkel. The Lower Rhine provides a haven for the giant manufacturing complexes of the petrochemical industry. Other branches of industry also make a substantial contribution to the pollution of the Rhine, in particular the potassium mines in Alsace, the paper and cellulose industry near Karlsruhe and the steel works in the Rhine-Westphalian industrial area. It is impossible

is not after all going to be built, as a result of a decision taken in June 1988 by the Swiss government.

In spite of the fact that the excess tonnage in Western Europe has gone up over the last two years to around ten million tons, the international Rhine fleet also remains a major culprit in the pollution stakes. This occurs primarily through the discharge of mineral oil products from the diesel engines of the barges (bilge oil), through substances that get into the water as a result of accidents during transport or loading, or through the extinguishing of fires, or through the unauthorized disposal of rubbish and waste-water. There is little danger to the skippers of dis-

to calculate the precise extent of the damage due to the discharge of radioactive substances and waste heat by nuclear power stations.

Nowhere else is there such a concentration of nuclear power stations as along the banks of the Rhine. Nine reactors are in operation or being built (Beznau, Leibstadt, Fessenheim, the Karlsruhe nuclear research centre, Philippsburg, Biblis, Mühlheim-Kärlich, Kalkar and Dodewaard). The reactor that was being planned at Kaiseraugst near Basle

Left, a less picturesque section of the Rhine. **Above**, a mural of the "fast breeder" at Kalkar, with the actual edifice in the background.

covery by the police. At night and in fog the patrol helicopters stay on the ground. It is not only irresponsible skippers who are to blame, but also the lack of disposal facilities on shore. Between Basle and Duisburg the situation is particularly critical. It is to be remedied - if the environmental politicians in Rhineland-Palatinate have their way - by central waste disposal facilities in Mainz.

Other polluters of the Rhine are households and agriculture, through their zealous use of chemical products. Housewifes are still prepared to pay more in order to have their washing "whiter than white". Every month pounds or even kilos of washing powder from each washing machine find their way into the waste-water. Measured against these quantities the problems due to other household chemicals are insignificant. Most local sewage plants are unable to cope with the chemical waste from private households as they have no facilities for the disposal of phosphates and nitrates. The sewage plant of Düsseldorf-Süd alone discharges 2.2 tons of phosphorous and 229 tons of nitrogen into the Rhine every year.

In spite of over-production, farmers continue to maximize the yield of their fields through the intensive use of pesticides and fertilizers. Every year the fields are sprayed with millions of tons of poison to kill insects,

pollutants were to be done away with. Around 50 types of fish were once found in the river, of which twelve have remained. Perch, barbel and roach are common, less prolific are eel, pike, gudgeon, ruffle, tench and zander.

As a result of the Sandoz accident, the entire eel population between Basle and the Loreley 400 kilometres downstream, which numbered 150 000, was destroyed. Thousands of grayling, pike and zander also died.

Even worse affected were small animals such as mussels, snails, crabs, flukes and flatworms, which were decimated over a stretch of several hundred kilometres. Their annihilation was not without consequence for the fish, that were reliant on the small

weeds and fungus. This method of dealing with pests does not only contaminate the soil and ground-water, but also the Rhine as a consequence of erosion. The liquid manure resulting from the fattening of pigs, chicken batteries and other mass animal farming is a further problem.

The use of the Rhine as a sewer has not been without its consequences for the ecological system of the river. Experts estimate that of the 700 to 800 species originally living in the Rhine, only ten percent have survived all the pollution. Although their number is slowly increasing again, there will never be a complete regeneration, even if all

animals for their nutrition. Experts expect the numbers of fish to decline still further.

The pollution of the Rhine, whether through the officially approved poisoning that goes on every day or through the repeated accidents - is having disastrous consequences not only for the river itself, but also for the North Sea. The carpets of algae, under which fish perished in vast numbers, and the demise of the seals in the summer of 1988 that brought a call for better protection of the North Sea, were largely due to the pollution flowing through the Rhine and into the sea. According to the German hydrographical institute, half of the 700,000 tons of nitrogen and 65,000 tons of phosphorus that enter the sea via the rivers comes from the Rhine. These substances provide nutrition for the algae, which in their turn starve the water - and the animal life it contains - of oxygen.

And while the seals succumbed to a virus, all the experts agree that the agent of the disease was only able to destroy them because their immune system had been weakened by the high quantities of poisonous substances to which their bodies had been subjected.

While the Rhine is no longer very important as a source of human nutrition, it does supply drinking water for some 30 million people. The waterworks are having to spend

more and more money on technical equipment capable of extracting the poisons from the water. Active carbon filtering can by no means remove all the poisonous substances from the water. The tiny carbon particles are powerless against nitrates. The bill is paid by the consumer, and he pays it twice over. The rising costs of processing drinking water are causing water charges to shoot up. According to the Cologne water authority, the price

Left, evening time in the Ruhr Basin. **Above**, river freight near the Dutch border.

of water in the cathedral city could be halved if they did not have to invest in expensive purification equipment.

The water is usually obtained as a bank filtrate. With this method, the gravel and sand layers of the banks act as a natural filter. In addition, micro-organisms break down at least some of the harmful substances in the river water as it seeps away. After some days, or sometimes after some years, according to the position of the drinking water well, this pre-purified river water is then pumped up and purified again by means of gravel and active carbon filters.

The natural purification of the bank filtrate has long been an inadequate method of coping with the flood of chemicals. Drinking water inspectors thus found around 600 organic chemicals, twenty of them carcogenic, in the bank filtrate taken from near the banks of the Rhine. Even after active carbon filtering the samples were still found to contain seven carcogenic substances.

It is not even the case that all the water authorities can meet their needs from bank filtrate. Demand is so great that some are forced to take their drinking water directly from the Rhine, necessitating the use of other, far more expensive processing methods. The Rhine water, drawn out with pumps, is first put through a basic purification process and enriched with oxygen. Then it is exposed to an artificial biological cycle: for several weeks fish, worms and micro-organisms do the "work" of biological purification, which is then followed by chemical purification.

The water authority managers are desperately worried about the prospect of the banks of the Rhine becoming so saturated with poisons that purification will no longer be possible. Even the mixture of Rhine and bank water with the apparently clean groundwater has in many places become pointless with the increasing contamination of the ground-water by the fertilizers and pesticides used by the farmers.

Up to now hardly any moves have been made to remedy the situation. Industry continues to discharge tons of harmful substances, sewage plants that remove phosphates and nitrates are still too expensive for most communities and even the farmers do not yet appear to see any reason to be more careful with their poisonous sprays.

TRAVEL TIPS

GETTING THERE

With a length of over 1300 kilometres, the Rhine flows through Switzerland, France, the Federal Republic of Germany and the Netherlands. For a short stretch it also borders on Austria. A large number of towns and cities provide easy access for trips along the river, whether by ship, by rail or by car.

BY AIR

The following airports are located within easy reach of the Rhine:

SWITZERLAND

Zürich-Kloten (international airport)

LIECHTENSTEIN

Flugcenter Schönauer (for round-flights and direct flights to Malbun), Gewerbeweg, FL-9490 Vaduz

FRANCE

Euro Airport Basle-Mulhouse-Freiburg (international airport)
Strasbourg-Entzheim

FEDERAL REPUBLIC OF GERMANY

International airports
Rhein-Main Airport Frankfurt am Main
Cologne-Bonn Airport
Düsseldorf Airport

Local Airports
Freiburg im Breisgau
Baden-Baden
Karlsruhe
Speyer
Mannheim
Essen Mülheim

THE NETHERLANDS

Amsterdam-Schiphol Airport
Rotterdam-Sestienhoven Airport

BELGIUM

Brussels International Airport

BY SHIP

The biggest operator of cruises on the Rhine is the Köln-Düsseldorfer Deutsche Rheinschiffahrt (Cologne - Düsseldorf Steamship Company), Frankenwerft 15, 5000 Köln 1. Tel: (0221) 20880. These are the main ports of call: Basle (Switzerland), Strasbourg (France), Speyer, Mannheim, Rüddesheim, Braubach, Koblenz, Cologne, Düsseldorf (Federal Republic of Germany), Rotterdam, Amsterdam (Netherlands).

BY RAIL

The major cities in Switzerland, France, The Federal Republic of Germany and the Netherlands are served by the fast and comfortable Inter City (IC) and Euro City (EC) trains, which normally run about once an hour. Smaller places are served either by local trains or bus.

BY CAR

If you want to make rapid progress with your own car, take the motorways, of which there is an extensive network in Switzerland, France, Germany and the Netherlands. There are also main roads along much of the River Rhine. One would be advised to obtain the necessary maps before setting out.

Leadfree petrol is available in all countries, although it is not quite so common in France. Here it would be advisable to check where leadfree petrol is available from your own automobile association. Fuel is somewhat cheaper in Germany and Holland than it is in France and Switzerland. Make sure that you have all the necessary papers before setting out, including an internationally recognized driver's licence.

Travel Essentials

VISA

For travelling through the countries of the Rhine, an identity card or passport is required by citizens of Liechtenstein, France, the Federal Republic of Germany, The Netherlands and Belgium. The same goes for most other European countries. For nationals of other countries a visa may well be required. Information can be obtained by contacting the consulates or embassies of the specific countries one intends to visit, or a travel agency or airline.

MONEY MATTERS

There are bureaus de change at most border crossings, should you not have enough of the local currency.

SWITZERLAND AND LIECHTENSTEIN

There are 100 centimes to one Swiss Franc. There are no limits on the amounts of local or foreign currency that can be brought in or taken out.

FRANCE

There are 100 centimes to the French Franc. There are no limits on the amount of local or foreign currency brought into the country. There is a limit of FF 5,000, or its equivalent in foreign currency (unless declared before arrival), which can be taken out.

AUSTRIA

There are 100 Groschen to the Austrian Schilling. There is no limit on the amount of foreign currency which can be brought into the country. 15,000 Schillings can be taken out.

FEDERAL REPUBLIC OF GERMANY

There are 100 pfennigs to the German Mark. There are no limits on the amounts of local or foreign currency brought in or taken out.

THE NETHERLANDS

There are 100 cents to the Dutch Gilder. There are no limits on the amounts of local or foreign currency brought in or taken out.

Note: On board the "KD" ships, the valid currency is the German Mark (DM). The larger ships all possess a bureau de change. Eurocheques up to a limit of DM 400 per cheque are accepted. Credit cards are not accepted. It is advisable to procure the money you need on dry land before setting out on a cruise.

HEALTH

There is sufficient medical care and facilities in all countries of the Rhine. Chemists and hospitals are generally easy to get to.

To call an ambulance in **Switzerland**. Tel:144. There is no universal number which can be called in **France**. You can get the Police de Secours by calling 17. In **Germany**, the emergency number to call in most cites is 112, which will get you the fire brigade. There is also no universal number which can be called in the **Netherlands**.

It is advisable to obtain comprehensive medical insurance in your own country before setting out. Amongst European countries, there is normally an agreement between the state health authorities, which then take over the costs for treating visitors, provided that the necessary health documents are presented. It may be that the visitor has to bear these costs himself and get them refunded by his state health authority on returning home.

WHAT TO WEAR

Between May and September it can get hot in the Rhinelands. Light casual clothing is the order of the day, although jackets, pullovers and coats should not be left at home. Some protection against rain should be brought along, whatever the season. Those wishing to visit the opera or theatre, should bring suitable formal clothing.

WHAT TO BRING

You can buy absolutely everything in all the countries of the Rhine, so it isn't too drastic if you forget your toothbrush, film, suntan lotion or fine French perfume. Nevertheless, there are certain articles which you definitely shouldn't forget: Travel documents, money, cheques and credit cards which are accepted by the big hotels, restaurants and shops.

Bring along a few assorted medicines and articles of first aid - depending on what you are going to be doing; protection against sun and rain. Those who intend walking through the vineyards or in open country should make sure they have a stout pair of shoes or boots. Bring swim wear if you intend swimming in Lake Constance, in the pools on the large "KD" ships, or in hotel swimming pools. Camera and film supply - film may be a lot cheaper at home, certainly a lot cheaper than in Switzerland!

Travellers from overseas should bring along a compact phrase book (French, German, Dutch). Don't forget an adapter for electric shavers, hairdryers and other appliances.

ANIMALS

Should you wish to travel with your cat or dog, this must have received an inoculation against rabies 30 days before entry into the countries of the Rhine. In addition, you need to be able to produce a certificate of ownership (licence) and a description of the animal, which can be made out by any vet. For further information about inoculations and travelling abroad with animals, contact the competent authority at home. Don't forget to check with the hotel whether they take animals. Many don't.

CUSTOMS

The customs regulations of European Community countries (Switzerland is not a member) are, to all intents and purposes, identical. No duty is levied on articles for everyday needs and for travelling - cameras, sports equipment, tents etc. Duty free are the following articles brought in from other EEC countries: 300 cigarettes or 150 cigarillos or 75 cigars or 400 grams of tobacco; 1.5 litres of spirit or four litres of wine; Other goods with a value of up to FF 1,030, DM 500, hfl 500, bfr 9,600. From countries outside the EEC, the following are duty free: 200 cigarettes or 100 cigarillos or 50 cigars or 250 grams of tobacco; 2 litres of wine or 1 litre of spirit; other goods to a maximum value of FF 230, DM 115, hfl 110, bfr 1,600. For people whose permanent abode is not in Europe, duty free are: 400 cigarettes or 200 cigarillos or 100 cigars or 500 grams of tobacco.

The following articles can be brought into Switzerland duty free: 200 cigarettes or 50 cigars or 250 grams of tobacco; goods up to a maximum value of sfr 100. Articles for everyday needs and for travelling are also duty free.

For a trip aboard a "KD" ship (Switzerland, France, Federal Republic of Germany, Netherlands), passports are deposited with the bursar on embarkation and given back at the end of the voyage.

TIPPING

Prices in hotels, restaurants, for the taxi, at the hairdressers, etc. are all inclusive of service. However, if you are happy with the service, it is normal to leave a tip of between 5 and 10 percent of the amount on the bill.

VALUE ADDED TAX

Value added tax (VAT) is levied in Switzerland (WUst), France (TVA), Federal Republic of Germany (MwSt) and in the Netherlands (BTW). The rate varies from country to country. Should you wish to export valuable items, get the necessary documents filled out in the shop and get these stamped on the border. Send the export stamped export documents back to the shop, and the value added tax will be refunded, less a small charge.

GETTING ACQUAINTED

POLITICS AND ECONOMY

The peoples living along the banks of the Rhine have fought for their freedom against both their own and foreign rulers. The fact that all the countries are now democracies is thanks to a whole series of struggles stretching right back into the mists of time. There were peasants' revolts, civil wars and revolution; the reformations of the 16th century, the revolts against Hapsburg domination in Switzerland and the Netherlands, and working class revolutions following the industrial developments of the 18th and 19th centuries. Germany suffered a complete regression to barbarism from 1933 to 1945, when only Switzerland and Liechtenstein were spared the conquests and occupation of the Third Reich. The fascists had taken such a hold over the body and soul of the people that this time freedom could not be achieved from within. It took allied forces from other lands to liberate the countries of the Rhine.

The economic order of the democracies along the Rhine is, without exception, governed by the capitalist system. The more vulnerable sections of the community are protected from the worst effects of the free market by the welfare state. The European Community will be complete with the advent of the Free European Market in 1992. Though they are not members, Switzerland and Austria are economically bound to the countries of the Common Market.

SWITZERLAND

The official name of Switzerland is the Swiss Confederation. It is a neutral country made up of 23 cantons with Bern as its capital. The total area is 41,293 square kilometres and the population is approximately 7 million. Due to the mountainous terrain, only a quarter of the land area can be used for agriculture. Cereals and fruit are the main crops, and wine is also produced wherever the terrain and climate allows. Dairy farming is very important, and the milk is processed into numerous varieties of cheese and used in the production of all that lovely Swiss chocolate. Industry plays an important role in the Swiss economy, too, machine building and precision tools being particularly important. The clocks and watches produced in Switzerland, 95 percent of which go for export, account for 45 percent of world production. The huge combines of the chemical industry produce everything from drugs to paint, plastic and fertilizer. Nothing need be said about the importance of banking in Switzerland.

LIECHTENSTEIN

The Principality of Liechtenstein lies between Austria and Switzerland. Its eleven parishes make up a total area of 160 square kilometres. The capital city is Vaduz. Agriculture includes fruit, wine, meat and dairy farming. There are a number of small but efficient industries, producing textiles and manufacturing machinery. For tax reasons the "head offices" of numerous firms from throughout the world are based in Liechtenstein. The principality is tied to Switzerland through customs and currency union.

AUSTRIA

The neutral country of Austria is officially known as the Republic of Austria. It is made up of nine states and its capital is Vienna. Approximately 8 million people live in a total area of 83,853 square kilometres. Almost half of this is exploited for agricultural production, including a great deal of dairy farming and wine cultivation. Forestry is also important. There is also a lot of heavy industry in Austria, notably iron and steel, whose growth has been assisted by the presence of locally occurring minerals, including ores and oil. Austria is the world's biggest producer of magnesium. The chemical and textile industries are also important.

FRANCE

La République Française consists of a total of 96 Départments. Paris is the capital of the centralized state which has a population of about 55 million. France is the most important wine producing country in the world, the export of wine and brandy playing a large role in the economy. Agriculture otherwise consists of cereals, sugar, milk products, fish and meat. Forestry is also an important factor for the agricultural side of the economy. Minerals include coal in the north-east, iron in Lorraine and Potassium in Alsace. The most important industries are iron and steel, chemicals and textiles, as well as the manufacturing of cars, ships and aircraft.

FEDERAL REPUBLIC OF GERMANY

After the Second World War, in 1949, two separate German states came into being. The German Democratic Republic (GDR) in the east, a member of the Warsaw Pact, and the Federal Republic in the west. For the moment at least, the capital of West Germany is Bonn which is situated on the Rhine. The Federal Republic is made up of 10 states and West Berlin, and its total area is 248,690 square kilometres. It has a population of some 66 million. As a result of pro-democracy campaigns in the GDR which reached their climax in the winter of 1989-90, and led to the opening of the Berlin Wall, a new democratically elected government took control of the country in April 1990. After the reunification of Germany due in October 1990, elections for the whole country will take place in December 1990. The united Germany will have a population of over 80 million and an area of 356,868 square kilometres.

Agricultural production includes a variety of crops. Wine is important, particularly on the Rhine, though there are other well-known wine producing areas. Industry is heavily export-oriented, and includes iron and steel, the manufacturing of automobiles, chemicals and electronic articles and oil processing. The service industries are expanding by leaps and bounds.

THE NETHERLANDS

The Kingdom of the Netherlands - Koninknjk der Nederlanden - is a constitutional monarchy governed by parliament. The capital is Amsterdam and the seat of parliament and government is in The Hague. The eleven provinces cover an area of 33,811 square kilometres and are inhabited by a total of some 15 million people. As well as Dutch, Fresian is also spoken. The production of food has an important place in the economy. Cattle, pigs and poultry are bred in enormous numbers; fruit, vegetables and flowers are grown outside as well as under the protection of glasshouses. Coastal and deep-sea fishing is also important. Oil and gas are the most important minerals.

TIME

The countries of the Rhine are all governed by Middle European Time (Greenwich Mean Time plus 1 = GMT + 1). Summer time, where the clocks are put forward for one hour, runs from the last weekend in March to the last weekend in September.

CLIMATE

The best time to travel along the Rhine is between April and October. By early summer the trees and bushes along the banks of the river have all blossomed into a blaze of colour.

The climate along the whole course of the Rhine is relatively mild, although in the mountains it can get very cool even in the summer. Immediately to the north of the mountains there is the frequently occurring phenomenon of Föhn, a warm, dry wind which, while affording great visibility, also causes sensitive people to get headaches and feel generally off colour.

It is particularly mild around Lake Constance, allowing fruit and vegetables to flourish. Spring starts early here and autumn arrives relatively late. June is the rainiest month, and July the hottest. Between rain and sun, mist can cause hindrance to shipping. The Upper Rhine also possesses a mild climate with relatively little precipitation.

Warm summers and mild winters accompany the Upper Rhine on its journey through Alsace. The lowlands of the Upper Rhine have the mildest climate in Germany, with especially little rain. Much loved is the Kaiserstuhl, the large volcanic hill rising above the Rhine Plain between Freiburg and Colmar, where the long hours of sunshine allow the cultivation of especially good wine.

The large differences in temperature within the Federal Republic are displayed by the varying times in which the trees start to blossom. Between Basle and Freiburg this normally takes place between 10th and 20th of April, while to the north, and beyond the Rhine Basin, the trees generally blossom some four weeks later. The Middle Rhine is also characterised by a mild climate with little rainfall, the best conditions for producing excellent wines, such as those of Rhine-Hessen.

The influence of the Gulf Stream makes itself particularly apparent in the regions of the Lower Rhine; the winters here are generally very mild. The nearer one gets to the North Sea, the more windy it gets. While the winters are mild, the summers are not especially warm.

Certainly, whenever one chooses to travel along the Rhine, an umbrella, a warm jacket, sunglasses and light clothing will all come in handy.

ELECTRIC CURRENT

In all countries of the Rhine, current is A.C. 220 volts

WEIGHTS AND MEASURES

The metric system is used in all countries of the Rhine.

Linear Measures
The unit is the metre (m).
1 metre= 100 centimetres (cm) = 1000 millimetres (mm)
1000 metres = 1 Kilometre (km)
1 inch = 2.54 cm
1 foot = 0.305 m
1 yard = 0.914 m
1 statute mile = 1760 yards = 1609.34 m

Square Measurement
The units are hectares and square metres.
1 square Kilometre (sqkm) = 100 hectares (ha) = 1,000,000 square metres
1 hectare (ha) = 10,000 square metres
1 square inch = 6.4516 square centimetres
1 square yard = 9 square feet = 0.836 square metres
1 acre = 4046.7 square metres = 0.40467 hectares
1 square mile = 640 acres = 2.59 square kilometres

Body Measurements
The unit is the cubic metre
1 cubic metre = 1,000,000 cubic centimetres
1 cubic yard = 27 cubic feet = 0.765 cubic metres

Measures of Capacity
The unit is the litre (l).
1 cubic metre = 1000 litres
1 imperial pint = 0.57 litres

Weights
The unit is the kilogramme (kg)
1 ton (t) =1000 kg
1 kilogramme = 1000 grammes (g)
1 ounce = 28.35 g
1 lb = 453.6 g

BUSINESS HOURS

The times given below are only a rough guide. In the larger towns and cities, as well as in tourist spots, there is often no midday break; the shops are open right through the day.

SWITZERLAND

Shops
Monday to Friday 8/8.30 a.m. - 6.30 p.m., Saturday 8/8.30 a.m. - 4/5 p.m.. Some shops are closed on Monday morning.

Banks
Monday to Friday 8.30 a.m. - 4.30 p.m.. In smaller towns and communities the banks close at lunchtime, from 12.00 -2 p.m..

PRINCIPALITY OF LIECHTENSTEIN

Shops
Monday to Friday 8 a.m. - 12.00, 1.30 p.m. - 6.30 p.m., Saturday 8 a.m. - 4 p.m..

Banks
Monday to Friday 8 a.m. - 12.00, 1.30 p.m. - 4.30 p.m..

Post
Vaduz - Monday to Friday 8 a.m. - 12.00, 1.45 p.m. - 6 p.m., Saturday 8 a.m. - 11 a.m.
Schaan - Monday to Friday 7.45 a.m. - 12.00, 2 p.m. - 6.15 p.m..

Triesenberg - Monday to Friday 8 a.m. - 12.00, 2 p.m. - 6 p.m., Saturday 8 a.m. - 11 a.m.

AUSTRIA

Shops
Monday to Friday 8 a.m. - 12.00, 2 p.m. - 6 p.m., Saturday 8 a.m. - 12.00. In the centres of the large towns and cities the most important shops do not close at midday.

Banks
Monday, Tuesday, Wednesday, Friday 8 a.m. - 12.30 p.m, 1.30 p.m. - 3 p.m., Thursday 8 a.m. - 12.30 p.m, 1.30 p.m. - 5.30 p.m..

Post
Monday to Friday 8 a.m. - 12.00, 2 p.m. - 6 p.m., Saturday 8 a.m. -12.00.

FRANCE

Shops
There is no fixed closing time for shops in France. In general business hours are from 9.30 a.m. - 6.30 p.m. Monday to Friday with a midday break from 12.00 - 2 p.m.. The large shopping centres on the outskirts of the towns are usually open from 10 a.m. - 10 p.m.. Most food stores, especially those nn tourist centres, are also open on Sunday until 1 a.m. In many places shops are closed on Monday mornings or even the whole day on Monday.

Banks
Monday to Saturday 9.30 a.m. - 12.00, 2 p.m. - 4 p.m.. Some banks are closed on Monday and others on Saturday.

Post
Monday to Friday 9 a.m. - 7 p.m., Saturday 9 a.m. - 12.00., The main post offices in the larger towns and the telegraph services are open 24 hours a day.

FEDERAL REPUBLIC OF GERMANY

Shops
Monday to Friday 9/10 a.m. - 6/6.30 p.m.. On Thursdays the main shops remain open until 8.30 a.m. Saturday 9/10 a.m. - 1/2 p.m.. In smaller towns and communities there is usually a midday break between 12.30 p.m. and 3 p.m..

Banks
Monday to Friday 8.15 a.m. - 1 p.m., 2 p.m. - 4 p.m.. On Tuesdays and Thursdays the banks stay open until between 5 p.m. and 6.30 p.m.. These banks might close on Fridays at 2 p.m..

Post
Monday to Friday 8/9 a.m. - 12.00, 3 p.m. - 6 p.m., Saturday 9 a.m. - 12.00. The main post offices in the larger towns are open 24 hours a day.

THE NETHERLANDS

Shops
Monday to Friday 8/8.30 a.m. - 5.30/6 p.m., Saturday 8/8.30 a.m. - 4/5 p.m.. In some places the shops are open until 9 p.m. on Thursdays and Fridays.

Banks
Monday to Friday 9 a.m. - 4/5 p.m.. On Thursdays and Fridays these can remain open until 9 p.m..

Post
Monday to Friday 8 a.m. - 5 p.m., Saturday 8.30 a.m. - 12.00.

PUBLIC HOLIDAYS

The calendar of public holidays varies slightly from country to country.

SWITZERLAND

1 January (New Years Day)
6 January (Epiphany)
Good Friday
Easter Monday
1 May (May Day)
Ascension Day
Whit Monday
Corpus Christi - mainly in Catholic communities
1 August (National Holiday)
1 November (All Saints Day)
Day of Prayer and Repentance
25 and 26 December (Christmas)

LIECHTENSTEIN

Liechtenstein adheres to all the Swiss public holidays and has in addition:

15 August (Assumption Day)
8 September (Conception Day)

FRANCE

1 January (New Years Day)
Good Friday (only in Alsace)
Easter Monday
1 May (May Day)
8 May (Liberation Day 1945)
Ascension Day
Whit Monday
14 July (National Holiday)
15 August (Assumption Day)
1 November (All Saints Day)
11 November (Armistice 1918)
25 December (Christmas)
26 December (Christmas) - only in Alsace

FEDERAL REPUBLIC OF GERMANY

1 January (New Years Day)
6 January (Epiphany) - only in Baden Württemberg and Bavaria
Good Friday
Easter Monday
1 May (May Day)
Ascension Day
Whit Monday
Corpus Christi - only in Baden Württemberg, Bavaria, Hessen, North Rhine Westphalia, Rhineland Palatinate and Saarland
15 August (Assumption Day) - only in Bavaria and Saarland
1 November (All Saints Day) - in Baden Württemberg, Bavaria, Hessen, North Rhine Westphalia, Rhineland Palatinate and Saarland
Day of Prayer and Repentance
25 and 26 December (Christmas)

THE NETHERLANDS

1 January (New Years Day)
Good Friday
Easter Monday
30 April (Queen's Day)
1 May (May Day)
Ascension Day
Whit Monday
25 and 26 December (Christmas)

RELIGION

The countries of the Rhine are dominated by both Protestants and Catholics. In eastern Switzerland, where the Rhine has its source, and in northern Switzerland, the people are predominantly Catholic, as indeed they are in Alsace in France. In Germany and the Netherlands the two balance each other out, although the people who live along the Rhine are mostly Catholic.

While most Catholic churches are open during the day, those of the Protestant faith close as soon as the service is over.

COMMUNICATIONS

MEDIA

Reading and listening to English in the countries of the Rhine is no great problem.

NEWSPAPERS

It is possible to obtain international newspapers in stations, airports and large hotels of major towns and cities. Kiosks and newsagents also often sell newspapers and magazines such as the Herald Tribune, Time, The Economist, The Times and The European.

TELEVISION AND RADIO

While an intimate knowledge of the languages is required to understand most of the programmes broadcast in the different countries on the Rhine an increasing use of cable and satellite television allows the reception of a number of English and American TV productions. Ask locally. The American and British Forces radio stations broadcast news and music in English as does Radio Luxembourg and the Voice of America. It is also possible to receive the BBC World Service.

POST & TELEPHONE & TELEX

The postal services are well developed in all countries of the Rhine. There are plenty of public telephones available, dotted around the landscape as well as in the cities. All restaurants, pubs, hotels, youth hostels and campsites have telephones. Telegrams can be sent from post offices and hotels. The larger hotels normally have telex and/or telefax facilities.

Important telephone numbers, such as directory enquiries, country and area codes can be found on the first pages of the telephone directory or posted up in the hotel.

EMERGENCIES

PERSONAL SAFETY

There are emergency telephones located on the motorways and the main roads in all countries, as well as on the mountain roads in Switzerland.

SWITZERLAND

Police: Tel: 117. Fire brigade: Tel: 118. Emergency breakdown service: Tel: 140.

FRANCE

The Police de Secours can be reached by calling 117. In case of a car accident one should call a 24 hours service on (05) 106106.

FEDERAL REPUBLIC OF GERMANY

In almost all of the country you can call 110 to get the police and 112 to reach the fire brigade and emergency ambulance service.

THE NETHERLANDS

There are no universal telephone numbers for police and fire brigade. In case of breakdown call (060) 888 or (070) 262611.

MEDICAL EMERGENCIES

There are no problems unless one happens to find oneself miles away from civilisation. Medical care is well developed in all countries bordering the Rhine. Chemists can be found everywhere. In larger places there is a notice on the door to say which chemist in the vicinity is open at night time.

There are no universal numbers for calling emergency medical and dental services in any country of the Rhine. Each city has its own number. If emergency care is necessary, enquire at the hotel, or ask any local person for assistance.

GETTING AROUND

ORIENTATION

Travelling along rivers is generally more straightforward than travelling through countries. There are only two directions one can take. The river Rhine is never more than 1 kilometre wide, although it is over a thousand kilometres long.

Whether you take the boat, the train, the car, or cycle at a more leisurely pace through the vineyards, or walk, the whole of the Rhine is accessible by some means or other.

Below are some especially interesting and beautiful trips which can be undertaken either on or along the Rhine. There is not room to print all the possibilities here; further information can be obtained from respective tourist information offices (see page 319 for addresses).

In the large cites along the Rhine, such as Basle, Strasbourg, Mainz, Wiesbaden, Cologne, Düsseldorf, Duisburg, Rotterdam and Amsterdam, city sightseeing tours will lead you to the places of interest.

Here are some ideas for some excursions on or near the river.

SWITZERLAND

With its picturesque old city, a particularly popular destination is **St. Gallen** which can easily be reached from lake Constance. You can also take the cable car to the summit of Säntis (2,500 metres).

The region around **Schaffhausen** is excellent walking country. For further information, contact: Vorstadt 2, CH-8200 Schaffhausen. Tel: (053) 85226 or 55141.

LIECHTENSTEIN

Vaduz - A popular outing is taking the chair lift to the top of Malbun-Sareiserjoch (2000m).

AUSTRIA

Bregenz - A good view of Lake Constance and the Alps that lie beyond is afforded from the top of Pfänder Mountain (1060 m), which can be reached by cable car.

Dornbirn - This is a good point from which to explore the Forest of Bregenz.

FRANCE

Strasbourg - From Rohan Palace it is possible to take a mini train through the old city. It is also possible to go sightseeing on Strasbourg's rivers and canals. Information can be obtained from: Port Autonome de Strasbourg, 15, rue de Nantes, F-67000 Strasbourg. Tel: 88841313.

If you have your own car take a trip out into the Vosges or further into the depths of Alsace.

FEDERAL REPUBLIC OF GERMANY

Lake Constance

On Lake Constance there are no less than 39 steamers of the White Fleet, a combined operation of the German, Austrian and Swiss railways, providing regular services. Special excursions can be taken during the high season which lasts from Easter to October. The timetable of the scheduled ships fits in with the arrival and departure times of the trains. In the winter time there are Advent and New Year cruises with dancing and music. Travellers can also take advantage of the "sail and explore" scheme. For further information contact the following addresses:

"Fahr Schiff und wandere" (sail and explore), Internationaler Bodensee Verkehrsverein, Schützenstraße 8, D-7750 Konstanz. Tel: (07531)22 232.

Deutsche Bundesbahn, Bodensee-Schiffsbetriebe, D-7750 Konstanz. Tel: (07531) 28 13 89.

Österreichische Bundesbahnen, Schiffahrtsstelle, A-6901 Bregenz. Tel: (05574) 22 868.

Schweizerische Bundesbahnen, CH-8590 Bahnhof Romanshorn

Schweizerische Schiffahrtsgesellschaft Untersee und Rhein, CH-8202 Schaffhausen. Tel: (053) 54 282.

Motorbootgesellschaft Bodman GmbH, D-7762 Bodman-Ludwigshafen. Tel: (077 73) 54 86.

Here are some of the itineraries: **Konstanz - Meersburg - Bregenz**: 3.5 hours. **Konstanz - Meersburg - Mainau - Überlingen**: 1.5 hours. **Überlingen - Bodman**: 1 hour. **Kreuzlingen - Konstanz - Reichenau - Schaffhausen**: 3.75 hours. **Rorschach - Romanshorn - Kreuzlingen - Mainau**: 2.5 hours. **Lindau - Rorschach**: 1 hour. **Rorschach - Reineck**: 1 hour.

Car ferries operate all the year round. There is an hourly service from Friedrichshafen to Romanshorn during the season, every two hours during the winter months; there is a service from Konstanz to Meersburg; between 6 a.m. and 7 p.m., it leaves every 15 minutes, between 7 p.m. and 10.30 p.m, every 30 minutes and thereafter every hour.

The High Rhine above Basle

There are regular ferry services on the stretch of the river from the **Rhine Falls** to **Rheinau**. Contact:

Ernst Mändli AG, Dorfstraße 207, CH-8212 Nohl am Rheinfall. Tel: (053) 21 588

- Bad Säckingen to Schwörstadt and Hauenstein (Easter to September). Contact:

G. Michmayr, Schaffhauser Straße 9, D-7880 Bad Säckingen. Tel: (077 61) 44 41

- The Basle ferry services include a daily trip to Rheinfelden at 2 p.m. from May to September. From May until October on

Thursdays and Sundays there is a ferry trip which takes a look at the port of Basle. Contact:
Basler Personenschiffahrtsgesellschaft AG, Marktgasse 5, CH-4051 Basle. Tel: (061) 25 24 00.

The Upper Rhine below Basle

Here, too, there are many ways of discovering the river on the water.

- A number of steamers operate out of Breisach from April to December. On Sundays there are two round trips and on Tuesdays aboard the "Weinland Baden", there is a round trip which includes wine tasting and a visit to a typical Baden wine cellar. There are further round trips on Mondays and Wednesdays from May until September. In the summer the steamers travel as far as Basle and Strasbourg. Contact:
Schiffahrtsbüro Ernst Kurella, Halbmondstraße 13, D-7814 Breisach. Tel: (076 67) 79 47.

- From March until December there are different excursions to be taken from Sasbach or Weisweil. You can travel through the locks to Strasbourg. There are romantic evening trips every second Saturday. The "Special Days" - Saturday, Sunday and holidays - include a trip on an old steam train over on the French side. At the end of August there is an impressive firework display. Contact:
Schiffsanlegestelle, D-7831 Sasbach. Tel: (076 42) 88 28.

- A very special experience can be had by embarking on a cruise offered by the luxury of the **Cologne-Düsseldorf Steamship Company**. These trips can last several days:
Basle to **Rotterdam** via **Strasbourg**, **Cologne** and **Antwerp** 4 days
Rotterdam to **Basle** 5 days
Basle - **Nijmegen** - **Amsterdam** 3 to 4 days

There is a romantic Rhine trip lasting two days from Frankfurt on the river Main to Cologne and vice versa. On top of that there are floating wine seminars, Christmas and New Year trips and special daily excursions. Contact any major travel agent or:
KD - Köln-Düsseldorfer, Deutsche Rheinschiffahrt AG, Frankenwerft 15, D-5000 Köln 1. Tel: (0221) 20 88 - 288.

The Season for all those trips lasts from Easter until the end of October.

Here are some agents of the Cologne-Düsseldorf Steamship Company:
KD German Rhine Line
Elsässer Rheinweg, CH-4051 Basle.
Rheinallee, D-5407 Boppard.
Rheinufer, D-5423 Braubach.
Burgplatz, D-4000 Düsseldorf.
Konrad-Adenauer-Ufer, D-5400 Koblenz.
Frankenwerft 15, D-5000 Köln 1.
Rheinallee, D-5330 Königswinter 1.
Kd German Rhine Line
Groenedaal 49a, NL-3011 Rotterdam.
Rheinufer, D-6220 Rüdesheim.
Albert-Schweitzer-Straße 2, D-6720 Speyer.
KD German Rhine Line, 31, Rue Molière, F-67550 Vendenheim.

The following companies also offer trips on the Rhine:
Bonner Personenschiffahrt, Brassertufer, D-5300 Bonn 1. Tel: (0228) 63 65 42.
Personenschiffahrt Feste Zons, D-4047 Dormagen-Zons. Tel: (02106) 42 149/42 349.

In May, June and September there are daily passenger services from Düsseldorf's Old City to Kaiserswerth. There are round trips to Duisburg and to Zons, the medieval fortified city.
Rheinische Bahngesellschaft AG, Hansaallee 1, D-4000 Düsseldorf-Oberkassel. Tel: (0211) 32 61 24.

In Duisburg it is possible to take a two-hour round tour of the port, which is the largest inland river port in the world.
Duisburger Hafenrundfahrt-Gesellschaft, Hedwigstraße 23-29, D-4100 Duisburg 1. Tel: (0203) 39 50.

In July and August there are cruises from Emmerich to Arnhem and Xanten.
Helmut Hell Schiffahrt GmbH&Co, Grollscher Weg 2, D-4240 Emmerich. Tel: (02822) 33 06.

WINE AND OTHER TOURS

The mild climate of the Rhine Basin enables vines to prosper and everywhere that wine is grown, there are cellars and pubs where you can taste it. The Rheingau-Riesling route is something particularly special; 65 kilometres of *Gemütlichkeit* and merriment on foot, by bike or by car.

Further wine growing areas worth close inspection are to be found in the region of the Kaiserstuhl, which is also famed for its cuisine. It is also well worth trundling along the German *Weinstraße* with all the full-bodied, tasty wine it offers. Don't drive under its influence! For lovers of red wines, a walk along the Ahr is a nice little detour, best made in the autumn when the sun bathes the reddened leaves of the trees and the vines on the hillsides. The tired wayfarer can find bounteous supplies of liquid refreshment, food, and time to rest his weary body at any of the numerous hosteleries to be found in the area.

Anybody interested in a more active holiday can get involved in picking the grapes. Ask around locally.

You can organise your own wine field trip in places such as Rüdesheim, Bingen, Bad Hönningen, Königswinter-Oberdollendorf, Boppard, Leutersdorf and St. Goarshausen. There is a special wine seminar in Oppenheim from the early August to the beginning of September. Contact:
Stadt Oppenheim, Merianstraße 2, D-6504 Oppenheim. Tel: (06133) 24 44.

There are further wine seminars available in St. Goarshausen, Oberwesel, Mainz, Bacharach and Rüdesheim. Information is available from local tourist offices.

Here are some special day trips you can undertake near the Rhine. The places are listed in alphabetical order.

Bad Breisig
Round flights from the airport at Mönchsheide.

Bad Honnef
The Three Hill Trek (Burg Reitersdorf - Löwenburg - Drachenfels). You can descend to the valley again using the rack railway or the path which snakes its way down through the vineyards to Bad Honnef. The walk takes about four hours.

Bacharach
There are many delightful walks which can be undertaken from the wine town of Bacharach. You can also explore the area by boat, bus or train. Information is available from the local tourist office.

Cleves
This is a great place for walking and cycling in the border regions to Holland. There are no hills! For further information contact:
Amt für Wirtschaftsföderung und Fremdenverkehr, Rathaus, D-4190 Kleve. Tel: (02281) 84 254.

Lake Constance
It is possible to visit the "Flower Island" Mainau from beginning of April to late autumn. Open daily 9 a.m. - 7 p.m.

Then you can have a look round the Old and New Castles in Meersburg (the Old Castle is open from March to October daily 9 a.m. - 6 p.m., and from November to February daily 10 a.m. - 5 p.m.; the New Castle is open from April to October 10 a.m. - 1 p.m. and 2 p.m. - 6 p.m.).

You can take the car ferry from Konstanz to Meersburg and then precede by bus to Unteruhldingen where you can see the reconstructed Stone Age village on stilts, and to Birnau. Unteruhldingen can be visited from April until October 9 a.m. - 7 p.m.. The Baroque church in Birnau can be visited every day.

Lake Constance to Basle
The largest ruined citadel in Germany is to be found at Hohentwiel. This is where the novel "Ekkehard" unravels, Joseph Viktor von Scheffel's 19th century bestseller. He was also the author of "The Trumpeter of Säckingen".

Düsseldorf
15 kilometres east of the city is the Neandertal, the site of the discovery of the remains of early man - the Neandertaler, who can now be seen on display in the museum. Outside it is possible to see European bison, wild horses and aurochs running around freely.

Freiburg
There is a cable car to the top of the 1300 metre high "Schauinsland" in the Black Forest. You can also make trips into the Black Forest and to the vineyards of the Kaiserstuhl.

Geisenheim
There are 14 circular hikes which are all very well marked. Ask the local tourist office for more details.

Heidelberg
Again, the tourist information office will inform you of the multiplicity of attractions and things to do in this beautiful city: **Heidelberg Verkehrsverein**, Friedrich-Ebert-Anlage 12, D-6900 Heidelberg. Tel: (06221) 10 821.

Karlsruhe to Worms
A few kilometres to the west of these cities runs the German Wine Road along the Pfilzerwald Nature Reserve. Among the many wine villages are Landau, Neustadt and Bad Dürkheim.

Koblenz
Northwest of Koblenz at the Laacher Lake lies Maria Laach, a famous monastery and centre of pilgrimage.

Krefeld
Here it is possible to travel by horse-drawn carriage, as in times of yore, along the routes taken by the old post coaches. **Fahrsport-Zentrum**, Gatzenstraße 48, D-4150 Krefeld-Verberg.

Neuwied, Bad Hönningen, Linz
From here you can travel up the Wiedtal in the Rhenish Westerwald, with its many windmills.

Nierstein
You can take many picturesque and varied walks through the vineyards. For further information contact the local tourist information office.

Romantic Rhine
There are many possibilities for walking and hiking between Mainz and Cologne. For details contact the relevant tourist information office (see page 319). One can also write to: **Fremdenverkehrsamt Rheinland Pfalz**, Löhrstraße 103-105, D-5400 Koblenz. Tel: (0261) 31079.

Rüdesheim
You can take a round flight over the Rhine Valley at weekends:
Flugplatz Ebental, Ebental Estate. Tel: (06722) 2426.

There are countless round trips, day and evening trips on the Rhine itself. For further information. Tel: (06722) 2962.

The wine field trip begins at the Ringmauer (Drosselgasse car park), goes up along the *Panoramaweg* and finishes at the wine museum in Brömserburg, which is open from April until the end of October, daily 9 a.m. - 12.30 p.m. and 1.30 p.m. - 6 p.m..

It is also possible to take the cable car up to the Niederwald Monument.

Rüdesheim-Assmannshausen
From here it is possible to take the cable car to the game park at the Falkenlust Hunting Lodge, and to take a walk with a view of the Rhine. If you don't come back to the point of departure, take the ferry back past the Mouse Tower.

St. Goarshausen
The path of the Loreley Castle Tour runs straight along the ridge from Kamp-Bornhofen. Contact: **Loreley-Burgen-Straße**, Dolkstraße, D-5422 St. Goarshausen. Tel: (06771) 351.

Upper Rhine Plain
Right of the Rhine below the slopes of the Odenwald, the picturesque B3 mountain road runs from Wiesloch via Nußloch and Lei-

men to Heidelberg. From there it continues further towards the north through the villages of Dossenheim, Schriesheim, Weinheim (with the castles Wachenheim and Windeck), Sulzbach, Hemsbach, Laudenbach and Heppenheim (with the Starkenburg Castle). Then past Bensheim and Auerbach with the Auerbacher Castle, to Bickenheim and Seeheim-Jugenheim and Heiligenberg Castle. The route continues through Malchen and Eberstadt with Frankenstein Castle where the monster is said to have lived, and on to Darmstadt. This region is Germany's "spring garden". Here blossom almonds, apricots, peaches and cherries when in other parts of the country the snow and ice have hardly begun to thaw. Every place on the *Bergstraße* is an attraction whatever the time of the year.

The low-lying pastures to the right of the Rhine near Lampertheim north of Mannheim extend right up to Lorsch. Here amongst the oxbow lakes of the Altrhein there is an extensive nature preserve. In the sandy soils asparagus grows particularly well.

Waldshut-Tiengen
Here lies beautiful walking country lying between 300 and 700 metres.

Worms
Part of the Nibelungen saga unravels here. Go over the Rhine bridge and follow the B 47 to the east, the Nibelungenstraße to Lorsch, where one can visit the Carolingian Palace from the year 764. From here to Odenwald, where Siegfried used to go hunting, and where he was murdered by Hagen.

THE NETHERLANDS

Amsterdam, the diamond city
Amsterdam is one of the most interesting cities in Europe, with all its bridges (over 100), its 7,000 protected buildings, its flower market at the Singel, its colourful goings on at the Leidsplein and the Rembrandtplein with all their night clubs, bars, pubs and cafés.

Kinderdijk
Nowhere else on earth is there such a large collection of windmills as in Kinderdijk; 19 solid mills stood here as early as 1740. Every Saturday afternoon in July and August the mills are started up, just like in the old days. In the second week of September the mills are even lit up in the evening. It is possible to visit the mills from the beginning of April until the end of September.

Rotterdam
Here one can go on a guided boat trip around the harbour, fly over the city itself, take in the mills and the Rhine delta and the fields of flowers.

BRIDGES AND FERRIES

Bridges across the Rhine are marked on all detailed maps. You may, however wish to get to the other side where there is no bridge, and here it is worth checking whether there is a ferry:

Ferries across the Rhine (car ferries are marked with *)

SWITZERLAND

Augst, Basle(3)

FRANCE

Rhinau* - Kappel (D)

FEDERAL REPUBLIC OF GERMANY

Romanshorn - Friedrichshafen (Lake Constance)*, Konstanz - Meersburg (Lake Constance)*, Rastatt - Seltz*, Leimersheim - Leopoldshafen*, Otterstadt - Brühl*. Altrip - Mannheim*, Eich - Gernsheim*, Mittelheim - Frei-Weinheim*, Mainz - Wiesbaden, Bingen - Rüdesheim*, Niederheimbach - Lorch*, Kaub - Bacharach, Oberwesel*, St. Goar - St. Goarshausen*, Bad Salzig - Kamp-Bornhofen, Boppard - Filsen*, Koblenz - Stolzenfels, Lahnstein, Andernach - Leutesdorf*, Brohl-Lützing - Rheinbrohl, Bad Breisig - Bad Hönningen, Linz - Remagen, Bad Kripp*, Oberwinter - Unkel, Bad Honnef - Remagen-Rolandseck*, Bonn - Mehlem.-Königswinter*, Bad Godesberg - Niederdollendorf*, Bonn - Beuel, Wesseling - Niederkassel, Rheinkassel - Leverkusen-Hitdorf*, Zons - Düsseldorf-Urdenbach*, Düsseldorf-Kaiserswerth - Meerbusch-Langst*, Rheinberg-Orsay - Duisburg-Walsum*, Xanten - Bislich.

THE NETHERLANDS

Pannerden, Wamel - Tiel, Loevestein, Woudrichem, Dordrecht, Rotterdam.

BY BICYCLE

It is possible to travel by bike along practically the entire length of the river. Stations are a good place to hire bicycles, and information can be obtained at the ticket offices. Here are some addresses.

AUSTRIA

A-6900 Bregenz
Fahrradverleih Drissner, Rheinstraße 64.
Kaufmann Roman, Brielgasse 40.

FEDERAL REPUBLIC OF GERMANY

D-5484 Bad Breisig
Autohaus Berlin, Zehnerstraße 51.
Günter Schmidgen, Schmittgasse 4.

D-5300 Bonn
Kurscheid KG, Römerstraße 4.

D-4047 Dormagen-Zons
Elisabeth Erkelen, Schloßstraße 45.

D-7800 Freiburg im Breisgau
Zweirad-Müller, Klarastraße 80.

D-6900 Heidelberg
Hauptbahnhof, Paketschalter.

D-7750 Konstanz
Rathaus, Brückengasse 2.
Rad-Lädle, Komturweg 2a.

D-5420 Lahnstein
Café Rheinterrassen, Blücherstraße 20.

D-8990 Lindau
Zwei-Rad-Center, next door to Inselhalle

D-6227 Oestrich-Winkel
Schaab, Hauptstraße 2.

D-7760 Radolfzell
Fahrradhaus Joos, Schützenstraße 14.
Fahrradladen Mees, Höllturmpassage 8.

WHERE TO STAY

HOTELS

The order of the countries follows the flow of the Rhine, and the places where hotels can be found are then ordered alphabetically. In the smaller towns and villages there are rarely luxury hotels, although this is made up for by their hospitality and cosiness. The following is not a complete list. The relevant tourist information offices will be able to provide further information, as well as assisting in reserving accommodation. Many hotels contain top-class restaurants.

SWITZERLAND

CH-4000 Basle
Hotel Basel, Münzgasse, CH-4051 Basle. Tel: (061) 25 24 23.
Hotel Drachen, Aeschenvorstadt 24, CH-4051 Basle. Tel: (061) 23 73 00.
Hilton International, Aeschengraben 31, CH-4002 Basle. Tel: (061) 22 66 22.

CH-8212 Neuhausen
Hotel Bellevue. Tel: (053) 22 21 21.

CH-8200 Schaffhausen
Hotel Fischerzunft. Tel: (053) 25 32 81.

CH-8260 Stein am Rhein
Hotel Closterhof. Tel: (054) 42 42 42.

LIECHTENSTEIN

FL-9497 Malbun.
Alpenhotel Malbun. Tel: (075) 21 181.

FL-9490 Vaduz
Hotel Löwen. Tel: (075) 21 408.
Hotel Vaduzerhof. Tel: (075) 28 484.
Parkhotel Sonnenhof, Mareestraße 29. Tel: (075) 21 192.

AUSTRIA

A-6900 Bregenz
Hotel Mercura, Platz der Wiener Symphoniker. Tel: (05574) 26 100.
Hotel Meßmer, Kornmarktstraße 16. Tel: (05574) 22 356.
Hotel Schwärzler, Landstraße 9. Tel: (05574) 22 422.
Hotel Weißes Kreuz, Römerstraße 5. Tel: (05574) 22 488.
A-6890 Lustenau, Sporthotel Huber, Erholungszentrum. Tel: (05577) 38 310.

FRANCE

F-67000 Strasbourg
Le Grand Hotel, 12, Place de la Gare. Tel: 88 32 46 90.
Hotel Hannons, 15, Rue du 22 Novembre. Tel: 88 32 16 33.
Hilton International, Avenue Herrenschmidt. Tel: 88 37 10 10.
Holiday Inn, 20, Place de Bordeaux. Tel: 88 35 70 00.
Hotel des Rohans, 17-19, Rue du Maroquin. Tel: 88 32 85 11.

FEDERAL REPUBLIC OF GERMANY

General room reservations: Beethovenstraße 69, D-6000 Frankfurt. am Main. Tel: (069) 75 721.

D-5470 Andernach
Hotel Fischer, Am Helwartsturm 4-6. Tel: (02632) 49 20 47.
Hotel Meder, Konrad-Adenauer-Allee 17. Tel: (02632) 42 632.

D-6533 Bacharach
Hotel Gelber Hof, Blücherstraße 26. Tel: (06743) 10 17.
Rhein-Hotel, Auf der alten Stadtmauer. Tel: (06743) 12 43.

D-5484 Bad Breisig
Kurhaus - Kurhotel, Koblenzer Straße 35. Tel: (02633) 97 311-15.
Rhein-Hotel, Rheinstraße 11. Tel: (02633) 96 067/8.

D-5462 Bad Hönningen
Kurparkhotel, Am Thermalbad. Tel: (02635) 49 41.

Hotel St. Pierre, Hauptstraße 138. Tel: (02635) 20 91.

D-5340 Bad Honnef
Hotel Seminaris, Alexander-von-Humboldt-Straße 20. Tel: (02224) 77 10.

D-7880 Bad Säckingen
Hotel Goldener Knopf, Rathausplatz 9. Tel: (07761) 60 78
Schneckenhalde, Schneckenhalde 12. Tel: (07761) 30 07.

D-6530 Bingen
Hotel Rheingau, Rheinkai 8. Tel: (06721) 17 496.
Germaniablick, Mainzer Str. 142. Tel: (06721) 14 773.

D-5300 Bonn
Kaiser Karl Hotel, Vorgebirgsstraße 56. Tel: (0228) 65 09 33.
Residenz Hotel, Kaiserplatz. Tel: (0228) 26 970.
Scandic Crown Hotel, Berliner Freiheit. Tel: (0228) 65 31 51.
Schloßparkhotel, Venusbergweg 27-31. Tel: (0228) 21 70 36.
Steigenberger Hotel, Bundeskanzlerplatz 1. Tel: (0228) 20 191.
Beethoven, Rheingasse 26. Tel: (0228) 63 14 11.
Rheinland, Berliner Freiheit 11. Tel: (0228) 65 80 96.

D-5407 Boppard
Bellevue Rheinhotel, Rheinallee 41. Tel: (06742) 10 20.
Hotel Rheinvilla, Rheinallee 51. Tel: (06742) 25 82.
Sport- und Kurhotel Klostergut Jakobsberg. Tel: (06742) 30 61.

D-4190 Cleves
Hotel Braam, Emmericher Straße 159. Tel: (02821) 90 90.

D-5000 Cologne
Altstadt-Hotel, Salzgasse 7. Tel: (0221) 23 41 24.
Dom-Hotel, Domkloster 2a. Tel: (0221) 20 240.
Excelsior Hotel Ernst, Trankgasse 1-5. Tel: (0221) 27 01.

Holiday Inn Crown Plaza, Habsburger-Ring 9-13. Tel: (0221) 20 950.
Inter-Continental, Helenenstraße 14. Tel: (0221) 22 80.
Hyatt Regency Köln, Kennedyufer 2a. Tel: (0221) 82 81 234.
Maritim Hotel Köln, Heumarkt 20. Tel: (0221) 20 270.
Ramada Renaissance Hotel, Magnusstraße 20. Tel: (0221) 20 340.

D-5040 Brühl
Hotel Brühler Hof, Uhlstraße 30. Tel: (02232) 42 711.
Rheinischer Hof, Euskirchener Straße 123. Tel: (02232) 33 021.

D-4220 Dinslaken
Hotel Garni, Bahnhofsplatz 9. Tel: (02134) 52 309.

D-4047 Dormagen
Romantik Hotel, Krefelder Straße 14-18. Tel: (02106) 41 041.
Zum Feldtor, Schloßstraße 40, in Zons. Tel: (02106) 54 41.

D-4000 Düsseldorf
Hotel Arcade, Ludwig-Erhard-Allee 2. Tel: (0211) 77 010.
Hotel Eden, Aderstraße 29-31. Tel: (0211) 38 970.
Esplanade Hotel, Fürstenplatz 17. Tel: (0211) 37 50 10.
Hilton International, Georg-Glock-Straße 20, in Golzheim. Tel: (0211) 43 770.
Hotel Inter-Continental, Karl-Arnold-Platz 5, in Golzheim. Tel: (0211) 45 530.
Hotel Nikko (with Japanese flair), Immermannstraße 41. Tel: (0211) 86 61.
Rheinstern Penta-Hotel, Emanuel-Leutze-Straße 17. Tel: (0211) 59 97-0

D-4100 Duisburg
Duisburger Hof, König-Heinrich-Platz 1. Tel: (0203) 33 10 21.
Novotel, Landfernmannstraße 20. Tel: (0203) 30 00 30.
Plaza Hotel, Dellplatz 1. Tel: (0203) 21 975.

D-6228 Eltville-Erbach
Hotel Tillmanns Erben, Hauptstraße 2. Tel: (06123) 40 14.

D-4240 Emmerich
Hotel Stadt Emmerich, Bahnhofstraße 26-28. Tel: (02822) 40 04.

D-7800 Freiburg im Breisgau
Colombi Hotel, Rotteckring 16. Tel: (0761) 31 415-9.
Rappen, Münsterplatz 13. Tel: (0761) 31 353.
Schwarzwälder Hof, Herrenstr. 43. Tel: (0761) 32 386.
Zum Roten Bären (the oldest inn in Germany), Oberlinden 12. Tel: (0761) 36 913.

D-6222 Geisenheim
Waldhotel, Marienthaler Straße 20. Tel: (06722) 60 77

D-6900 Heidelberg
Holiday Inn, Kurfürstenanlage. Tel: (06221) 16 10 41.
Parkhotel Atlantic, Schloßwolfsbrunnerweg 23. Tel: (06221) 10 856.
Penta Hotel, Vangerowstraße 16. Tel: (06221) 90 80.
Romantik Hotel Zum Ritter, Hauptstraße 178. Tel: (06221) 20 203.

D-5424 Kamp-Bornhofen
Hotel Rheinpracht, Rheinuferstraße 105. Tel: (06773) 265.

D-5425 Kaub.
Hotel Burg Gutenfels. Tel: (06774) 220.

D-5400 Koblenz
Hotel Brenner, Rizzastraße 32. Tel: (0261) 32 060.
Cityhotel Metropol, Schützenstraße 32. Tel: (06261) 37 702.
Hotel Hohenstaufen, Emil-Schüller-Straße 41-43. Tel: (0261) 37 081.
Scandic Crown Hotel, Julius-Wegeler-Straße 2. Tel: (0261) 13 60.
Weinhaus Merkelbach, Emser Straße 87, in Pfaffendorf. Tel: (9261) 73 234.

D-5330 Königswinter
Hotel Rheingold, Drachenfelsstraße 36. Tel: (02223) 23 048.

D-7750 Konstanz
Barbarossa, Obermarkt 8. Tel: (07531) 22 021.
Parkhotel am See, Seestraße 25. Tel: (07531) 51 077.

Hotel Seeblick, Neuhauser Straße 14. Tel: (07531) 54 018.
Steigenberger Inselhotel, Auf der Insel 1. Tel: (07531) 25 011.

D-4150 Krefeld
City-Hotel, Philadelphiastraße 63-65. Tel: (02151) 60 951.
Parkhotel Krefelder Hof, Ürdinger Straße 245. Tel: (02151) 58 40.

D-5420 Lahnstein
Dorint-Hotel Rhein-Lahn, Im Kurzentrum. Tel: (02621) 151.
Hotel Kaiserhof, Am Salhofplatz. Tel: (02621) 24 13.

D-5090 Leverkusen
City Hotel, Wiesdorfer Platz 8. Tel: (0214) 42 046.
Ramada Hotel, Am Büchelter Hof 11, in Wiesdorf. Tel: (0214) 38 30.

D-8990 Lindau
Hotel Bayerischer Hof.
Hotel Reutemann
Hotel Seegarten, Seepromenade. Tel: (08382) 50 55.
Hotel Bad Schachen, Bad Schachen. Tel: (08382) 50 11.
Hotel Gasthof Stift, Stiftsplatz 1 (Insel). Tel: (08382) 40 38/9.
Strandhotel Tannhof - Silence Hotel, Oeschländer Weg 24, Bad Schachen. Tel: (08382) 60 44.

D-5460 Linz
Hotel Berg Ockenfels. Tel: (02644) 20 71.
Hotel Gut Frühscheid, Roniger Weg. Tel: (02644) 14 41.

D-6700 Ludwigshafen
Best Western Hotel Excelsior, Lorientallee 16. Tel: (0621) 51 92 01.
Ramada Hotel, Pasadena-Allee 4. Tel: (0621) 51 93 01.
Regina Hotel, Bismarckstraße 40. Tel: (0621) 90 26.

D-6500 Mainz
Am Römerwall, Römerwall 53. Tel: (06131) 23 21 35.
Europa-Hotel, Kaiserstraße 7. Tel: (06131) 63 50.

Favorite Parkhotel, Karl-Weise-Straße 1. Tel: (06131) 82 091.
Hilton International, Rheinstraße 68. Tel: (06131) 24 50.

D-6800 Mannheim
Augusta Hotel, Augusta-Anlage 43. Tel: (0621) 41 80 01.
Gasthaus Goldene Gans, Tattersallstraße 19. Tel: (0621) 22 353.
Holiday Inn, Kurfürstenarkade. Tel: (0621) 10 71-180.
Mannheimer Hof, Augusta-Anlage 4-8. Tel: (0621) 45 021.
Maritim Parkhotel, Friedrichsplatz 2. Tel: (0621) 45 071.

D-5450 Neuwied
Park-Hotel, Am Carmen-Sylvia-Garten 6. Tel: (02631) 25 334.

D-6505 Nierstein
Rhein-Hotel, Mainzer Straße 16. Tel: (06133) 51 61.

D-6532 Oberwesel
Hotel Auf Schönburg. Tel: (06744) 70 27.
Hotel Römerkrug, Marktplatz 1, Tel.: (06744) 81 76.

D-6227 Oestrich-Winkel
Romantik Hotel Schwan, Rheinallee 5. Tel: (06723) 30 01.

D-7760 Radolfzell
Gasthof Adler, Seestraße 34. Tel: (07732) 34 73.
Zur Schmiede, Friedrich-Werber-Straße 22. Tel: (07732) 40 51.

D-5480 Remagen
Hotel Waldheide, Rheinhöhenweg 101, in Oberwinter. Tel: (02228) 72 92.

D-5456 Rheinbrohl
Hotel Zum Stern, Am Marktplatz. Tel: (02635) 26 20.

D-5401 Rhens
Hotel Königstuhl, Am Rhein 1. Tel: (02628) 22 44.

D-6220 Rüdesheim-Assmannshausen
Hotel Aumüller-Traube, Rheinstraße 6-9. Tel: (06722) 30 38.

Hotel Weingut Krone, Rheinuferstraße 10. Tel: (06722) 20 36.
Hotel Jagdschloß Niederwald, Auf dem Niederwald 1. Tel: (06722) 10 04.

D-5401 St. Goar
Hotel Rheinfels, Heerstraße 69. Tel: (06741) 312.
Hotel Zur Post, Bahnhofstraße 3. Tel: (06741) 339.
Schloß-Hotel auf Burg Rheinfels, Schloßstraße 47. Tel: (06741) 20 71.

D-5422 St. Goarshausen
Pohl's Rheinhotel Adler. Tel: (06771) 26 13.

D-5485 Sinzig-Bodendorf
Kurhaus Spitznagel, Weinbergstraße 29. Tel: (02642) 42 492.

D-6720 Speyer
Goldener Engel, Mühlturmstraße 1 A. Tel: (06232) 76 732.
Graf's Hotel Löwengarten, Schwerdstraße 14. Tel: (06232) 71 051.
Trutzpfaff, Webergasse 5. Tel: (06232) 78 399.

D-6531 Trechtingshausen
Hotel Burg Reichenstein. Tel: (06721) 61 01.

D-5463 Unkel
Rheinhotel Schulz, Vogtgasse 4-7. Tel: (02224) 23 02.

D-7890 Waldshut-Tiengen
Hotel Kaiser, Bismarckstraße 24 (Waldshut). Tel: (07751) 22 17.
Hotel Bercher, Bahnhofstraße 1 (Tiengen). Tel: (07741) 61 066.

D-4230 Wesel
Hotel Rheinterrassen, An der Rheinpromenade 9. Tel: (0281) 21 198.
Zur Aue, Reeser Landstraße 14. Tel: (0281) 21 000.

D-6200 Wiesbaden
Aukamm-Hotel, Aukammallee 31. Tel: (06134) 57 60.
Holiday Inn, Bahnhofstraße 10-12. Tel: (06134) 16 20.
Hotel Im Park, Danziger Straße 104, in Sonnenberg. Tel: (06134) 54 11 96.

Penta-Hotel, Auguste-Victoria-Straße 15. Tel: (06134) 37 70 41.

D-6520 Worms
Hotel Boos, Mainzer Straße 5. Tel: (06241) 47 63.
Nibelungen Hotel, Martinsgasse 16. Tel: (06241) 69 77.

THE NETHERLANDS

Netherlands reservations centre, Postbus 404, NL-2260 AK Leidschendam. Tel: (070) 20 25 00

Amsterdam
ACCA Hotel, Van de Veldestraat 39, NL-1071 CW Amsterdam. Tel: (020) 66 25 262.
Amstel Inter-Continental, Professor Tulpplein 1, NL-1018 GX Amsterdam. Tel: (020) 22 60 60.
Amsterdam Ascot, Damrak 95-98, NL-1012 LP Amsterdam. Tel: (020) 26 00 66.
Hilton Amsterdam, Apollolaan 138-140, NL-1077 BG Amsterdam. Tel: (020) 78 07 80.

Arnhem
Golden Tulip Rijnhotel, Ouderlangs 10, NL-6812 CG Arnhem. Tel: (085) 43 46 42.

Nijmegen
Atea Hotel, Stationsplein 19, NL-6512 AB Nijmegen. Tel: (080) 23 88 88.
AMS Hotel Belvoir, Gr. v. Roggenstraat 101, NL-6522 AX Nijmegen. Tel: (080) 23 23 44.

Rotterdam
Hilton International, Weena 10, NL-3012 CM Rotterdam. Tel: (010) 41 44 044.
Novotel Schiedam, Hargalaan, NL-3118 JA Schiedam. Tel: (010) 47 13 322.
Savoy Hotel, Hoogstraat 81, NL-3011 PJ Rotterdam. Tel: (010) 41 39 280.
Hotel Traverse,'s Gravendijkwal 70-72, NL-3014 EG Rotterdam. Tel: (010) 43 64 040.

Schiphol
Hilton International, Herbergierstraat 1, NL-1118 ZK Schiphol. Tel: (020) 60 34 567.

Tiel.
Hotel Tiel, Ln v. West Royen 10, NL-4003 AZ Tiel. Tel: (03440) 22 020.

Utrecht
Holiday Inn, Jaarbeursplein 24, NL-3521 HR Utrecht. Tel: (030) 91 05 55.
Scandic Crown Hotel, Westplein 50, NL-3531 BC Utrecht. Tel: (030) 92 52 00.

Zierikzee
Hotel Mondragon, Havenplein 21, NL-4301 JG Zierikzee. Tel: (01110) 13 051.

CAMPING

There is a large selection of campsites in all countries. Camping in undesignated areas is illegal.

SWITZERLAND

Swiss Camping- und Caravan Club, CH-6000 Luzern. Tel: (041) 23 48 22.

CH-9499 Altenrhein
Idyll. Tel: (071) 42 42 13.

CH-9430 St. Margrethen
Bruggerhorn. Tel: (071) 71 22 01.

CH-8246 Schaffhausen
Strandbad Rheinwiesen. Tel: (053) 29 33 00.

CH-8260 Stein am Rhein
Grenzstein. Tel: (054) 41 23 79.

LIECHTENSTEIN

FL-9487 Bendern
Camping Bendern. Tel: (075) 31 465.

FL-9495 Triesen
Mittagsspitze. Tel: (075) 22 105.

AUSTRIA

A-6900 Bregenz
Camping Lamm, Mehrerau. Tel: (05574) 31 301.
Camping Weiß (neu-Amerika). Tel: (05574) 35 771.
Seecamping, Bodangasse. Tel: (05574) 31 395.
Freizeitcamp Mexico, Hechtweg 4. Tel: (05574) 33 260.

FRANCE

Touring Camping Caravaning France, 8, Rue Lucien Sampaix, F-75010 Paris. Tel: 1 42 40 76 09.

FEDERAL REPUBLIC OF GERMANY

German Camping Club, Mandlstraße 28, D-8000 München 40. Tel: (089) 33 40 21.

D-6533 Bacharach
Camping am Rheinufer, Strandbadweg. Tel: (06743) 17 52, 13 90.

D-5484 Bad Breisig
Camping Rheintalstraße 75. Tel: (02633) 96 349.
Camping Rheineck, Vinxtbachtal. Tel: (02633) 95 645.

D-5462 Bad Hönningen
Camping Thermalbad. Tel: (02635) 23 22.

D-6530 Bingen
Camping Hindenburgbrücke, Mainzer Straße. Tel: (06721) 17 160.

D-5300 Bonn
Camping Siebengebirgsblick, Rolandswerth. Tel: (0228) 78 26.

D-5407 Boppard-Bad Salzig
Camping Sonneneck, on the B9. Tel: (06742) 21 21.

D-5401 Brey
Camping Die kleine Rheinperle, on the B9 between Boppard und Koblenz. Tel: (02628) 88 60.

D-5000 Cologne
Camping Berger, Uferstraße 53a (Rodenkirchen). Tel: (0221) 39 24 21.
Camping Waldbad, Peter-Baum-Weg (Dünnwald). Tel: (0221) 60 33 15.
Jugendzeltplatz, Alfred-Schütte-Allee (Poll). Tel: (0221) 83 59 89.
Städtischer Familienzeltplatz, Weidenweg (Poll). Tel: (0221) 83 19 66.

D-4047 Dormagen
Camping Pitt-Jupp, Stürzelberg. Tel: (02106) 42 210.
Camping Strandterrasse, Stürzelberg. Tel: (02106) 71 717.

D-4000 Düsseldorf
Camping Lütticher Straße. Tel: (0211) 59 14 01.
Camping Unterbacher See. Tel: (0211) 899-2038.
Camping Meerbusch-Langst, car ferry Kaiserswerth. Tel: (02150) 25 02.

D-4100 Duisburg
Camping Entenfang. Tel: (0203) 76 01 11.

D-6228 Eltville
Camping an der Brückenschenke, Hattenheim. Tel: (06723) 28 27.

D-4240 Emmerich
Camping Wildweg 2-8. Tel: (02828) 25 24.

D-7800 Freiburg im Breisgau
Camping Hirzberg, Kartäuserstraße 99. Tel: (0761) 35 054.
Camping Möslepark. Tel: (0761) 72 938.
Camping St. Georg, Basler Landstraße 62. Tel: (0761) 43 183.

D-6222 Geisenheim
Camping am Rheinufer. Tel: (06722) 85 15.

D-6900 Heidelberg
Camping Heide. Tel: (06223) 21 11.
Camping Neckartal, Schlierbach. Tel: (06221) 80 25 06.

D-4132 Kamp-Lintfort
Camping Altfeld, Altferlder Straße. Tel: (02842) 47 04.

D-5425 Kaub
Camping am Elsternband, Blücherstraße. Tel: (06774) 560.

D-7640 Kehl
Campingplatz der Freundschaft. Tel: (07851) 26 03.

D-5400 Koblenz
Camping Rhein-Mosel, Schartwiesenweg. Tel: (0261) 80 24 89.

D-7750 Koblenz
Camping Fließhorn, Dingelsdorf. Tel: (07533) 52 62.
Camping Klausenhorn, Dingelsdorf. Tel: (07533) 63 72.

Camping Am Wasserwerk. Tel: (07531) 31 388.
Camping Mainau-Litzelstetten. Tel: (07531) 44 321.

D-5420 Lahnstein
Camping Burg Lahneck. Tel: (02621) 27 65.
Camping an der Lahnmündung, Sandgasse 8. Tel: (02621) 83 90.
Camping Wolfsmühle, Hohenrhein 77. Tel: (02621) 25 89. Jugendzeltplatz im Süßgrund, Friedrichssegen. Tel: (02621) 17 52 41/2.

D-5458 Leutesdorf
Camping Marienberg, Haus 4. Tel: (02631) 72 446.

D-8990 Lindau
Camping am See, Zech. Tel: (08382) 72 236.
Camping Gitzenweiler Hof, Oberretnau. Tel: (08382) 54 75.
Camping Hammergut, Reutin. Tel: (08382) 74 688.

D-6223 Lorch-Bodental
Camping Suleika, between Assmannshausen and Lorch, approached from Rheinuferstraße. Tel: (06726) 94 64.

D-6800 Mannheim
Camping Strandbad. Tel: (0621) 85 62 40.

D-4040 Neuss
Camping Grimlinghausen. Tel: (02101) 39 868.

D-5450 Neuwied
Camping in der Au (meadow), Altwied.

D-6532 Oberwesel
Camping Schönburg. Tel: (6744) 245.

D-7760 Radolfzell
Camping Böhringen. Tel: (07732) 36 05, 38 53.
Camping Markelfingen. Tel: (07732) 10 611.
Camping Mettnau. Tel: (07732) 12 197, Naturfreunde-Camping Markelfingen.

D-5480 Remagen
Camping Goldene Meile. Tel: (02644) 22 222.

D-6220 Rüdesheim-Assmannshausen
Camping Ebental. Tel: (06722) 25 18.
Camping Rheinanlagen (Rüdesheim). Tel: (06722) 25 28.

D-6531 Trechtingshausen
Camping Marienort, Am Morgenbach. Tel: (06721) 61 33.

D-7890 Waldshut-Tiengen
Camping Schlüchttalterrassen (Waldshut). Tel: (07441) 33 66.

D-4230 Wesel
Camping Grav-Insel, Bislicher Straße. Tel: (0281) 79 21.

D-6200 Wiesbaden
Camping Maarau. Tel: (06134) 43 83.

D-6520 Worms
Camping Nibelungenbrücke. Tel: (06241) 24 355.

D-4232 Xanten
Camping Bislicher Insel, Dreeveld Estate. Tel: (02802) 20 10.

THE NETHERLANDS

Netherlands Camping Club, Wolterstraat 99, NL-2871 ZM Schoonhoven. Tel: (01823) 21 44.

Amsterdam
Camping Amsterdamse Bos, Kleine Noordijk 1, NL-1432 CC Amsterdam. Tel: (020) 41 68 68.
Gaaspercamping, Loosdrechtdreef 7, NL-1108 AZ Amsterdam. Tel: (020) 96 73 26.
Camping De Badhoeve, Uitdammerdijk 10, NL-1026 CP Durgerdam. Tel: (02904) 294.
Jeugdcamping Vliegenbos, Meeuwenlaan 138, NL-1022 AM Amsterdam. Tel: (020) 36 88 55.
Jeugdcamping Zeeburg, Zuider Ijdijk 44, NL-1095 KN Amsterdam. Tel: (020) 94 44 30.

Arnhem
Camping Kemperbugerweg 77, NL-6816 RW Arnhem. Tel: (085) 43 16 00.

Nijmegen
Camping De Kwakkenberg, Luciaweg 10, NL-6523 NK Nijmegen. Tel: (080) 23 24 43.

Otterlo
Camping Beek en hei, NL-6731 Otterlo. Tel: (08382) 14 83.

Rotterdam
Camping, Kanaalweg 84, NL-3041 JE Rotterdam. Tel: (010) 41 59 772.

Utrecht
Camping De Berekuil, Arienslaan 5, NL-3573 PT Utrecht. Tel: (030) 71 38 70.

Zierikzee
Camping Grote, Zelkeweg 10, NL-4301 NJ Zierikzee. Tel: (01110) 13 716.

YOUTH HOSTELS

Because the Rhine is such a popular area for cycling and hiking, there are a large amount of youth hostels to cater for the traveller. Sometimes youth hostels are located in fine old buildings, such as the castle at Lauffen on the Rhine Falls and the lighthouse in Konstanz.

SWITZERLAND

Youth Hostel Association of Northwest Switzerland, St.-Alban-Rheinweg 170, CH-4006 Basel. Tel: (061) 42 77 37.

Youth Hostel Association of East Switzerland-Liechtenstein, Postfach 116, CH-8887 Mels. Tel: (085) 25 020.

CH-4052 Basle
Jugendherberge St.-Alban-Kirchrain 10. Tel: (061) 23 05 72.

CH-8447 Dachsen
Jugendherberge Schloß Laufen, on the Rhine Falls. Tel: (053) 29 61 52.

CH-8200 Schaffhausen
Jugendherberge Belair, Randenstraße 65. Tel: (053) 25 88 00.

CH-8260 Stein am Rhein
Jugendherberge Stein am Rhein. Tel: (054) 41 12 55.

LIECHTENSTEIN

Jugendherberge Schaan-Vaduz, Untere Rüttigasse 6, CH-9494 Schaan. Tel: (075) 25 022.

AUSTRIA

A-6900 Bregenz
Jugendherberge, Belruptstraße 16 a. Tel: (05574) 22 867.

FRANCE

Féderation Unie des Auberges de Jeunesse, 27, Rue Pajol, F-75018 Paris. Tel: 1 42 41 59 00.

FEDERAL REPUBLIC OF GERMANY

Deutsches Jugendherbergswerk, Bismarckstraße 8, D-4930 Detmold. Tel: (05231) 74 010

D-6533 Bacharach
Jugendburg Stahleck, Schloßberg. Tel: (06743) 12 66.

D-5340 Bad Honnef-Selhof
Jugenherberge, Selhofer Straße 106. Tel: (02224) 71 300.

D-5000 Cologne
Jugendgästehaus, An der Schanz 14 (Riehl). Tel: (0221) 76 70 81.
Jugendherberge, Siegesstraße (Deutz). Tel: (0221) 81 47 11.

D-4000 Düsseldorf
Jugendherberge, Düsseldorfer Straße 1. Tel: (0211) 57 40 41.

D-4100 Duisburg
Jugendherberge, Kalkweg 148 e (Wiedau). Tel: (0203) 72 41 64.

D-7800 Freiburg im Breisgau
Jugendherberge, Kartäuserstraße 151. Tel: (0761) 67 656.

D-6900 Heidelberg
Jugendherberge, Tiergartenstraße. Tel: (06221) 41 20 66.

D-5400 Koblenz
Jugendherberge auf der Festung Ehrenbreitstein. Tel: (0261) 73 737.

D-7750 Konstanz
Jugendherberge im Otto-Moericke-Turm, Zur Allmannshöhe 18. Tel: (07531) 32 360.

D-8990 Lindau
Jugendherberge, Herbergsweg 11. Tel: (08382) 58 13.

D-6800 Mannheim
Jugendherberge, Rheinpromenade 21. Tel: (0621) 82 27 18.

D-6220 Rüdesheim
Jugendherberge am Kreuzberg. Tel: (06722) 27 11.

D-5401 St. Goar
Jugendherberge, Bismarckweg 17. Tel: (06741) 388.

D-6200 Wiesbaden
Jugendherberge, Blücherstraße 66. Tel: (06121) 48 657.

THE NETHERLANDS

Niederländische Jeugdherbergs Centrale, Professor Tulpplein 4, NL-1018 GX Amsterdam. Tel: (020) 55 13 155

Arnhem
Jeugdherberg Alteveer, Diepnbrocklaan 27, NL-6815 AH Arnhem. Tel: (085) 42 01 14.

Amsterdam
Jeugdherberg Stadsdoelen, Kloveniersburgwal 97, NL-1011 Amsterdam. Tel: (020) 24 68 32.
Jeugdherberg Vondelpark, Zandpad 5, NL-1054 GA Amsterdam. Tel: (020) 83 17 44.

Dordrecht
Jeugdherberg De Hollandse Biesbosch, Baanbroekweg 25, NL-3313 LP Dordrecht. Tel: (078) 21 13 11.

Rhijnauwen
Jeugdherberg, Rhijnauwenselaan 14, NL-3891 HH Rhijnauwen. Tel: (03405) 61 277.

Rotterdam
City hostel, Rochussenstraat 107-109, NL-3015 EH Rotterdam. Tel: (010) 43 65 763.

FOOD DIGEST

CUISINE AND RESTAURANTS

The inns and restaurants listed below are typical for the region concerned. In addition to these places there are many hotels which contain good quality restaurants. We would advise you to reserve a table whenever possible.

SWITZERLAND

Switzerland doesn't only offer a great variety of famous cheeses (Emmentaler, Appenzeller, Gruyère), which go particularly well with the Swiss wines and beers, but also a great number of delicious types of sausage: *Klöpfer* (Basle), *Schüblinge* (St Gallen), *Panti* and *Knackerli* (Appenzell). On just about every menu you can find *Geschnetzeltes* (veal in cream sauce) and *Rösti* (fried grated potato). A speciality of Schaffhausen is *Bölletünne* (onion cake). The numerous lakes and rivers further endow the fine Swiss cuisine with multifarious species of fish.

The best known Swiss dishes, of course, are cheese fondue and raclette. Those partaking of cheese fondue dunk a piece of white bread affixed to a long fork into melted cheese to which white wine and cherry juice has been added for further aroma. With raclette, slices of special raclette cheese are melted in a specially designed raclette grill and eaten with baked potato. Pickled onions, gurkins, corn on the cob and paprika are usually served with both dishes.

Switzerland also boasts a great variety of tempting sweets and deserts, including wonderful cakes and pastries filled with fresh fruit. Swiss chocolate, of course, is world renowned. On top of all this, the Swiss are masters at making fruit juice from plums, cherries and pears. *Enzian* is a high quality drink made from the roots of the yellow gentian flower, and *Grappa* is made out of the skins of the grapes left behind after wine fermentation.

Which brings us back to wine. Most wine produced in the Alpenrhein region is red or rosé. The best known are: Fläsher, Jeninser, Malanser, and Maienfelder. Fine wines also come from further downstream as well, from the High Rhine north of Basle. These include: Hallauer, Osterfinger, Rheinhalder (from the region around Schaffhausen), and the wines from the Argau and Basle.

CH-4000 Basle
Brauerei und Restaurant Fischerstube, Rheingasse 45. Tel: (061) 69 26 635
Gifthüttli (historic inn), Schneidergasse 11. Tel: (061) 25 16 56.
Les Quatres Saisons, Clarastraße 43. Tel: (061) 69 18 044.
Rôtisserie des Rois (in Hotel Drei Könige), Blumenrain 8. Tel: (061) 25 52 52.
Safran-Zunft, Gerbergasse 11. Tel: (061) 25 19 59.
Topas (koscher cuisine), Leimenstraße 24. Tel: (061) 22 87 00.
Am Alten Stückli (historic wine cellar), Barfüsserplatz 1. Tel: (061) 25 15 92.
CH-Schaffhausen
Gerberstube (16th century inn), Bachstraße 8. Tel: (053) 25 21 55.
Schaefli (near the boat pier). Tel: (053) 25 11 44.
Zum Sittich, Vordergasse 43. Tel: (053) 25 13 72.

FL-9488 Schellenberg
Wirtschaft zu Löwen. Tel: (075) 31 162.

FL-9490 Vaduz
Gasthof Löwen (historic hotel with a view of the castle). Tel: (075) 21 408.
Restaurant Torkel (in the royal vineyards). Tel: (075) 24 410.

AUSTRIA

Here one can find the most delicious puddings and sweets. *Käsespätzle* (flower dumplings with cheese), *Krautspätzle* (flower dumplings with Sauerkraut), *Kaiserschmarr'n* (a kind of pancake cut into pieces and served with stewed fruit), cottage cheese strudel and apple strudel. Dumplings or potatoes go well with a spicy, juicy stew

(gulasch), accompanied by a glass of Heuriger (new wine) or a grüner Veltiner (white wine), or a glass of one of the many different brews of beer. Here are some restaurants:

A-6900 Bregenz
Gasthof Adler, Vorklostergasse 66. Tel: (05574) 31 788.
Montfort (café, restaurant), Bahnhofstraße 15. Tel: (05574) 22 186.

A-6912 Hörbranz
Kronen-Stuben (Austrian national cuisine), Lindauer Straße 48. Tel: (05573) 23 41.

A-6911 Lochau
Landgasthof Haggen, Haggen 1. Tel: (05574) 22 926.

FRANCE

There is little that needs to be said about the quality of the French cuisine and the importance the French attach to eating. The French enjoy their food like practically no other country on earth. Meals, which often last for hours, normally consist of numerous courses, of soup, vegetables and meat, nothing overcooked, all accompanied by generous quantities of wine. There is also a continuous supply of baguette, just to make sure that by the end of the meal you are well satisfied, particularly if you have managed to get through the cheese or even the gâteau which are normally served towards the end, washed down by more wine. A glass of fine cognac or a digestive normally rounds off the feast.

The Alsace wines are famous, particularly for high quality white wines, the chalky soil being well-suited to the variety of grapes that are grown in the region. Some of the best-known are Riesling, Silvaner, Weißklevener, Grauklevener, White Burgundy, Muscadet, Pinot Blanc, Tokay d'Alsace, Gewürztraminer, and Pinot Noir.

Back to food: The French like to eat fresh produce. Local vegetables and salads are prepared like only the French know how, with cream, herbs and mild oils. The meat is not necessarily the best in the world, but the French seem to know how to cook it. Poultry and fish are both very well represented on French menus. Of course there are specialities of the Alsace region. Strasbourg whole liver paté (*Paté de foie gras*), snails (*escargots*), Strasbourg sausage salad onion cake, Sauerkraut (*choucroute*), chicken in white wine (*coq au Riesling*), *Baeköffa* (a stew consisting of different meats, potatoes, onions and white wine, baked in the oven). Although the strong Munster cheese may not be to everybody's taste, there are a number of other fine cheeses to choose from. *Guglhupf* (yeast cake) is a further speciality. The beer from Alsace is every bit as renowned as the flavoursome fruit schnapps - the strawberry, the plum and the mirabelle. Some restaurants in Strasbourg:

F-67082 Strasbourg
A la Petite Alsace, 23, Rue du Bain-aux-Plantes. Tel: 00 35 03 69.
Ami Schulz, 1, Ponts Convests. Tel: 88 32 76 98.
Arsenal, 11, Rue de l'Abreuvoir. Tel: 88 35 03 69.
Maison des Tanneurs, 42, Rue du Bain-aux-Plantes. Tel: 88 32 79 70.
Termnus Gruber, La Cour de Rosemont, 10, Place de la Gare. Tel: 88 32 87 00.

FEDERAL REPUBLIC OF GERMANY

In Germany, lunch, normally consisting of meat, vegetables, potatoes and sauces, is traditionally the main meal of the day. It is usually accompanied by beer, so lets begin there.

German beer varies greatly in its alcohol content. While a normal brew contains about 5.5%, *Starkbier* (strong beer) can contain up to 16% or even more. There are two basic types of beer in Germany, top-fermented and bottom-fermented beer. A top-fermented beer is where the yeast rises to the top during the fermentation process. Fermentation takes place at a temperature of 15 - 20 degrees Celsius. In places like Düsseldorf and Cologne, there are pub breweries which produce top-fermented beer, known as *Altbier* (brewed the old way), the *Kölsch* served in Cologne being an example. At one time all beer brewed in Germany used to be of this variety. However, most beer now brewed in Germany is bottom-fermented beer. Here, the yeast sinks to the bottom during a fermentation that takes place at the lower temperature of 4 to 9 degrees. All German export beer (e.g. Dortmunder), as well as Pils, is of this type.

So what delicacies do the Germans along the Rhine prefer? The people of the Palatinate have a special penchant for beef broth. In Rhine Hessen there is *Handkäs mit Musik*, cheese with onion rings, vinegar, oil and plenty of pepper. There is also *Spundekäs zu Woi* (plug cheese with wine). It gets its name "plug" after the stoppers used for the wine casks, for it resembles these in shape. It is formed out of cottage cheese, egg yellow, onions, chopped cucumbers and salt and pepper. Chops and sauerkraut are also a great favourite. In Rüsesheim, a very special drink is on offer - the "Rüdesheim coffee". It is coffee with a shot of local brandy, topped with cream and powdered chocolate.

In Cologne one can get *Halven Hahn*, a rye bread roll served with mature Gouda. Then there is *Kölsch Kaviar* - rye bread and black pudding. A further delight is the *Sauerbraten*, marinated beef in a sweet and sour sauce. On the Lower Rhine the traveller can expect to come across such delicacies as buckwheat pancakes.

In the region around Lake Constance, there is a great choice of fish prepared in a whole variety of ways. The fruit for which the area is famous is also used to make fruit juices. The region, particularly around Meersburg and Konstanz, belongs to the Baden viticulture area, and is indeed famous for its wines, both red and white.

A number of well known wine growing areas stretch along the Rhine; those of Baden, Hessen, Rhineland Palatinate, Rhine Hessen, the Rhinegau, and the Nahe, the Moselle, and the Ahr rivers. Most of the wine produced is white. In October and November, after the harvest, the *Federweiße*, the new wine which goes to the head very easily, is ready for drinking. It goes very well with onion cake and fresh walnuts.

German wine is divided into three qualities: table wine, *Qualitätswein* and *Qualitätswein mit Prädikat*. The latter includes wine produced from the late harvests, like the *Beerenauslese* and the *Trockenbeerenauslese*. Most red wine on the Rhine is produced in Assmannshausen. This full-bodied wine goes particularly well with the *Assmannshäuser Rotweinkuchen*. The ingredients are as follows:

6 eggs
300g butter

150g sugar
100g honey
the pulp of a vanilla stick
1/8l Assmannshausen Late Burgundy
1.5 tsp. cinnamon
1.5 tsp. cocoa powder
150g grated bitter chocolate
300g flour
1 packet of baking powder

Beat the eggs, butter, sugar, honey and vanilla. Add the wine and then the cinnamon, cocoa and the chocolate. At the end mix the flour with the baking powder and fold it in. Put the mixture into a greased cake dish and cook in the oven on medium heat for forty to fifty minutes. It tastes delicious.

In every small town and village along the Rhine, it is possible to find nice cosy pubs and restaurants. In the larger cities there is a busy pub life, especially in the older parts of town. Here is a choice of typical inns and restaurants.

D-6533 Bacharach
Kurpfälzische Münze (historic wine house and restaurant), Oberstraße 72-74. Tel: (06743) 13 75.
Gutsausschank Zur Traube, Blücherstraße 59. Tel: (06743) 14 39, 17 17.
Weinhaus Altes Haus, Oberstraße 61. Tel: (06533) 12 09.

D-5484 Bad Breisig, Ab Acht im Schwan,
Vogelsangstraße 6. Tel: (02633) 92 44

D-5300 Bonn
Am Tulpenfeld, Heussallee 2-10. Tel: (0228) 21 90 81.
Bonner Eßzimmer, Wachsbleiche 26. Tel: (0228) 63 86 68.
Em Höttche (historic inn), Markt 4. Tel: (0228) 65 85 96.
Rheinhotel Dreesen, Rheinstraße 45-49. Tel: (0228) 82 020.
Restaurant "Natürlich", Rosenstraße 34. Tel: (0228) 69 10 00, **Union-Säle**, Restaurant im Konrad-Adenauer-Haus, Friedrich-Ebert-Allee 73-75. Tel: (0228) 54 44 01.
Weinhäuschen, Fährstraße 26, in Mehlem. Tel: (0228) 34 22 35.
Zur Kerze (nighttime restaurant), Königstraße 25. Tel: (0228) 21 07 69.

D-5301 Bonn-Bad Godesberg
Zum Aennchen (wine bar), Aennchenplatz 2. Tel: (0228) 31 20 51.

D-5407 Boppard
Rheinlust, Le Gourmet, Kanne, Rheinallee 27-30. Tel: (06742) 30 01.
Weingut Felsenkeller (belongs to the local estate), Mühltal 21. Tel: (06742) 21 54.

D-5401 Brey
Zum Alten Fritz, Am Rathaus. Tel: (02628) 23 32.

D-5040 Brühl
Kaiserbahnhof (wine and *Altbier* cellar), Alter Bahnhof. Tel: (02232) 25 581.
Kupferkanne (new German cuisine), Kölner Straße 50-51. Tel: (02232) 42 675.
Zum Steinfass, Steingasse 2, Brühl-Badorf. Tel: (02232) 34 177.

D-4190 Cleves
Altes Landhaus Zur Mühle, Tiergartenstraße 68. Tel: (02821) 17 147.
Petersilchen, Opschlag 10. Tel: (02821) 18 939.
Historischer Weinkeller, Mehlgasse 16. Tel: (0261) 46 26.

D-5000 Cologne
Altstadt-Päffgen, Heumarkt 62. Tel: (0221) 21 97 20.
Deutsches Bierhaus, Roonstraße 33. Tel: (0221) 24 01 881.
Früh am Dom, Am Hof 12-14. Tel: (0221) 23 66 16, 21 26 21.
Haus Töller (ancient *Kölsch* pub), Weyerstraße 96. Tel: (0221) 21 40 86.
Sprößling (vegetarian restaurant), Mozartstraße 9. Tel: (0221) 23 21 24.
Zum Treppchen, Kirchstraße 15, in Rodenkirchen. Tel: (0221) 39 21 79.
Zur Tant (protected half-timber building), Rheinbergstraße 49, in Porz. Tel:(02203) 81 883.

D-4220 Dinslaken
Dinslaker Köpi-Haus (Ale house).
Kartoffelkiste (historic inn), Rathaus. Tel: (02134) 13 523.

D-4047 Dormagen-Zons
Gasthof Stadt Zons, Feste Zons, Rheinstraße 14. Tel: (02106) 46 608.

D-4000 Düsseldorf
Haus Deichgraf, In den großen Banden. Tel: (0211) 72 40 31.
Restaurant Hofkonditorei Bierhoff, Oststraße 128. Tel: (0211) 36 03 36.
Im Füchschen, Ratinger Straße 28. Tel: (0221) 84 062.
Schloßturm, Mühlenstraße 2. Tel: (0211) 32 03 36.
Schneider-Wibbel-Stuben, Schneider-Wibbel-Gasse 5-7. Tel: (0211) 80 000.
Zum Schiffchen, Hafenstraße 5. Tel: (0211) 13 24 21.
Zum Uerige (top-fermented beer pub brewery), Bergerstr. 1. Tel: (0211) 84 455.

D-4240 Emmerich
Altes Gasthaus Christ, by the church. Tel: (02822) 70 303.

D-7800 Freiburg Alte Weinstube Zur Traube, Schusterstraße 17. Tel: (0761) 32 190.
Greiffenegg-Schlößle, Schloßbergring 3. Tel: (0761) 32 728.
Oberbirch's Weinstuben (Baden wine and game dishes), Münsterplatz. Tel: (0761) 37 530.
Schloßbergrestaurant Dattler, Schloßbergbahn. Tel:80761) 31 729.

D-6900 Heidelberg
Altdeutsche Weinstube, Hauptstraße 224. Tel: (06221) 21 138.
Alter Kohlhof (regional specialities), Kohlhof 5. Tel: (06221) 21 915.
Destille (meeting place in the Old City), Untere Straße 6. Tel: (06221) 22 808.
Goldener Hecht (traditional pub), Steingasse 2. Tel: (06221) 26 984.
Kupferkanne, Hauptstraße 127. Tel: (06221) 21 790.
Traube (ancient wine cellar), Rathausstraße 75. Tel: (06221) 37 37 92.
Vegetarian Restaurant, Kurfürsten-Anlage 9. Tel: (06221) 22 814.

D-5424 Kamp-Bornhofen
Restaurant auf Burg Sterrenberg. Tel: (06773) 323.
Restaurant-Café at Burg Liebenstein. Tel: (06773) 308.

D-5400 Koblenz
Im Stüffje, Hohenzollernstraße 5. Tel: (0261) 32 486.

Weindorf Koblenz, Julius-Wegeler-Straße (on the Rhine promenade). Tel: (0621) 31 680, 44 257.
Westerwälder Bauernstube, Clemensstraße 16. Tel: (0261) 34 210.

D-5330 Königswinter
Weinhaus Zur Mühle, Lindenstraße 7, in Oberdollendorf. Tel: (02223) 21 813.

D-7750 Konstanz, Restaurant Staader Fährhaus, Fischerstraße 30. Tel: (07531) 33 118.
Zum Küfer Fritz (wine bar), Sallmannsweilergasse. Tel: (07531) 22 198.
Zum Pfannkuchen, Kreuzlinger Straße. Tel: (07531) 33 118.

D-4150 Krefeld
Dachsbau (house of beers), Hubertusstraße 70. Tel: (02151) 77 44 44.
Herbst Pitt (typical Krefeld restaurant), Marktstraße 105. Tel: (02151) 77 36 93.

D-5420 Lahnstein
Gasthaus Zum Schwanen, Johannesstraße 9. Tel: (02621) 78 49.
Wirtshaus an der Lahn, Lahnstraße 8. Tel: (02621) 72 70.
Zum Anker, Schwarzgasse 4. Tel: (02621) 28 79.

D-8990 Lindau
Brauerei-Gasthof Steig, Steigstraße 31. Lindau-Reutin. Tel: (08382) 78 066.
Gasthaus Zum Sünfzen, Maximilianstraße 1. Tel: (08382) 58 65.

D-5460 Linz
Kurfürstliche Burggastronomie (feasting like in the Middle Ages), Burgplatz 4. Tel: (02644) 70 21.

D-6700 Ludwigshafen
Biermuseum (local specialities), Berliner Straße 21. Tel: (0621) 51 56 76.
Goldener Weinberg (historic inn), Lorien. Tel: (0621) 51 92 51.
Sonnenschein Weinstuben, Ludwigsplatz 10. Tel: (0621) 51 86 77.

D-6800 Mannheim
Alte Münz (Palatinate specialities), Fußgängerzone "Planken". Tel: (0621) 28 262.
Bierbrezn - Weinstadl, Collinistraße 3. Tel: (0621) 10 11 36.

Heller's Vollwert-Restaurant, Kaiserring. Tel: (0621) 15 35 25.
Evening Star (cocktail bar), Augusta-Anlagen 43-45. Tel: (0621) 41 80 01.
Zum Ochsen (oldest restaurant in Mannheim), Hauptstraße 70, in Feudenheim. Tel: (0621) 79 20 65.

D-6505 Nierstein
Gutsschänke im Oberdorf, Oberdorfstraße 28. Tel: (06133) 58 541.

D-6227 Oestrich-Winkel
Hallgarten, Hallgartener Zange (highest restaurant in the Rhingau, 600 metres). Tel: (06723) 20 74.
Oestrich Hotel Schwan (Rhenish specialities), Rheinallee 5. Tel: (06723) 30 01.
Winkel Graues Haus (regional cuisine, large wine cellar), Graugasse 10. Tel: (06723) 26 19.
Haus am Strom, Gänsgasse 13. Tel:806723) 22 50.

D-7760 Radolfzell
Basilikum (gourmet restaurant), Löwengasse 30. Tel: (07732) 56 776.
Mettnau-Stube (fish specialities), Strandbadstraße 23. Tel: (07732) 13 644.
Restaurant Strandcafé, Strandbadstraße 102. Tel: (07732) 16 50.

D-5480 Remagen
Weinhaus Restaurant St. Urban, Alte Straße 15. Tel: (02642) 31 11.
Restaurant du Maitre - Hotel Waldheide, Rheinhöhenweg 101, in Oberwinter. Tel: (02228) 72 92.
Zum Rolandbogen, Rolandswerth. Tel: (02228) 372.
Rosalkas Restaurant, Rolandseck, in the artists' station. Tel: (02642) 77 39.

D-6220 Rüdesheim-Assmannshausen
Historisches Altes Rathaus (wine restaurant), Lorcher Straße 8. Tel: (06722) 20 51.
Weinlokal Alte Dorfschänke, Niederwaldstraße 7. Tel: (06722) 23 83.

There are many wine bars and pubs in the Drosselgasse.

D-6720 Speyer
Rhein-Restaurant Hammer, Rheinallee 2. Tel: (O6232) 24 333.
Zum Domnapf (a listed building), Domplatz 1. Tel: (06232) 75 454.

Zur alten Münze (wine bar), Korngasse 1 a. Tel: (06232) 79 703.

D-4230 Wesel
Weinstube Berliner Tor, Berliner-Tor-Platz. Tel: (0281) 24 822.
Zur Aue (Lower Rhine specialities), Reeser Landstraße 14. Tel: (0281) 26 11.

D-6200 Wiesbaden
Bebop (jazz pub), Saalgasse 9. Tel: (06121) 52 87 24.
Die Ente vom Lehel (gourmet restaurant), Kaiser-Friedrich-Platz 3. Tel: (06121) 13 36 66.
Mövenpick, Sonnenbergstraße 2. Tel: (06121) 52 40 05.
Quatre Saisons (wine pub), Wilhelmstraße 53. Tel: (06121) 37 32 25.
Saladin (vegetarian restaurant), Schützenhofstraße 3. Tel: (06121) 30 10 77.
Wiesbadener Ratsbräu (rustic bierkeller), Schloßplatz 6. Tel: (06121) 30 00 23.

D-6520 Worms.
Bacchus (fish specialities), Obermarkt 10. Tel: (06241) 69 13.
Gießenbrücke (Old German cuisine), Rheinstraße 43. Tel: (06241) 24 891.
La Madrague (New German cuisine), Kämmerstraße 71. Tel: (06141) 27 620.
Sudpfanne (Palatinate specialities), Hagenstraße 18. Tel: (06141) 21 144.
Rôtisserie Dubs (gourmet restaurant), Kirchstraße 6, in Rheindürkheim. Tel: (06242) 20 23

THE NETHERLANDS

No more wine is produced in the wilder reaches of the Lower Rhine. Instead, the Dutch produce Genever out of juniper berries. For most people in this part of the world the day begins with a *Kopje Koffie*. Beer is normally drunk with the meal and in the afternoon, tea is often served. After the evening meal, one might drink Advocaat. The North Sea is source of a great variety of fish - in May is herring time. April to September is the time for shell fish which are to be found served up in every restaurant and many snack bars. Meat is mostly roasted. The cheese for which the country is famous is enjoyed far beyond its borders.

Around five hundred restaurants are marked with a blue sign meaning that they serve a reasonably-priced tourist menu. The price is the same in all restaurants although the individual cooks actually decide on the menu.

Amsterdam
Schepp, Linaeusstraat 210. Tel: (020) 93 81 04.
Le Saumon, Rokin 115. Tel: (020) 27 52 83.
Restaurant Excelsior, Niuwe Doelenstraat 2-8. Tel: (020) 23 48 36.

Nijmegen
In de Boterwaag, Grote Markt 26. Tel: (080) 23 07 57.

Rotterdam
Beluga an de Maas, Haringvliet 92 b. Tel: (010) 41 36 717.
Captain's Cabin, Calandstraat 8 a. Tel: (010) 43 66 849.
Engels, Stationsplein 45. Tel: (010) 41 19 550.
La Vilette, Westblaak 160. Tel: (010) 14 86 92.
Parkheuvel, Heuve Ilaan. Tel: (010) 36 05 30.

Tiel
Lotus (Asian specialities), West Luidensestraat 49. Tel: (03440) 15 702.

Utrecht
CR Ons Eiland, Marco Polo Laan 2. Tel: (030) 88 02 15.
Het Glazen Huis, Marienplaatz 24. Tel: (030) 31 84 85

THINGS TO DO

NATURE RESERVES

There is a great choice of nature reserves and parks, where it is still possible to see nature undisturbed.

AUSTRIA

Fußach
Between the "new" and the "old" Rhine at Lake Constance lies one of the largest sweet water swamps in Europe, with 2000 hectares of reeds and rushes in which almost 500 species of bird make their nest.

FEDERAL REPUBLIC OF GERMANY

Brühl
The woodland and lake district of the Kottenforstville Nature Park is not only good for walking, but also provides the possibility for fishing, swimming and rowing.

Cologne
On the right bank of the Rhine in Deutz there is the Rhine Park. There are game parks in Brück and Dünnwald.

Dormagen
In Delhoven the Tannenbusch Nature Reserve is surrounded by a game park and a geological park.

Emmerich
Nature Reserve Knauheide north of Elten.

Freiburg im Breisgau
Taubergießen Nature Reserve lies north of the city on the confluence with the river Eltz. Wild grapes still grow here on the Rhine meadows.

Gernsheim
The 16-kilometre long arm of the Altrhein, no longer attached to the river itself, surrounds the Kühkopf Nature Reserve. Peduncular oaks and elms provide cover for many rare species of water fowl.

Hammerstein
Opposite the town and in the river lies the island of Hammersteiner Werth with its recreation area.

Konstanz
The Wollmatinger Ried lies in the lowlands west of the town.

Mannheim
Another nature reserve is the Mannheim Reißinsel. There is also the Ketscher Rheininsel which lies some 15 kilometres to the south of the city.

Oestrich-Winkel
The Rheininsel Fulderaue with its recreation area lies facing the town .

Radolfzell
On the Mettnau Penninsular there is a nature and bird reserve

Waldshut-Tiengen
Here is the Wutach-Gauchach Nature Reserve.

Wesseling
The Entenfang ("duck catch") Nature Re-

serve provides nesting and for rare water fowl.

Wiesbaden
There is a recreation area on Maaraue Island at the confluence with the Main River.

THE NETHERLANDS

The large National Park De Hoge Veluwe lies north of the Rhine near Arnhem.

BOTANICAL & ZOOLOGICAL GARDENS

Many interesting hours can be enjoyed by looking at indigenous and more exotic species of flora and fauna.

SWITZERLAND

Basle
Basle Zoological Gardens, Viaduktstraße/ Binningerstraße. Open daily in summer 8 a.m. - 6.30 p.m., in winter 8 a.m. - 5.30 p.m.

FEDERAL REPUBLIC OF GERMANY

Bendorf
Butterfly Garden, Schloßpark Saynl. Open daily in summer 9 a.m. - 6 p.m., in winter 9 a.m. - 5 p.m.

Bonn
Botanical Gardens. Meckenheimer Allee 171. Open May to September 9 a.m. - 6 p.m., October to April 9 a.m. - 4 p.m.
Waldau Game Park, Venusberg.

Duisburg
Duisburg Zoo, Mülheimer Straße 273. Open daily 8.30 a.m. until dark.

Heidelberg
Botanical Gardens, Im Neuenheimer Feld 340. Open Monday to Thursday, Sundays and holidays 9 a.m. - 12.00 and 1 p.m. - 4 p.m., closed on Friday and Saturday.

Cologne
Botanical Gardens, Amsterdamer Straße 36. Open daily from 8 a.m. until dusk.
Forest Botanical Gardens, Schillingsrotter Weg. Open Summer daily until 8 p.m., winter Saturday and Sunday until dusk.
Zoo, Riehler Straße 173. Open daily 9 a.m. - 6 p.m.

Konstanz
The large island of Reichenau is an island of fruit and vegetables. At one time wine used to be grown here.

Krefeld
Botanical Gardens, Schönwasserpark. Open daily 8 a.m. - 6 p.m. in summer, 1. November to 1. February Monday to Thursday 9 a.m. - 3 p.m., Friday 9 a.m. - 12.00.
Krefelder Zoo, Uerdinger Straße 37. Open daily in summer 8 a.m. - 6 p.m., in winter 8 a.m. until dark.

Mannheim
Luisenpark
Herzogenriedpark
Forest Park

Neuwied
Neuwied Zoo, Waldstraße 160. Open daily 9 a.m. - 6 p.m.

Remagen
Wildpark Rolandseck. Open daily in Summer 9 a.m. - 6 p.m., in winter until dusk.

Unteruhldingen
Mainau Island on Überlinger See is the flower island with tropical and sub-tropical vegetation.

THE NETHERLANDS

Arnhem
Burger's Safari Park, Delenseweg. Open daily in summer 9 a.m. - 5 p.m., in winter 9 a.m. - 4.30 p.m.
Burger's Zoo, Schelmseweg 85. Open daily 9 a.m. - 8 p.m.

Rotterdam
Diergaarde Blijdorn, Van Aerssenlaan 49. Open daily 9 a.m. - 5 p.m.

PLEASURE PARKS

There are a great many parks which are fun for all the family.

SWITZERLAND

Lipperswil. Conny-Land is the Lake Costance recreation park with Europe's largest dolphinarium.

FEDERAL REPUBLIC OF GERMANY

Brühl, "Phantasialand" - the land of unlimited possibilities, Berggeiststraße 31-41, Open daily from 1. April to 31. October from 9 a.m.

Freiburg in Breisgau, The Europa-Park, an adventure and theme park, is situated in Rust between Freiburg and Kehl, Open daily from 1. April to 16. October from 9 a.m.

Rüdesheim, A park on the Lach for games and sporting activities.

Speyer, The Holiday Park in the direction of Haßloch offers a great variety of things to do.

Wiesbaden, Between Wiesbaden and Schlangenbad the Taunus-Wunderland opens its doors to a fairytale world, Open daily 9 a.m. - 6 p.m.

SIGHTSEEING

As many of the cities on the Rhine can look back on a long history, they offer a great deal in terms of old buildings, alleyways, churches and cathedrals and palaces. Here is a reminder of some of the better-known places worth visiting.

SWITZERLAND

Basle, Town Hall, Spalentor, Minster, Old City, The world famous zoo, The Roman excavations in Augst (12 kilometres east of the city).

Schaffhausen, Old City, Munit Fortress, Rhine Falls (3 kilometres away, Europe's largest waterfall, boat trips to the base of the falls).

LIECHTENSTEIN

The dwarf state between Switzerland and Austria. **Vaduz** (picturesque Old City).

AUSTRIA

Near **Dornbirn** is the Rappenlochschlucht and the Alplochschlucht, a ravine with a 120 metre high waterfall.

FRANCE

Colmar, Matthias Grünewald's Isenheimer Altar in the Unterlinden Museum.

Mulhouse, Place de la Réunion, the market square in the old city, Town Hall - Hotel de Ville, Europe Tower on Europe Square.

Strasbourg, The Cathedral of Our Lady, Haus Kammerzell opposite the cathedral, The Tanners Quarter, Rohan Palace, Stag's Apothecary,Old Town Hall.

FEDERAL REPUBLIC OF GERMANY

Bacharach, Stahleck Castle (youth hostel with great views), Chapel of St Werner.

Bad Hönningen, Arenfels Castle.

Bingen, Burg Klopp (nice views), Mouse Tower, Chapel of St Rochus.

Bendorf, Castle Sayn on the Kehrburg, containing the St Hubertus Bierkeller.

Bonn, Town Hall on the market place, Collegiate Church, Open daily from 7 a.m. to 7 p.m., Pilgrimage Chapel (with staircase by Balthasar Neumann) Poppelsdorf Castle (containing the University's natural science collection), Bundeshaus (visits only allowed after prior application), Beethoven House (museum), Hofgarten.

Bad Godesberg, Godesburg ruins, Redoute Castle, Braubach, Marksburg (with an impressive weapons collection and a nice view from the tower).

Brühl, Augustenburg Castle, with the staircase by Balthasar Neumann, Falkenlust Hunting Lodge, situated in a pleasant park. Open from 9 a.m. - 12.00, 2 p.m. - 4 p.m.. Jewish cemetery, on the corner of Kölnstraße and Schildgesstraße.

Cleves, Swan's Castle, home of Lohengrin the Knight of the Holy Grail. Open daily April to October 11 a.m. to 5 p.m., November to March Saturdays and Sundays 11 a.m. to 5 p.m.

Cologne, Cathedral, containing the Shrine of the Tree Magi, Church of Our Lady of the Assumption, City Gates, Romanesque Churches.

Dinslaken, Castle with drawbridge, watermills and windmills.

Dormagen-Zons, Historic windmill inside the medieval fortified city, Rhine Tower.

Düsseldorf, Altstadt "the longest bar in the world", Apart from beer there are many monuments including the Jan Wellem equestrian statue by Gabriel de Grupello, Hofgarten, Jägerhof Castle, Rhine Tower (234 metres high), Benrath Château.

Duisburg, Abbey Church Duisburg-Hamborn.

Eltville, Wine Cellars in the erstwhile Cistercian Monastery (Kloster Eberbach). Open 1 April to 30 September 10 a.m. - 6 p.m., Saturday and Sunday 11 a.m. to 4 p.m. Tel: (067323) 42 28.

Emmerich, Rhine Bridge, the longest suspension bridge in Germany.

Freiburg, Old City, Minster (with Altarpiece by Hans Baldung), Old Town Hall.

Geisenheim, Schönborn Castle, Johannisberg Castle, Castle Schwarzenstein.

Heidelberg, Old City, Castle (with the famous Heidelberg Vat), University Library (with the Great Heidelberg Songbook).

Kamp-Bornhofen, Liebenstein Castle, Sterrenberg Castle.

Kaub, Gutenfels Castle, with the Castle Hotel, Pfalzgrafenstein Castle (guided tours available).

Koblenz, Ehrenbreitstein Fortress which can be reached by chairlift, containing the Provincial Museum of Koblenz, Stolzenfels Castle (daily tours), Towers of the old Roman wall, Old castle, Elector's Castle, Deutches Eck.

Königswinter, Drachenburg. Open in summer 10 a.m. to 6 p.m., Drachenfels (the rack railway operates from January to November), Heisterbach Monastery.

Konstanz, Old Town, including the "Sacristan's House" ("Haus zur Kunkel").

Lahnstein, Lahneck Castle.

Lindau, Harbour, with its old and new lighthouse, Convent.

Linz, Ockenfels Castle, colourful half-timbered houses, Town Hall, the oldest still in use in the Rhineland Palatinate.

Lorch, Nollig Castle, good views.

Mainz, St Martins Cathedral, Old City, St Stephen's Church, with stained glass panels by the contemporary artist Marc Chagall, "Kupferberg" sparkling wine cellars, seven floors underground; tours and tasting by appointment.

Mannheim, Elector's Palace, Synagogue, Art Nouveau buildings around Friedrichsplatz.

Neuwied, Rommersdorf Abbey, Altwied Castle ruins, Neuwied Castle.

Niederheimbach, Sooneck Castle.

Oberwesel, Church of Our Dear Lady, Schönburg Castle.

Oestrich-Winkel, "Graues Haus", the oldest stone-built cottage in Germany, Brentano House, where Goethe used to stay, Historic wooden crane, the hallmark of the town.

Oppenheim, St Catherine's Church, one of the finest Gothic churches on the Rhine.

Radolfzell, Old Town, Church of Our Dear Lady, Castle on the island of Mettnau.

Remagen, Church and Monastery of St Apollinaris, Remagen Bridge, Rolandsbogen.

Rheinbrohl, Hammerstein ruins, Rheindiebach, Fürstenberg Castle ruins.

Rüdesheim, Drosselgasse, Rhine jollity on the Romantic Rhine, Niederwald Monument, accessible on foot or by cable car, Brömserburg, the Museum of the History of German Wines.

Speyer, Altpörtel, the "old gate", Jewish Baths, Cathedral. Open from 1. April to 30 September 9 a.m. - 5.30 p.m., Saturday 9 a.m. to 4 p.m., Sunday 1.30 p.m. to 4.30 p.m.

St Goar, Rheinfels Castle. Open April to September 9 a.m. - 6 p.m., October 9 a.m. - 5 p.m.

St Goarshausen, Castle "Katz" (tours not possible), Mouse Castle (tours possible), Loreley.

Trechtingshausen, Rheinstein Castle, with its large weapons collection, Reichenstein Castle, Falkenstein Castle, Castle Hotel.

Wesel, Old water workings on the Lippe; the steam engine plant is a monument to technology, Church of St Willibrord.

Wiesbaden, Old City, Old Town Hall, Palace, Greek Chapel on the Neroberg (nice views), State Theatre, Pump Room.

Worms, Holy Sand, the oldest Jewish cemetery in Europe, Luther Memorial, Cathedral of St Peter and Paul, with the Baroque High Altar by Balthasar Neumann (April to October, 8 a.m. - 6 p.m.).

THE NETHERLANDS

Dortrecht, In the east wing of the erstwhile Augustinian Monastery, is the assembly hall where the Dutch under William of Orange decided to rebel against the ruling Spanish; Dortrecht became the seat of the revolutionary government which was successful in wresting independence.

Rotterdam, Euromast and Space Tower, City Library, to view the works of Erasmus, Waalhaven, Diamond Center.

Utrecht, St Michael's Cathedral, with the highest and most splendid church tower in the Netherlands.

CULTURE PLUS

MUSEUMS

There is an abundance of museums along the length of the Rhine, catering for just about everybody's interests. In most countries they are open from Tuesday to Sunday 10 a.m. - 5 p.m., in France from Wednesday to Monday.

SWITZERLAND

Arbon
Historical Museum of the City.

Arenenberg
Napoleon Museum, Mannenbach-Salenstein.

Augst
Roman Museum (Augusta Raurica, the oldest Roman colony on the Rhine), Giebenacher Straße 17.

Basle
Basle Antique Museum and the Ludwig Collection, St. Albangraben 5.
Architecture Museum, Pfluggässlein 3.
Basle Papermill, Swiss Paper Museum und, Museum of Writing and Printing, St.-Alban-Tal 37.
Basle Industrial Museum, Spalenvorstadt 2.
Basle History Museum, Steinenberg 4.
Musical Instrument Collection, Leonhardstraße 8.
Collection of Coaches and Sleds, Brüglingen.
Jewish Museum of Switzerland, Kornhausgasse 8.
Museum des Films, Blauenstraße 49.
Museum of Contemporary Art, St.-Alban-Rheinweg 60.
Museum of Anthropology and Swiss Folklore Museum, Augustinergasse 2.
Natural History Museum, Augustinergasse 2.

Navigation Museum "Unser Weg zum Meer", Rheinhafen Kleinhüningen.
Swiss Pharmaceutical History Museum, Pfluggässlein 3.
Swiss Fire Brigade Museum, Kornhausgasse 18.
Swiss Sport Museum, Missionsstraße 28.
City and Cathedral Museum, Unterer Rheinweg 26.

Berneck
"Haus zum Torggel" (wine museum).

Buchs
Castle Werdenberg and Rhine Museum.

Chur
Bündner Art Museum, Postplatz.
Bündner Nature Museum, Masaserstraße 31.
Cathedral Museum, Hof 19.
Rätisches Museum (archaeology, history, folklore), Hofstraße 1.

Disentis
Collection in the Benedictine Abbey.

Keuzlingen
Fire Brigade Museum, Konstanzer Straße 39.
Museum of Local History and Culture Haus Rosenegg, Bärenstraße 6.
Dolls Museum Jeannine, Schloßgut Girsberg.
Telephone, Telegraph and Radio Museum, Löwenstraße 12.

Laufenburg
Museum zum Schiff, Fischergasse.

Neuhausen
Fishery Museum, Rosenbergstraße 17.

Rheinfelden
Burgen-Modell-Museum (models of castles), Rindergasse 9.
Fricktaler Museum, Marktgasse.
Oldtimer Museum, in the erstwhile Hotel des Salines.

Rorschach
Museum of Local History and Culture in the corn exchange, Hafenplatz.

Sargans
Museum Sarganserland and Castle Museum, in the castle.

Schaffhausen
All Saints Museum (early history, history, nature), Klostergasse 1
Old Weapons Collection in the Munot Tower.

Splügen
Museum of Natural History and Culture Rheinwald, Oberdorfplatz 65.

Steckborn
Museum of Natural History and Culture am Untersee, Turmhof.
Sewing Machine Museum, Bernina-Näh-maschinen-Fabrik.

Stein am Rhein
Monastery Museum St.Georgen.
Dolls Museum, Schwarzhorngasse 136.

Trun
Oberländer Talmuseum - Museum Sur-silvan.

Zillis
Schamser Talmuseum, near the church.

LIECHTENSTEIN

Schaan
Schaaner Village Museum, Landstraße 19.

Triesenberg
Walser Museum of Natural History and Culture, in the centre of the village.

Vaduz
Museum of Stamps, Städtle 17.
Liechtenstein National Art Collection, (permanent exhibition of Peter Paul Rubens), Städtle 37.
Liechtenstein Provincial Museum, Städtle 43.

AUSTRIA

Bregenz
Vorarlberg Country Museum, Kornmarkt 1,
Military Museum, in the Martins Tower.

Hard
Museum of Natural History and Culture, Mittelweiherburg.

Hohenems
Hohenems Palace (where the Nibelungen saga was found).

Open air Museum Sägemühle (sawmill).

Lustenau
Embroidery Museum, Pontenstraße 20.

FRANCE

Colmar
Musée Bartholdi, 30, Rue des Marchands.
Musée d'Unterlinden (Grünewald's Isen-heimer Altar), 1, Place d'Unterlinden.
Musée d'Histoire Naturelle, 11, Rue Turenne.

Huningue
Musée d'Histoire Locale, Rue des Boul-angers.

Marckolsheim, Musée du Memorial de la Ligne Maginot, Route du Rhin.

Mulhouse
Musée de l'Impression sur Etoffes, 3, Rue des Bonnes-Gens.
Musée de la Chapelle Saint-Jean, Grand-Rue.
Musée des Beaux-Arts, 4, Place Guil-laume.
Musée du Sapeur-Pompier (fire brigade), 2, Rue Alfred Glehn.
Musée Francais du Chemin de Fer (rail-ways), 2, Rue Alfred de Glehn.
Musée Historique, Hotel de Ville, Place de la Réunion.
Musée Minéralogique, 3, Rue Alfred Werner.
Musée National de l'automobile, 192, Avenue de Colmar.

Neuf-Brisach
Musée Vauban, 7, Place de la Porte de Belfort.

Sessenheim
Memorial Goethe.

Strasbourg
Cabinet des Estampes (stamp collection), 5, Place du Château.
Collection de l'Institut d'Egyptologie de L'Université, Palais de L'Université.
Musée Alsacien, 23, Quai Saint-Nicolas.
Musée Archéologique, Château de Rohan, 2, Place du Château.
Musée d'Art Moderne, Ancienne Douane,

1, Rue du Vieux-Marché-aux-Poissons.
Musée de Moulages, Université de Strasbourg.
Musée de L'Oeuvre Notre-Dame, 3, Place du Château.
Musée des Arts Décoratifs, Château de Rohan, 2, Place du Château.
Musée des Beaux-Arts, Château de Rohan, 2, Place du Château.
Musée Historique, Grand Boucherie, 3, Rue de la Grande-Boucherie.
Musée Zoologique de L'Université et de la Ville, 29, Boulevard de la Victoire.

FEDERAL REPUBLIC OF GERMANY

Allensbach
Museum of Natural History and Culture, Rathausplatz.

Andernach
Town Museum, Haus von der Leyen, Hochstraße 97.

Bad Breisig
Dolls Museum, Koblenzer Straße 31.

Bad Honnef
Bundeskanzler-Adenauer-Haus, Konrad-Adenauer-Straße 80, Rhöndorf.

Bad Säckingen
Hochrheinmuseum (Museum of the High Rhine), in the castle.
Mineral Museum, Villa Berberich, Parkstraße 1, Bad Säckingen
Museum of Natural History and Culture (clock und trumpet collection) in the castle.

Bendorf
Municipal Museum Bendorf (iron objects), Kirchplatz.
Turmuhren-Museum (clocks), in Castle Sayn.

Bingen
Museum of Natural History and Culture, Burg Klopp.

Bodman
Bodman-Museum (prehistorical), Town hall.

Bonn
Akademisches Kunstmuseum (antique sculptures), Am Hofgarten 21.

Ernst-Moritz-Arndt-Haus (dedicated to the publisher and patriot), Adenauerallee 79.
Beethoven-Haus, Bonngasse 20.
Frauen-Museum (women's museum), Im Krausfeld 10.
Museum of Natural History and Culture Beuel, Steinerstraße 36.
Mineralogical-Petrological Museum, Poppeldorfer Castle, Meckenheimer Allee 171.
Alexander König Museum (animals and their world), Adenauerallee 150-164).
Stamps Exhibition of the German Post Office, Heinrich-von-Stephan-Straße 1.
Rhenish Provincial Museum (history and art), Colmantstraße 14-16.
Schumann Haus (dedicated to the composer), Sebstianstraße 182.
Municipal Art Museum, Rathausgasse 7.

Boppard
Municipal Museum Boppard (pre- and early history, furniture collection), Kurtrierische Burg.

Braubach
Castle Museum Marksburg and German Castles Association, Marksburg.

Breisach
Breisgau-Museum of pre- and early history, Münsterbergstraße 21.

Brühl
Max-Ernst-Kabinett (dedicated to the surrealist), Bahnhofstraße 21, Castle Augustusburg, Castle Falkenlust.

Cleves
Mill Museum, Donsbrüggen.
City Museum Haus Koekkoek (Lower Rhine art), Kavariner Straße 33.

Cologne
Agfa-Foto-Historama, History of Photography Collection, Bischofsgartenstraße 1.
Cutlery Museum Bodo Glaub, Burgmauer 68.
Archiepiscopal Diocese Museum, Roncalliplatz 2.
Herbig-Haarhaus-Lackmuseum (East Asian and European lacquerwork), Vitalisstraße 198-226.
Cologne City Museum, Zeughausstraße 1-3.
Museum of East Asian Art, Universitätsstraße 100.

Museum Ludwig (art from 1900 to the present day), Bischofsgartenstraße 1.
Rautenstrauch-Joest-Museum (culture and art of non-European peoples), Ubier-Ring 45.
Roman-Germanic Museum, Roncalliplatz 4.
Schnütgen-Museum (church art), Cäcilienstraße 29.
Theatre Museum of Cologne University, Castle Wahn.
Wallraf-Richartz-Museum (painting from 1300 to 1900, Sculpture from 1800 to 1900), Bischofsgartenstraße 1
Customs Museum, Neuköllner Straße 1.

Dinslaken
Museum of Local History and Culture, Brückstraße 31.

Dormagen
District Museum Zons (Art Nouveau, temporary exhibitions), Burg Friedestrom, Schloßstraße 1, Zons.
Missions Museum, Knechtsteden Abbey.

Düsseldorf
Dumont-Lindemann-Archives, Theatre Museum of the State capital Düsseldorf, Jägerhofstraße 1.
Goethe Museum
Heinrich-Heine-Institut, Bilker Straße 12-14.
Hetjens Museum, German Ceramics Museum, Schulstraße 4.
Düsseldorf Art Museum, Ehrenhof 5.
North Rhine Westphalia Art Collection, Grabbeplatz 5.
State Museum of People and Science (society and economy), Ehrenhof 2.
Löbbecke Museum und Aqua Zoo, Kaiserswerther Straße 380 (in the *Nordpark*).
Memorial to the Victims of National Socialism, Mühlenstraße 29
Museum of Natural History and Culture Benrath, Benrather Schloßallee 104.
Navigation Museum in the Castle Tower.
City Museum, Bäckerstraße 7-9.
City Arts Centre, Grabbeplatz 4.

Duisburg
Wilhelm-Lehmbruck-Museum (Complete works of the sculptor, modern art), Friedrich-Wilhelm-Straße 40.
Museum of German Inland Shipping, with the old paddle steamers "Oscar Huber" the dredger "Minden", Dammstraße 11, Ruhrort.

Museum of the Lower Rhine, Friedrich-Wilhelm-Straße 64.

Eltville
Gutenberg Memorial (dedicated to the inventor of printing), Burgstraße 1.
Museum of Natural History and Culture, Burgstraße 1.
Kloster Eberbach, Schwalbacher Straße 56-62.

Emmerich
Rheinmuseum (Navigation Museum), Martinikirchgang 2.

Freiburg im Breisgau
Augustiner Museum (art from the Middle Ages to the present day), Salzstraße 32.
Kleines Stuckmuseum, Liebigstraße 11.
Natural History Museum, Gerberau 32.
Museum of Modern Art, Marienstraße 10 a.
Museum of Local History, Wenzingerhaus, Zum schönen Eck.
Museum of pre- and early History, Colombischlößle, Rotteckring 5.
Anthropology Museum, Gerberau 32.
Chamber of Tin Figures, Schwabentor.

Friedrichshafen
Municipal Lake Constance Museum (art collection from Lake Constance from the Middle Ages to the present day).
Zeppelin Wing (history of airships), Adenauerplatz 1.

Gernsheim
Museum of Natural History and Culture, Schöfferplatz.

Hagnau
Dolls and Toys Museum, Neugartenstraße 20.

Heidelberg
Antique Museum, Marstallhof 4.
Bonsai-Museum, Mannheimer Straße 401.
German Apothecary Museum, Ottheinrichsbau.
Heidelberg Castle.
Elector of the Palatinate Museum (art from the Middle Ages to the present day), Hauptstraße 97.
Museum of Geology, Im Neuenheimer Feld 234.
Museum of Sacred Art and Liturgy, Jesuit Church, Richard-Hauser-Platz.

Textile Museum Max Berk, Brahmsstraße 8.
Anthropology Museum, Hauptstraße 235.
Zoological Museum, Im Neuenheimer Feld 230.

Ingelheim
History Museum, Rathausplatz.

Kamp-Bornhofen
Raft and Ship Museum, Town Hall.

Karlsruhe
Provincial Museum of Baden, Palace.
Open Air Museum (old windmills), An der Pfinz.
Folklore Collection, Erbprinzenstraße 13.
Upper Rhine Poetry Museum, Röntgenstraße 6, Durlach.
National Art Gallery, Hans-Thoma-Straße 2-6.
City Gallery in the Prinz-Max-Palais, Karlstraße 10.
Karlsruhe Transport Museum, Werderstraße 63.

Kaub
Blücher Museum (Blücher's Headquarters 1813/1814), Metzgergasse 6.

Kehl
Hanauer Museum, Friedhofstraße 5.

Koblenz
Beethoven Memorial (in his mother's birthplace), Warmbachstraße 204.
Haus Metternich (modern art), Münzplatz.
Provincial Museum of Koblenz, Ehrenbreitstein Citadel.
Middle Rhine Museum, Altes Kaufhaus, Florinsmarkt 15.
Castle Museum in Castle Stolzenfels.

Königswinter
Nibelungen Hall (with dragon's cave and reptile zoo), Drachenfelsstraße 107-111.
Siebengebirge (Seven Hills) Museum, Kellerstraße 16.

Konstanz
Lake Constance Nature Museum, Katzgasse 5.
Hus-Museum (dedicated to the Reformer Jan Hus, who was burned here as a heretic), Hussenstraße 64.

Rosgartenmuseum (art and culture of the Lake Constance area), Rosgartenstraße 5.
City Wessenberg Gallery, Wessenbergstraße 41.

Krefeld
German Textiles Museum, Andreasmarkt 8.
Kaiser-Wilhelm-Museum (art and culture from Gothic to present day), Karlsplatz 35.
Museum Burg Linn (hunting lodge).
Lower Rhine Museum, Albert-Steeger-Straße 19 a.
Museum Haus Lange, Museum Haus Esters (temporary exhibitions), Wilhelmshofallee 31-97.

Lahnstein
Museum in the Witches Tower (history), Salhofplatz.

Langenargen
Museum Langenargen (1200 years of art), Marktplatz 20.

Leverkusen
City Museum, Castle Morsbroich, Gustav-Heinemann-Straße 80.

Lindau
Peace Museum, Lindenhofweg 25, Schachen.
City Art Collection in Haus zum Cavazzen, Marktplatz.

Linz
Musica Mechanica (Music Museum), Burgplatz 4.

Ludwigshafen
City museum, Town Hall.
Wilhelm-Hack-Museum and City Art Collections, Berliner Straße 23.
Schillerhaus, Schillerstraße 6, Oggenheim.

Mainz
Episcopal Cathedral and Diocese Museum, Domstraße 3.
Gutenberg Museum (history and art of printing), Liebfrauenplatz 5.
Provincial Museum (paintings, old objects), Große Bleiche 49-51.
Natural History Museum, Mitternacht/Reichklarastraße.
Roman Germanic Central Museum, Elector's Palace.

Mannheim
Provincial Museum for Technology and Labour, Friedensplatz.
Museums Ship Mannheim.
Museum of Art and Local History (archaeology, ethnology and natural history), Zeughaus, C5.
City Art Gallery Mannheim, Moltkestraße 9.

Meersburg
Old Castle Meersburg with Castle Museum.
German Newspaper Museum, Schloßplatz 15.
Dornier Museum (aeroplanes), in the New Castle.
Museum of Natural History and Culture, New Castle.
Viticulture Museum, Vorburggasse.

Moers
Ducal Museum in the Castle, Kastell 9.
Gallery "Peschkenhaus", Meerstraße 1.

Neuss
Clemens-Sels-Museum (art and history), Am Obertor.

Neuwied
Hansa-Lloyd-Goliath Automobile Museum, Hermannstraße 49.
District Museum Neuwied (history, art), Raiffeisenplatz.
Museum Monrepos (Museum for the history of the Ice Ages), Neuwied 13.

Niederheimbach
Castle Sooneck (art, history, weapons).

Nierstein
Paleontological Museum, Town Hall.
Shipping Museum, Town Hall.

Oberwesel
Museum of Natural History and Culture, Town Hall.

Oestrich-Winkel
Brentanohaus (historical rooms, Goethe memorial), Am Lindenplatz 2.

Oppenheim
German Viticulture Museum, Wormser Straße 49.

Philippsburg
Fortress und Weapon History Museum, Schlachthausstraße 2.
Museum of Natural History and Culture, Hieronymus-Nopp-Straße.

Radolfzell
City Museum, Tegginger Straße 16.

Reichenau
Museum of Natural History and Culture, Ergat 1.
Treasury of the Minster, Burgstraße 1.

Remagen
Peace Museum The Bridge of Remagen, Rhine bank.
Gallerie Rolandshof with Sculpture Park.
Roman Museum, Kirchstraße.
Künstlerbahnhof (artist's station) Rolandseck (Hans-Arp-collection).

Rheinbach
Glass Museum, Vor dem Voigtstor 23.

Rüdesheim
Ferdinand Freiligrath Museum (dedicated to the poet), Hotel Krone, Assmannshausen.
Siegfrieds Mechanical Music Box, Oberstraße.
Oldtimer Museum "Man and his Car", Rheinallee 7 und 8, Assmannshausen.
Wine Museum Brömserburg, Rheinstraße 2.

Salem
Baden Marches Museum, Castle.
Fire Brigade Museum, Castle.

St. Goar
Local Historical Collection Castle Rheinfels, Rhineland Palatinate Doll, Teddy Bear und Toy Museum "Loreley", Sonnengasse 8.

Schwetzingen
Castle, Theatre and park.

Speyer
Cathedral and Diocese Museum, Domplatz 11.
History Museum the Palatinate (with Wine Museum), Domplatz.

Trechtingshausen
Castle Reichenstein (history and industry).

Überlingen
Photography Museum, Münsterstraße 27.
Weapons Museum, Historisches Zeughaus, Seepromenade.
Town Museum, Krummebergstraße 30.

Waldshut-Tiengen
Museum of Natural History and Culture, Alte Metzig, Kaiserstraße, Waldshut.

Wasserburg
"Museum im Malhaus" (dedicated to women persecuted as witches, history, fruit cultivation).

Weil
Museum of Natural History and Culture, Lindenplatz.

Weißenthurm
Eulenturm-Museum (geology, industry, history), Turmhof.

Wesel
Local History Museum Bislich, Dorfstraße, City Museum.

Wiesbaden
Dotzheimer Museum, Römergasse, Dotzheim.
Women's Museum, Nerostraße 16.
Provincial Museum of Wiesbaden (art from the Middle Ages to the present day, old objects, natural sciences), Friedrich-Ebert-Allee 2.

Worms
Judaica Museum, Raschi-Haus, Hintere Judengasse 6.
Museum of the City of Worms, Andreasstift, Weckerlingplatz.
Stiftung Kunsthaus Heylshof (art and handicrafts), Stephansgasse 9.

Xanten
Archaeological Park und Regional Museum Xanten, Trajanstraße 4, Kurfürstenstraße 7-9.
Cathedral Museum.

THE NETHERLANDS

Arnhem
Elektrum Museum (electronics), Klingelbeekseweg 45.
Local Museum of Archaeology, Art and Handicrafts, Utrechtseweg 87.
Museum Bronbeek (colonial history), Velperweg 147.
Museum Grenadiers und Jagers (Museum of the Grenadier Guards), Onder de Linden 101.
Nederlands Openluchtmuseum (Dutch open air museum), Schelmseweg 89.
De Watermolen (water mills, culture and nature), Zijpendaalseweg 24 a.

Bennekom
Jijk- en Luistermuseum (mechanical musical instruments), Kerkstraat 1.

Berg en Dal
Africa Museum (open air museum), Postweg 6.

Dordrecht
Dordrechts Museum (art), Museumstraat 40.
Museum Simon van Gijn (art, handicrafts and toys), Nieuwe Haven 29.

Grossbeek
Befreiungsmuseum 1944 (Liberation museum), Wylerbaan 4.

Heilig Land Stichting
Heilig Land Stichting (biblical open air museum), Profetenlaan 2.

Nijmegen
Nijmegen Museum Commanderie von Sint-Jan (history, modern art), Franse Plaats 3.
Velorama (bicycle museum), Franse Plaats 3.

Oosterbeek
Airborne Museum Hartenstein (Battle of Arnhem, 1944), Utrechtseweg 232.

Otterlo
Rijksmuseum Kröller-Müller (Vincent van Gogh, art of the 19th and 20th centuries), Houtkampweg 6.

Rhenen
Streekmuseum Het Rondeel (history), Kerkstraat 1.

Rotterdam
History Museum De Dubbelde Palmboom, Voorhaven 12.
History Museum Schielandshuis, Korte Hoogstraat 31.
Marine Infantry Museum, Maaskade 119.

Maritime Museum Prins Hendrik, Leuvehaven 1.
Museum Boymans-van Beuningen (art from the Middle Ages to the present day), Mathenesserlaan 18-20.
Museum Hendrik Chabot (dedicated to the artist), Berglustlaan 12.
Anthropology Museum, Willemskade 25.
Museum Stoomdepot (steam engines and locomotives), Giessenweg 82.
Nature Museum, Villa Dijkzigt, Westzeedik 345.
Openbaar Vervoer Museum (museum of public transport), Schinkelstraat 172.
Stichting Openlucht Binnenvaartmuseum (open air museum of sailing vessels), Koningsdam 1.
Toy-Toy Museum (toys), Groene Wetering 41.

Utrecht
Anatomical Museum, Janskerkhof 3 a.
Central Museum (history, art, culture), Agnietenstraat 1.
Hedendaagse Art (contemporary art), Achter de Dom 12-14.
Koffie- en Theekabinet en Pijpenkamer van Douwe Egberts (coffee, tea and tobacco), Keulsekade 143.
Historical Costume Museum, Loeff Berchmakerstraat 50.
Kruideniersmuseum Erven Betje Boerhave (colonial goods), Hoogt 6.
Museum Rijks Munt (coin museum), Leidseweg 90.
National Museum van Speelklok tot Pierement (mechanical musical instruments), Buurkerkhof 10.
Nederlands Spoorswegmueseum (railway museum in a former station), Johan van Oldenbarneweltlaan 6.
Provincial Museum (prehistoric, Roman and Middle Ages art), Agnietenstraat 1.
Rijksmuseum het Catharijneconvent (Christian culture), Nieuwe Gracht 63.
University Museum, Biltstraat 166.
Zoological Museum, Plompetorengracht 9.

Wageningen
Museum of Agricultural Machinery, Droevendaalsesteeg 50.

Wijk bij Duurstede
Kantonaal en Stedelijk Museum (history), Volderstraat 15.

Here is a list of some of the main theatres and opera houses to be found along the Rhine:

SWITZERLAND

Basle
Goethe Stage, Dornach. Tel: (061) 72 40 41.
Theatre and Comedy, Theaterstraße 7. Tel: (061) 22 11 33.

AUSTRIA

Bregenz
Festival Theatre and lakeshore stage, Platz der Wiener Symphoniker. Tel: (05574) 25 969.
Theatre for Vorarlberg, Kornmarktplatz. Tel: (05574) 22 870.

FEDERAL REPUBLIC OF GERMANY

Bonn
Bonnaoptikum, political satire cabaret, Graurheindorfer Straße 23. Tel: (0228) 35 33 35.
Opera House, Am Boeselagerhof 1. Tel: (0228) 72 83 87.
Theatre, Am Michaelshof 9, (0228) 82 080.

Cologne
Opera House, Offenbachplatz. Tel: (0221) 22 18 400.
Theatre, Offenbachplatz. Tel: (0221) 22 18 400.
Theatre Millowitsch, Aachener Straße 5. Tel: (0221) 25 17 47.

Dinslaken
Castle Theatre, Althoffstraße. Tel: (02134) 66 406.
Civic Hall, Althoffstraße 2. Tel: (02134) 59 44.

Düsseldorf
Das Kom(m)ödchen, cabaret, Kunsthalle, Hunsrückenstraße. Tel: (0211) 32 54 28.
German Opera on the Rhine, Heinrich-Heine-Allee 16 a. Tel: (0211) 13 39 49.
Düsseldorf Theatre, Gustav-Gründgens-Platz 1. Tel: (0211) 36 30 11.
Philipshalle, Siegburger Straße 15. Tel: (0211) 89 92 679.

Duisburg
City Theatre. Tel: (0203) 39 041.

Mercator-Halle, König-Heinrich-Platz. Tel: (0203) 33 90 26.
Rheinhausen-Halle, Beethovenstraße 20, Rheinhausen. Tel: (02135) 71 58.
Rhein-Ruhr-Halle, Walter-Rathenau-Straße 1 a. Tel: (0203) 54 337.

Emmerich
City Theatre, Grollscher Weg. Tel: (02822) 70 978.

Freiburg
Freiburg Theatre, Bertoldstraße 46. Tel: (0761) 34 874.

Heidelberg
Theatre. Tel: (06221) 20 519.

Karlsruhe
Baden Provincial Theatre, Baumeisterstraße 11. Tel: (0721) 60 202.

Koblenz
Rhenish Philharmonic, Elsterhofstraße. Tel: (0261) 39 00 50.
City Theatre, Deinhardplatz. Tel: (0261) 34 629.

Konstanz
City Theatre, Konzilstraße 11. Tel: (07531) 20 07 50.
South-west German Philharmonic, Oberer Konzilsaal. Tel: (07531) 63 031.

Krefeld
City Theatre, Theaterplatz 3. Tel: (02151) 16 87.

Ludwigshafen
Pfalzbau, Berliner Straße 30. Tel: (0621) 69 40 01.

Mainz
Theatre of the State Capital, Gutenbergplatz. Tel: (06131) 12 33 65/6.
Mainz Forum Theatre and Cabaret, Münsterstraße 5. Tel: (06131) 23 21 21.

Mannheim
National Theatre. Tel: (06121) 24 844.

Neuwied
Provincial Stage Rhineland Palatinate. Tel: (02631) 22 288.

Castle Theatre, Schloßstraße 1, (02631) 78 63 85.

Wiesbaden
Hessen Provincial Theatre, Wilhelmstraße. Tel: 806121) 13 23 25.
Cabaret, Karlstraße 15. Tel: (06121) 30 99 91.
Rhein-Main-Halle, Friedrich-Ebert-Allee/ Rheinstraße. Tel: (06121) 14 40.

THE NETHERLANDS

Amsterdam
Stopera, Music Theatre, Waterlooplein, Tickets and Programme from advanced booking office, Stationsplein 10.

FESTIVAL CALENDAR

Festivals have been celebrated since time immemorial on both banks of the Rhine. Spring festivals and summer festivals, old city festivals and street festivals, wine- and vintner festivals, fairs and marksmen's festivals, theatre and music festivals, carnival fairs and parades - the people who live on the Rhine always find an excuse for merriment. We have listed up some of the fairs and festivals; the local tourist offices (see addresses on page 319) will be happy to provide you with more details of events.

SWITZERLAND

Basle, Basle Fastnacht (the Monday following Shrove Tuesday); Reformation Festival and Fair in September.
Schaffhausen, Schaffhauser Fastnacht (end of January/beginning of February); International Bach Festival (every three years in the first week of spring); International Street Musician Meeting (every two years in the early summer); Schaffhauser Music Week (Rock and Pop in December).

AUSTRIA

Bregenz, International Music and Theatre Festival (March); Bregenz Spring Festival (ballet, opera and concerts in May); Bregenz Festival (opera, concerts held in July and August).
Hohenems, Schubert Music Festival (June).

FRANCE

Colmar, Fastnacht (January); Folklore Festival (June); Alsace Wine Fair (August); Sauerkraut Festival (September).

Mulhouse, Fastnacht (January); Summer Festival (June); October Festival.

Strasbourg, "Son et Lumière" in front of the Cathedral (April to October); Music Festival (June); Dance Festival (July); Alsace Folklore in the courtyard of Rohan Castle (June to August); Musica (contemporary music, September).

FEDERAL REPUBLIC OF GERMANY

Andernach, Festival of 1000 Lamps (September).

Assmannshausen, Red Wine Festival (Ascension).

Bad Breisig, Summer Nights Festival (July); Onion Market (September).

Bad Hönningen, Summer Nights Festival (July).

Bingen, Rochus Festival (3rd weekend in August).

Bingen-Rüdesheim, Firework display "the Rhine in Flames" (1st Saturday in July).

Bonn, International Beethoven Festival (every three years, 1992, 1995 etc.).

Boppard, Rhine Bank Festival (July).

Braubach, Rose Festival (July).

Brühl, Concerts in Castle Augustusburg (further information: Kölner Kammerorchester e.V, Schloßstr. 2, D-5040 Brühl Tel: (02232) 43 902/43 21 83.

Cologne, Carnival (February/March).

Dattenberg, Castle Festival (July).

Dormagen-Zons, Medieval Jousting etc. before the city walls of Zons (June to September)

Freiburg, International Marquis Music Festival, Mundenhof (July); Freiburg Wine Festival on the Cathedral square (June); Theatre Festival (June/July).

Heidelberg, Castle Festival (July to August); Firework display (beginning of September).

Ingelheim, International Festival (Art and Culture on the Main River).

Koblenz-Braubach, Firework display (2nd weekend in August).

Mühlheim, Rhine Procession (June).

Konstanz, Lake Festival with firework display (July/August); Lake Constance Festival (May/June).

Krefeld, Flax Market at Castle Linn (Whitsuntide); Serenade in the great hall of Castle Linn (further information: Kultur der Stadt Krefeld, Von-der-Leyden-Platz, Rathaus, D-4150 Krefeld. Tel: (02151) 86 25 55/6.

Lindau, Lake Constance Festival (May/June).

Mainz, Mainz Fastnacht (1 January until Ash Wednesday); Open Air Festival on the Citadel (Music and cabaret, Whitsuntide); Johannisnacht - in honour of the inventor of printing Johannes Gutenberg (July); Mainz Wine Market (August/September).

Mannheim, International Organ Festival and May Market (May); cultural events in summer; International Film Week (autumn).

Meersburg, International Castle Concerts (June).

Nierstein, The Nierstein Vintner Festival (1st weekend in August); Day of the Open Wine Cellar (3rd weekend in September).

Oberwesel, Nights of 1000 Lights (September).

Radolfzell, The Lord of Radolfzell Festival - procession and festival in honour of the town's patron (3rd Sunday in July); The Mooser Regatta with decorated boats on the lake (on the following Monday).

Remagen, Promenade Festival (May); Wine Festival (September).

Speyer, Brezel Festival (2nd weekend in July); Rhine Bank Festival (August)

St. Goarshausen-St. Goar, Firework display (3rd weekend in September).

Wiesbaden, International May Performances, guest performances in the Hessen State Theatre, International Riding Tournament in the Park of Bieberich House (Whitsuntide); Wine Festival (August); Vintner Festival (autumn).

Worms, *Backfischfest*, the largest wine festival and fair on the Rhine (last weekend in August).

THE NETHERLANDS

In many places National Windmill Day (May) and the Holland Festival (June).

NIGHTLIFE

Every major city has its night club district, with bars, cabaret, variety shows, discos. Most hotels should be able to give you detailed information on these kinds of activities.

CASINOS

For those who can't resist, there are a number of Casinos on, or within easy reach of, the Rhine.

AUSTRIA

Bregenz, casino, Platz der Wiener Symphoniker.

FEDERAL REPUBLIC OF GERMANY

Lindau, Lindau casino.
Karlsruhe, The German casino capital is not far away in **Baden Baden.**
Mannheim/Ludwigshafen, Casino in **Bad Dürkheim.**
Wiesbaden, Casino in the Pump House.
Koblenz, Casino in **Bad Ems.**

THE NETHERLANDS

Amsterdam, Casino.
Rotterdam, Casino, Weena 10.

SHOPPING

WHAT TO BUY

You can buy tourist *kitsch* in countless shops along the Rhine. Here is a selection of the kinds of items it is worth buying for taking home in the different countries of the Rhine.

SWITZERLAND

Wine; cheese; spirits; chocolate; air-dried meat (*Bündnerfleisch*), Handicrafts; lace and embroidery from St Gallen; clocks and watches.

LIECHTENSTEIN

Stamps; wines; pottery; carvings out of roots (*Wurzelschnitzereiarbeiten*).

AUSTRIA

Wine; handicrafts; embroidery; silver jewellery.

FRANCE

Wine; cheese; liver and meat paté; pastries; fruit brandies; ceramics from Alsace; perfume.

FEDERAL REPUBLIC OF GERMANY

Wine and wine glasses and goblets (*Römer*), earthenware and glass beer mugs; Cuckoo Clocks from the Black Forest area.

THE NETHERLANDS

Flower bulbs (tulips; daffodils etc.). However, it is only possible to export these when they are cleared by a "certificate of health", and therefore it is probably less complicated to order through a merchant. Wooden clogs; Delft porcelain; silver jewellery; diamonds.

In all of the larger cities on or near the Rhine you can shop in the quaint "Old Cities" or in more modern pedestrian precincts and shopping malls. In the smaller places, if there are large shopping centres, they tend to be located outside town, where there used to be nothing but meadows.

Here are some of the best-known shopping centres:

FEDERAL REPUBLIC OF GERMANY

Cologne, Hohestraße/Schildergasse.
Düsseldorf, The "Kö", the Königsallee, is one of the most famous shopping streets in the world. It is also one of the most expensive!

THE NETHERLANDS

Rotterdam, Beursplein.
Lijnbaan, Binnenwegplein.
Utrecht, Hoog Catharijne, one of the largest shopping centres in Europe with a total area of 250,000 square metres. There is a large choice of all kinds of goods, from all corners of the world.

SPORTS

In just about every place on the Rhine there are modern facilities for swimming, tennis and generally keeping fit.

Winter ports are possible in the Alps, in the Black Forest, the Vosges and the German Highlands (Rhenish Uplands), to the left and to the right of the river. Fishing is only allowed with a permit, which can be obtained from the local tourist association. However, the increasing pollution of the Rhine has led to a drastic reduction in the numbers of fish, although this situation is not so serious along the stretches above Basle.

On certain stretches of the Rhine, and on Lake Constance, windsurfing and waterskiing are possible. In addition, one can hire motorboats and sailing boats. In Holland, all craft capable of going faster than 16 km/h need to be registered. Insurance is also necessary. Post offices handle the registration bureaucracy. A more peaceful way of seeing the Rhine is by canoe or kajak.

The German Canoe Club or the ADAC, the German Automobile Association, can provide further details as well as the necessary map material.

Golf courses are located in most of the large cities and tourist centres, although golf on the continent is not as widespread as it is in England or America.

FEDERAL REPUBLIC OF GERMANY

D-5300 Bonn
Segel- und Motorbootschule (sailing school), Freizeitpark Rheinaue.
Privat Segelflughafen (gliding club).

D-5205 St. Augustin 2
Bonner Reit- und Fahrverein (riding club, Im Erlengrund 15.
International Riding Club, Domhofstraße 25.

D-4100 Duisburg
Wedau-Sportpark, south of the city - rowing, ice-skating, waterskiing and swimming.

D-7800 Freiburg im Breisgau
Ballooning, hanggliding, gliding.

D-5400 Koblenz
Fitness and sport at the **recreation park** on the B9.

D-6500 Mainz
Ice-skating rink, Dr.-Martin-Luther-King-Weg.

D-6800 Mannheim
Badisch-Pfälzischer-Flugsportverein (flying club), Neuostheim Airport.

D-7760 Radolfzell
Drachenflugschule (hanggliding school) Stanko Petek, Mägdebergstraße 3.
Sailing school at Haus Bodenseereiter.

D-6200 Wiesbaden
Kaiser-Friedrich-Bad (public baths), a sightseeing attraction from 1910, Langgasse 38-40.
Henkell-Kunsteislaufbahn (ice -skating rink), Hollerborn/Nixenstraße.

SPECTATOR SPORTS

It is possible to watch sporting events throughout the year: skiing in the mountains; water sports on the river and Lake Constance; golf competitions and tennis tournaments; hanggliding contests. The national sport of most countries along the Rhine, notably Germany, is football. Some of the best-known stadiums and clubs of the Federal League are to be found along the Rhine, for example in Düsseldorf, Cologne and Mannheim. There are also a host of local football teams playing in regional leagues.

FEDERAL REPUBLIC OF GERMANY

D-4000 Düsseldorf
Rennbahn Grafenberg (picturesque racecourse), Wagnerstraße 26
Rheinstadion (the home of Fortuna Düsseldorf Football Club).
Eisstadion (The home of the DEG, Düsseldorf's legendary ice-hockey club).

D-5000 Cologne
Pferderennbahn (racecourse), Scheibenstraße, Weidenpesch.
Stadion Müngersdorf (home of Cologne Football Club), Aachener Straße.

D-4150 Krefeld
Municipal ice-skating rinks, Rheinlandhalle, Westparkstraße 126, and Werner-Rittenberger-Halle, Westparkstraße 120.
Grotenburg Stadion, Tiergartenstraße 165.
Galopp-Rennbahn im Stadtwald (racecourse).

D-6800 Mannheim
Eisstadion Mannheim, Bismarckstraße.

PHOTOGRAPHY

In the countries of the Rhine you can photograph everything except military installations. Film material is available in every town and city. Even if they are only small villages, the tourist centres are also not wanting in this regard. In the larger towns there are 24-hour developing services, or sometimes faster.

LANGUAGE

English and German are the predominant means of communication in most of the tourist centres along the Rhine.

SWITZERLAND

Near the source of the Rhine, where the Vorderrhein and Hinterrhein flow, is the canton of Grisons (Graubünden) where Rhaeto Romanisch is spoken in a number of different dialects. Further to the North *Schwyzerdütsch* is the common tongue spoken. This is a Swiss dialect of German which is very difficult or even impossible for Germans to understand. The written language is German.

LIECHTENSTEIN AND AUSTRIA

Here the official language is German, though again this is spoken in different dialects.

FEDERAL REPUBLIC OF GERMANY

Again, a great variety of dialects are spoken along the Rhine. English is taught as a compulsory language at school, and many German people can speak the language quite well. Communication should not be a problem.

FRANCE

Although the official language of the country is French, the people of Alsace speak *Elsässerditsch*. As with *Schwyzerdütsch*, this is a Germanic language, although it still sounds like a totally foreign language to German native speakers. The amount of French people who can or will speak English in France is much less than in Germany. Communication without a basic knowledge of French might be a problem.

THE NETHERLANDS

Dutch is spoken in the Netherlands, though many natives can speak at least two foreign languages - English and German and often French as well. This is the country where as an English native speaker one will have the least communication problems.

USEFUL ADDRESSES

TOURIST INFORMATION

(Fremdenverkehrsamt, Verkehrsamt, Verkehrsbüro, Verkehrsverein)

SWITZERLAND

CH-4001 Basle
Verkehrsbüro Basel, Blumenrain 2, Schifflände. Tel: (061) 25 50 50.

CH-4310 Rheinfelden
Verkehrsbüro, Marktgasse 61. Tel: (061) 87 55 20.

CH-8201 Schaffhausen
Tourist Information, Vorstadt 2. Tel: (053) 25 51 41.

CH-8260 Stein am Rhein
Verkehrsbüro, Oberstadt. Tel: (854) 41 28 35.

CH-8027 Zürich
Niederländisches Büro für Tourismus (NBT), Talstraße 70. Tel: (01)21 19 482.
Schweizerische Verkehrszentrale, Bellariastraße 38. Tel: (01) 20 23 737.

LIECHTENSTEIN

FL-9497 Malbun
Verkehrsbüro. Tel: (075) 26 577.

FL-9490 Vaduz
Fremdenverkehrszentrale, Postfach 139. Tel: (075) 21 443.

AUSTRIA

A-6900 Bregenz
Fremdenverkehrsamt der Landeshauptstadt Bregenz
Fremdenverkehrsverband Bodensee/Rheintal, Inselstraße 15. Tel: (05574) 23 391.

A-1010 Vienna
Deutsche Zentrale für Tourismus e.V, Schubertring 12. Tel: (0222) 53 27 92.
Niederländsiches Büro für Tourismus (NBT), c/o KLM, Kärntner Straße 12. Tel: (0222) 52 35 25.

FRANCE

F-67082 Strasbourg
Office du Tourisme de Strabourg et de sa région, Palais des Congrès. Tel: 88 32 57 07.

F-75002 Paris
Office National Allemand du Tourisme, 4, Place de l'Opéra. Tel: (01) 40 20 01 88.

FEDERAL REPUBLIC OF GERMANY

Deutsche Zentrale für Tourismus e.V, Beethovenstraße 60, D-6000 Frankfurt/Main 1. Tel: (069) 75 720.

D-6220 Assmannshausen (Rüdesheim-Assmannshausen)
Verkehrsverein. Tel: (06722) 22 25.

D-6533 Bacharach
Verkehrsamt. Tel: (06743) 12 97.

D-5484 Bad Breisig
Verkehrsamt, Albert-Mertes-Straße 11. Tel: (02633) 92 55.

D-5462 Bad Hönningen
Verkehrsamt, Neustraße 2 a. Tel: (02635) 22 73.

D-5340 Bad Honnef
Verkehrsamt-Kurverwaltung, Hauptstraße. Tel: (02224) 18 41 70.

D-7880 Bad Säckingen
Kurverwaltung GmbH, Waldshuter Straße 20. Tel: (07761) 51 316.

D-5407 Bad Salzig
Verkehrsamt Boppard, - Außenstelle Bad Salzig-. Tel: (06742) 62 97.

D-5630 Bingen
Verkehrsamt, Rheinkai 21. Tel: (06721) 14 269.

D-5300 Bonn
Tourist-Information, Cassius-Bastei, Münsterstraße 20. Tel: (0228) 77 34 66.

D-5407 Boppard
Städiches Verkehrsamt, Karmeliterstraße 2. Tel: (06742) 10 319.

D-5423 Braubach
Verkehrsamt, Rathausstraße 8. Tel: (02627) 203.

D-7814 Breisach
Städtisches Verkehrsamt, Postfach 11 29. Tel: (07667) 83 227.

D-5040 Brühl
Amt für Wirtschaft und Verkehrsförderung, Rathaus. Tel: (02223) 345.
Informationszentrum, Uhlstraße 7. Tel: (02223) 79 243.

D-4190 Cleves
Amt für Wirtschaftsförderung und Fremdenverkehr, Rathaus. Tel: (02821) 84 267.

D-5000 Cologne
Verkehrsamt, Unter Fettenhennen 19. Tel: (0221) 22 13 391.

D-4220 Dinslaken
Stadtverwaltung, Wilhelm-Lantermann-Straße 69. Tel: (02134) 66 222.

D-4047 Dormagen
Fremdenverkehrsamt, Schloßstraße 37. Tel: (02106) 53 519.

D-4000 Düsseldorf
Touristinformation, Heinrich-Heine-Allee 24. Tel: (0211) 89 92 346.
Verkehrsverein, Konrad-Adenauer-Platz. Tel: (0211) 35 05 05.

D-4100 Duisburg
Tourist Information, Königstraße 53. Tel: (0203) 28 32 189.

D-6228 Eltville
Verkehrsamt, Schmittstraße 2. Tel: (06123) 50 91.

D-4240 Emmerich
Fremdenverkehrsamt, Martinikirchgang 2. Tel: (02822) 75 331.

D-5465 Erpel
Verschönerungs- und Verkehrsverein, Bergstraße 12. Tel: (02644) 59 85, 12 21.

D-7800 Freiburg im Breisgau
Tourist-Information, Rotteckring 14. Tel: (0761) 21 63 289.

D-6222 Geisenheim
Verkehrs- und Verschönerungsverein, Rüdesheimer Straße 48. Tel: (06722) 80 21.
Verkehrsamt, Rathaus. Tel: (06722) 70 10.

D-6900 Heidelberg
Verkehrsverein, Friedrich-Ebert-Anlage 2. Tel: (06221) 10 821.

D-6148 Heppenheim
Fremdenverkehrsamt Bergstraße-Odenwald, Landratsamt. Tel: (06252) 15 321.
Verkehrsverein, Großer Markt 1. Tel: (06252) 13 171.

D-6507 Ingelheim
Stadtverwaltung, Neuer Markt 1. Tel:
(06132) 78 20.
Verkehrsverein, Rathausplatz 5. Tel:
(06132) 70 41.

D-5454 Kamp-Bornhofen
Verkehrsamt, Rheinuferstraße 34. Tel:
(06773) 360.

D-5425 Kaub
Verkehrsamt, Metzgergasse 26. Tel: (0774)
222.

D-7640 Kehl
Verkehrsamt, Marktplatz. Tel: (07851) 88
226.

D-5400 Koblenz
Fremdenverkehrsamt, Verkehrspavillion.
Tel: (0261) 12 93 06.
Tourist-Information, Konrad-Adenauer-
Ufer. Tel: (0261) 12 92 207.
Niederländisches Büro für Tourismus
(NBT), Laurenzplatz 1-3. Tel: (0221) 23 62 62.

D-5330 Königswinter
Verkehrsamt, Drachenfelsstraße 7. Tel:
(02223) 21 048.

D-7750 Konstanz
Tourist Information, Bahnhofplatz 13. Tel:
(07531) 28 43 76.

D-4150 Krefeld
Verkehrsverein, Theaterplatz. Tel: (02151)
29 290.

D-5420 Lahnstein
Städtisches Verkehrsamt, Stadthallenpas-
sage. Tel: (02621) 17 542.

D-7887 Laufenburg
Information Verkehrsamt, Am Zoll. Tel:
(07763) 5171.
Verkehrsamt, Hauptstraße 3. Tel: (07763)
41 40.

D-5458 Leutesdorf
Verkehrs- und Verschönerungsverein,
Hauptstraße 42. Tel: (02731) 72 227.

D-8990 Lindau
Verkehrsverein, Am Hauptbahnhof. Tel:
(08383) 50 22.

D-5460 Linz
Verkehrsamt, Rathaus. Tel: (02644) 25 26.

D-6223 Lorch
Städtisches Verkehrsamt, Markt 5. Tel:
(06726) 317.

D-6700 Ludwigshafen
Informationspavillion, Am Hauptbahnhof.
Tel: (0621) 51 20 35.

D-6500 Mainz
Verkehrsverein, Bahnhofstraße 15. Tel:
(06131) 23 37 41.

D-6800 Mannheim
Tourist Information, Bahnhofplatz 1. Tel:
(0621) 10 10 11.

D-6120 Michelstadt
Fremdenverkehrsverband Odenwald-
Bergstraße-Neckartal, Marktplatz 1. Tel:
(06061) 666.
Verkehrsamt, Marktplatz 1. Tel: (06061)
74 146.

D-5450 Neuwied
Touristikgemeinschaft Naturpark Rhein-
Westerwald, Augustastraße 8. Tel: (02631)
80 32 14.
Verkehrsamt, Kirchstraße 50. Tel: (02631)
80 22 60.

D-6505 Nierstein
Verkehrsverein, Bildstockstraße 10. Tel:
(06133) 51 11.

D-6532 Oberwesel
Verkehrsamt, Rathausstraße 3. Tel: (06744)
15 22.

D-6227 Oestrich-Winkel
Verkehrsamt. Tel: (06723) 27 74.

D-7760 Radolfzell
Verkehrsamt, Marktplatz 2. Tel: (07732)
38 00.

D-5480 Remagen
Verkehrsamt, Bachstraße 2. Tel: (02642)
20 10.

D-5342 Rheinbreitbach
Verkehrsverein, Rheinstraße 28. Tel:
(02224) 71 250.

D-5401 Rhens
Fremdenverkehrsamt, Rathaus. Tel:
(02628) 751.

D-6220 Rüdesheim
Städtisches Verkehrsamt, Rheinstraße 16.
Tel: (06722) 29 62.

D-5485 Sinzig
Verkehrsamt. Tel: (02642) 41 031.

D-5401 St. Goar
Verkehrsamt, Heerstraße 120. Tel: (06741)
383.

D-5422 St. Goarshausen
Verkehrsamt, Bahnhofstraße 8. Tel:
(06771) 427.
Verkehrsverein Loreley-Burgen-Straße,
Dolkstraße 11. Tel: (06771) 80 115.

D-6720 Speyer
Verkehrsamt, Maximilianstraße 11. Tel:
(06232) 14 396.

D-6531 Trechtingshausen
Verkehrsverein. Tel: (06721) 64 11.

D-5463 Unkel
Städtisches Verkehrsamt, Linzer Straße 6.
Tel: (02224) 33 09.

D-7890 Waldshut-Tiengen
Verkehrsamt, Postfach 19 41. Tel: (07751)
16 14 (Waldshut). Tel: (07741) 30 11 (Tiengen).

D-4230 Wesel
Weseler Verkehrsverein, Franz-Etzel-Platz
4. Tel: (0281) 24 498.

D-5047 Wesseling
Amt für Wirtschaftsförderung, Rathaus.
Tel: (02236) 701-254.

D-6200 Wiesbaden
Verkehrsbüro, Postfach 38 40. Tel: (06121)
31 28 45, 37 43 53.

D-6520 Worms
Verkehrsverein, Neumarkt. Tel: (06241)
25 045.

D-4232 Xanten
Verkehrsverein. Tel: (02801) 37 283.

THE NETHERLANDS

NL-6811 KL Arnhem
VVV Arnhem, Stationsplein 45. Tel: (085)
42 03 30.

NL-2594 AV Den Haag
National Bureau voor Tourisme, Bez-
uidehoutseweg 2. Tel: (070) 70 81 41 191.

NL-3311 JW Dordrecht
VVV Dordrecht, Stationsweg 1. Tel: (031)
78 13 28 00.

NL-6711 AV Ede
VVV Ede, Achterdoelen 36. Tel: (08380)
14 444.

NL-6511 TD Nijmegen
VVV Nijmegen, St. Jorisstraat 72. Tel: (080)
22 54 40.

NL-3012 AR Rotterdam
VVV Rotterdam, Studhuisplein 19. Tel:
(010) 13 60 00.
Coolsingel 67. Tel: (010) 41 36 006.

NL-4001 KX Tiel
VVV Tiel, Korenbeursplein 4. Tel: (03440)
16 441.

NL-3511 Utrecht
VVV Utrecht, Vredenburg 90. Tel: (030)
31 41 32.

ART/PHOTO CREDITS

INDEX

NOTES